A Nation Without Prisons

A Nation Without Prisons

Alternatives to Incarceration

Edited by
Calvert R. Dodge

Lexington Books
D.C. Heath and Company
Lexington, Massachusetts
Toronto   London

Chapter 4 is from *Prison Without Walls: Report on New York Parole* by the Citizen's Inquiry on Parole and Criminal Justice, Inc., © 1975 by the Citizen's Inquiry on Parole and Criminal Justice, Inc., excerpted and reprinted by permission of Praeger Publishers, Inc., New York.

Library of Congress Cataloging in Publication Data

Dodge, Calvert R.
    A nation without prisons.

    1. Corrections—United States. 2. Rehabilitation of criminals—United States. 3. Correctional institutions—United States. I. Title.
HV9304.D62   365.6'1'0973   74-16928
ISBN 0-669-96438-7

Second printing November 1976.

Published simultaneously in Canada.

Printed in the United States of America.

International Standard Book Number: 0-669-96438-7

Library of Congress Catalog Card Number: 74-16928

To

Judge Horace Holmes, James Carmany,
Carl Larson, and Edward Marck.

While working for one I learned the power
of innovation and creativeness in changing
law-offenders' lives.

While working with the other I learned the
power of persuasion in changing the system
from within.

While a student of the third I learned that
each of us makes little difference to
changing society, but together we have
the "power" to change society equal to
that of a nuclear bomb.

As a partner of the fourth I've
learned the value of "confrontation,"
"truth," and "openess" in
developing constructive human growth.

Contents

List of Figures   ix

List of Tables   xi

Foreword   xiii

Acknowledgments   xv

Introduction   xviii

Part I: *Overviews*

Chapter 1   **Major Institutions**
                 Corrections Task Force, National
                 Advisory Commission on Criminal
                 Justice Standards and Goals   3

Chapter 2   **Toward a New Criminology**
                 Eugene Doleschal and Nora Klapmuts   37

Chapter 3   **The Dissolution of the Training Schools**
                 In Massachusetts
                 Andrew Rutherford   57

Part II: *Alternatives*

Chapter 4   **Prisons Without Walls: Summary Report**
                 on New York Parole
                 Citizens' Inquiry on Parole and
                 Criminal Justice, Inc.   79

Chapter 5   **Community Alternatives to Prison**
Nora Klapmuts   101

Chapter 6   **Volunteers in Probation: Not Just a Band-Aid Story**
Judge Keith J. Leenhouts   133

Chapter 7   **Instead of Prison**
Michael J. Mahoney   147

Chapter 8   **Wilderness Training as an Alternative to Incarceration**
Joseph Nold and Mary Wilpers   155

Chapter 9   **M-2 (Man-to-Man) Job Therapy**
Richard J. Simmons, ed.   171

Chapter 10   **The Halfway House as an Alternative**
Calvert R. Dodge   197

Chapter 11   **The How and Why of Partners**
Robert Moffitt   213

Part III: *Conclusions*

Chapter 12   **A Nation Without Prisons: Dream or Reality?**
Calvert R. Dodge   233

Appendix   251

Author Index   257

Subject Index   259

About the Editor   265

List of Figures

6-1   NIMH and Royal Oak Municipal Court
       Research Grant, July 1968   143

9-1   Job Therapy of Washington Localized
       Community-Based Corrections—Client
       Services   188

9-2   Community Correctional Programs—Job
       Therapy   189

9-3   Comparison of Success Rates Between
       Various Groups   195

List of Tables

1-1   Date of Opening, State Maximum Security
        Prisons Still in Operation   6

1-2   Population of State Correctional
        Facilities for Adults, by Security
        Classification of Inmates   7

1-3   Comparative Use of State Correctional
        Institutions   24

3-1   Number and Percentage of Persons Committed
        to State Prisons and County Jails by
        Year and Age   66

3-2   Placement of Delinquents in Residual
        Services in Massachusetts, 1973   70

4-1   Released and Returned as Violator—Same
        Year, by Method of Release   89

9-1   Phase I, Job Preparation—Phase II Job
        Start   190

9-2   Personalized Service Contracts   191

Foreword

When Kentucky Manpower Development, a private nonprofit corporation which seeks to improve human service programs, expanded its program focus to include the criminal justice system, early research and analysis noted significant paradoxical concerns within the correctional area. Although essentially operated for rehabilitative purposes, this nation's federal and state correctional facilities for law-offenders fail miserably, in that approximately three-fourths of today's over 200,000 inmates will be returned to prison after being discharged or paroled. While criminologists, the National Advisory Commission on Criminal Justice Standards and Goals, and others are recommending a policy of not building new major correctional institutions, the federal government and several states are approving and/or constructing new prisons. Accordingly, a determining influence for the preparation of this book was the need to consider alternatives to this nation's disturbing and ineffective procedures for incarceration of offenders.

A Nation Without Prisons presents a broad overview of various schools of thought pertaining to effective rehabilitation of offenders. Recognizing that this country's correctional system has failed and is ready for change, several selected alternatives are discussed and suggested, not as *the answer*, but to stimulate thought and action in a wide search for a new direction in corrections. The book concludes with the call for a new order of criminology to replace the existing outdated and inappropriate system, which fails to meet requirements of this age.

In presenting the contributions of participating authors, Calvert Dodge reviews several selected programs that have proved successful as alternatives to prison. The editor utilized the closing of youth institutions in Massachusetts, delimiting of correctional institutions in Wisconsin and Washington, and other innovative efforts in his call for a multiapproach solution to problems inherent in this nation's failure-oriented system of prisons.

Ideas presented in this book may be criticized by those who consider the alternatives as either not new, too radical, or superficial. Others may claim that specific circumstances or situations make replication of the demonstrated activities impractical. Nevertheless, few will question the failure of our existing prison system and the need to explore every possible method for its replacement. Kentucky Manpower Development hopes that this book will stimulate action toward this goal.

Earl E. Staton
Executive Director
Kentucky Manpower Development, Inc.

Acknowledgments

Each contributor, though deep in his own efforts to help bring about change in our corrections system, found the time to put together valuable information and ideas and to share them with the readers of this book.

To those who have invented new ideas or changed the old in our corrections system but whose efforts are not reported in this book . . .

To the staff of the Kentucky Manpower Development organization who helped edit, type, and bring it together, especially Annette Craig . . .

To Milton Rector of the National Council on Crime and Delinquency and Norman Carlson, Director of the Federal Prison System, who both believe in changing the system, but in different ways, for their input . . .

To the criminologists and others who suggested changes in the book's contents, and criticized it . . .

I express my gratitude.

Introduction

Both long empirical experience and controlled research in institutions reveal a dramatic and important fact: Prison is simply not, and from all evidence cannot be, conducive to the rehabilitation of offenders, and it is not a deterrent to most people who commit crime.

Is there reason, then, for hope that America might lead the world away from the use of cages for criminals, as we led the world two hundred years ago to prisons as a more humane penalty than death, corporal punishment, mutilation, and banishment? I believe there is. The time-honored assumption that everyone who commits a crime must be imprisoned is now being challenged. Not the least among its challengers are the courts themselves, some of which have begun to ask whether today's prisons can lawfully carry out their responsibility.

In addition to purely legal challenges, both criminal justice officials and concerned citizens are looking at our collective experience of rehabilitation in prison, and they are appalled at what they see. Offenders come into prison, are maintained at considerable public expense, only to emerge years later less able to assume a useful place in society than before they were admitted, In view of our goals, what could be a more self-defeating process?

A Nation Without Prisons provides substantial evidence that there are alternatives for offenders that are more effective than incarceration. It provides judges, legislators, and citizen leaders with examples of the kind of program that can substantially reduce prison populations in every state. It says, in effect, that for both youth and adult offenders there is no compelling reason for imprisonment.

There is an exception to this rule, of course—the dangerous offender. We need to know how to identify this type of offender better. Using criteria of dangerousness such as those developed by the National Council on Crime and Delinquency would allow surer classification of offenders who require secure confinement and those who do not. Every day judges make such determinations of dangerousness. But their decisions quite often are based on personal experience, sketchy probation reports, or purely intuitive judgments. This is too poor a basis upon which to make a decision that may put a man or woman behind bars for many years.

There are still penologists whose faith passeth all understanding, and who still hope for transformation of the prison into a truly rehabilitating facility. They have not hesitated to experiment widely to reach their goal. Thus far, their experiments have shown that prison, no matter how small, clean, or centrally located, is ineffective in reforming the offender.

Orwellian programs such as the Federal Bureau of Prison's START project, which used behavioral modification in so questionable a manner as to elicit a public outcry, have yet to prove their value. The results have been deeply disappointing, and it is no wonder that the Bureau has terminated START. Other approaches that involve psychosurgery, involuntary use of drugs, or aversion therapy are no more constructive than beating or starving a prisoner. And we know from the past that such tactics do not work either.

It is regrettable that some correctional authorities have confused measures that make an offender tractable in prison with those which rehabilitate him in the community. These are not the same goals. All too often a compliant inmate who sticks to every prison rule may become a vicious criminal upon release.

The various programs described in this book are, in my judgment, a better approach to helping those who commit crime than the prison programs, psychiatric or otherwise. Certainly they are more humane, and usually far less costly. But even these programs, useful as they are, are just the beginning of a search for alternatives to prison. They have pointed a direction, and in this respect they are most valuable. But they have not yet provided the definitive road map we are seeking.

More research is needed in developing noninstitutional programs. More imaginative thinking is needed to produce acceptable punitive sanctions which have the potential of reforming offenders and deterring repeated crimes. In this connection, correctional authorities will do well to keep an eye on the British Criminal Justice Act of 1972. This law permits an English court to sentence a defendant to perform service in the community in lieu of imprisonment. It may well be that the wave of the future lies in this type of penalty, rather than in the latest mode of behavioral modification.

The alternatives to prison described in this volume should encourage correctional specialists to develop new and more effective ways of dealing with the offender. But at the very least, a review of these programs will impress upon the reader the fact that community treatment has its pioneers and experimenters, and that they are not working in vain.

Milton G. Rector
President
National Council on Crime and Delinquency

Crime has become a malignant enemy in America's midst. . . . We must arrest and reverse the trend toward lawlessness. . . . We can not tolerate an endless, self-defeating cycle of imprisonment, release, and reimprisonment which fails to alter undesirable attitudes and behavior. We must find ways to help the first offender avoid a continuing career of crime.

—Lyndon Johnson
in his message to
Congress, March 8, 1965

Part I: Overviews

1

Major Institutions[a]
Corrections Task Force[b]
National Advisory Commission on Criminal Justice Standards and Goals

The term "major institutions" as used in this chapter does not refer to size, but to state-operated penal and correctional institutions for juveniles, youths, and adults (as distinguished from detention centers, jails, work farms, and other types of facilities, which in almost all states are operated by local governments). Names used for major institutions differ from state to state. Institutions for juveniles carry such names as youth development centers, training schools, industrial schools, and state homes. Institutions for adults variously are called prisons, penitentiaries, classification and reception centers, correctional institutions, reformatories, treatment centers, state farms, and so forth. Altogether there are about 200 major juvenile and 350 major adult correctional institutions in the United States.

This chapter also discusses maximum, medium, and minimum security institutions. It is difficult to make clear-cut distinctions, however, in view of the enormous diversity. Generally the terms refer to relative degrees in the use of security trappings and procedures. All three security classifications may be used, and usually are, in the same institution. Moreover, maximum security in one state may be considered only medium security in another. Some so-called minimum security institutions might actually be considered medium security by some authorities. The terminology—maximum, medium, minimum—is as imprecise as the wide variety of names that may be used formally to designate individual institutions. The terms indicate the rough classifications traditionally used.

Historical Perspective

Institutionalization as the primary means of enforcing the customs, mores, or laws of a people is a relatively modern practice. In earlier times, restitution, exile, and a variety of methods of corporal and capital punishment, many of them unspeakably barbarous, were used. Confinement was used for detention only.

The colonists who came to North America brought with them the harsh penal codes and practices of their homelands. It was in Pennsylvania, founded by William Penn, that initial attempts were made to find alternatives to the

[a]Reprinted by permission of the General Counsel, LEAA, U.S. Department of Justice.

[b]A list of the names of the Corrections Task Force appears at the end of this chapter.

3

brutality of British penal practice. Penn knew well the nature of confinement because he had spent six months in Newgate Prison, London, for his religious convictions.

In the Great Law of Pennsylvania, enacted in 1682, Penn made provisions to eliminate to a large extent the stocks, pillories, branding iron, and gallows. The Great Law directed "that every county within the province of Pennsylvania and territories thereunto belonging shall . . . build or cause to be built in the most convenient place in each respective county a sufficient house for restraint, labor, and punishment of all such persons as shall be thereunto committed by laws."

In time William Penn's jails, like those in other parts of the New World up to and including the present, became places where the untried, the mentally ill, the promiscuous, debtors, and myriad petty offenders were confined indiscriminately.

In 1787, when the Constitutional Convention was meeting in Philadelphia and men were thinking of institutions based on the concept of the dignity of man, the Philadelphia Society for Alleviating the Miseries of Public Prisons was organized. The society believed that the sole end of punishment is to prevent crime, and that punishment should not destroy the offender. The society, many of whose members were influential citizens, worked hard to create a new penology in Pennsylvania, a penology which to a large degree eliminated capital and corporal punishment as the principal sanctions for major crimes. The penitentiary was invented as a substitute for these punishments.

In the first three decades of the nineteenth century, citizens of New York, Pennsylvania, New Jersey, Massachusetts, and Connecticut were busy planning and building monumental penitentiaries. These were not cheap installations built from the crumbs of the public treasury. In fact, the Eastern State Penitentiary in Philadelphia was the most expensive public building constructed in the New World to that time. States were extremely proud of these physical plants. Moreover, they saw in them an almost utopian ideal. They were to become stabilizers of society. They were to become laboratories committed to the improvement of all mankind.[1]

When these new penitentiaries were being planned and constructed, practitioners and theorists held three factors to be the primary contributors to criminal behavior. The first was environment. Report after report on offenders pointed out the harmful effects of family, home, and other aspects of environment on the offender's behavior. The second factor usually cited was the offender's lack of aptitude and work skills. This quality led to indolence and a life of crime. The third cause was seen as the felon's ignorance of right and wrong because he had not been taught the Scriptures.

The social planners of the first quarter of the nineteenth century designed prison architecture and programs to create an experience for the offender in which (1) there would be no injurious influences, (2) the offender would learn the value of labor and work skills, and (3) he would have the opportunity to learn about the Scriptures, and accept from them the principles of right and wrong that would then guide his life.

Various states pursued this triad of purposes in one of two basic methods. The Pennsylvania system was based on solitary confinement, accompanied by bench labor within one's cell. There the offender was denied all contact with the outside world except that provided by the Scriptures, religious tracts, and visits from specially selected exemplary citizens. The prison was designed painstakingly to make this kind of solitary experience possible. The walls between cells were thick, and the cells themselves were large, each equipped with plumbing and running water. In the cell were a workbench and tools. In addition, each cell had its own small walled area for solitary exercise. The institution was designed magnificently for its three purposes: elimination of external influences; provision of work; and opportunity for penitence, introspection, and acquisition of religious knowledge.[2]

New York's Auburn system pursued the same three goals, by a different method. Like the Pennsylvania system, it isolated the offender from the world outside and permitted him virtually no external contact. However, it provided small cells in which the convicts were confined only on the Sabbath and during nonworking hours. During working hours inmates labored in factorylike shops. The contaminating effect of the congregate work situation was eliminated by a rule of silence. Inmates were prohibited from communicating in any way with other inmates or the jailers.

The relative merits of these two systems were debated vigorously for half a century. The Auburn system ultimately prevailed in the United States, because it was less expensive and because it lent itself more easily to production methods of the Industrial Revolution.

But both systems were disappointments almost from the beginning. The awful solitude of the Pennsylvania system drove men to insanity. The rule of silence of the Auburn system became increasingly unenforceable, despite regular use of the lash and a variety of other harsh and brutal punishments.

Imprisonment as an instrument of reform was an early failure. This invention did, however, have some notable advantages. It rendered obsolete a myriad of sanguinary punishments, and its ability to separate and hold offenders gave the public a sense of security. It also was thought to deter people from crime by fear of imprisonment.

Imprisonment had many disadvantages, too. Principal among them was the phenomenon that so many of its "graduates" came back. The prison experience often further atrophied the offender's capacity to live successfully in the free world. The prison nevertheless has persisted, partly because a civilized nation could neither turn back to the barbarism of an earlier time nor find a satisfactory alternative. For nearly two centuries, American penologists have been seeking a way out of this dilemma.

Types of Institutions

Maximum Security Prisons

For the first century after invention of the penitentiary most prisons were built to be internally and externally secure. The early zealots who had dreamed of institutions that not only would reform the offender but also would cleanse society itself were replaced by a disillusioned and pragmatic leadership that saw confinement as a valid end in itself. Moreover, the new felons were seen as outsiders—Irishmen, Germans, Italians, and Negroes. They did not talk or act like "Americans." The prison became a dumping ground where foreigners and blacks who were not adjusting could be held outside the mainstream of society's concern. The new prisons, built in the most remote areas of the states, became asylums, not only for the hardened criminal but also for the inept and unskilled "un-American." Although the rhetoric of reformation persisted, the be-all and end-all of the prison was to hold.

From 1830 to 1900 most prisons built in the United States reflected that ultimate value—security. Their principal features were high walls, rigid internal security, cagelike cells, sweatshops, a bare minimum of recreation space, and practically nothing else. They kept the prisoners in and the public out, and that was all that was expected or attempted.

Many of these prisons were constructed well and have lasted long. Together they form the backbone of our present-day correctional system. As Table 1-1 shows, 56 of them, remodeled and expanded, still are in use. They currently house approximately 75,000 of the 110,000 felons in maximum security facilities. Today 56 percent of all state prisoners in America are in structures built to serve maximum security functions (see Table 1-2).

Any attempt to describe the "typical" maximum security prison is hazardous.

Table 1-1
Date of Opening, State Maximum Security Prisons Still in Operation

Date of Opening	Number of Prisons
Prior to 1830	6
1831 to 1870	17
1871 to 1900	33
1901 to 1930	21
1931 to 1960	15
1961 to date	21
Total	113

Source: American Correctional Association, 1971 Directory of Correctional Institutions and Agencies of America, Canada and Great Britain (College Park, Md.: ACA, 1971).

Table 1-2
Population of State Correctional Facilities for Adults, by Security Classification of Inmates

Classification	Inmates	Percent of Total Population
Maximum	109,920	56
Medium	57,505	30
Minimum	28,485	15
Total	195,910	100

Source: ACA, 1971 Directory and poll taken by the American Foundation's Institute of Corrections, which contacted the head of every State department of corrections.

One was constructed almost two centuries ago. Another was opened in 1972. The largest confines more than four thousand inmates, another fewer than sixty.[3] Some contain massive undifferentiated cell blocks, each caging as many as five hundred men or more. Others are built in small modules housing fewer than sixteen. The industries in some are archaic sweatshops, in others large modern factories. Many provide absolutely no inside recreation space and only a minimum outside, while others have superlative gymnasiums, recreation yards, and auditoriums. Some are dark, dingy, depressing dungeons, while others have many windows and are sunny. In one the early warning system consists of cowbells strung along chicken wire atop the masonry wall, while in others closed circuit television and sensitive electronic sensors monitor the corridors and fences.

Maximum security institutions are geared to the fullest possible supervision, control, and surveillance of inmates. Design and program choices optimize security. Buildings and policies restrict the inmate's movement and minimize his control over his environment. Other considerations, such as the inmate's individual or social needs, are responded to only in conformity with security requirements. Trustworthiness on the inmate's part is not anticipated; the opposite is assumed.

Technology has brought much to the design and construction of these institutions, and development of custodial artifacts has far outpaced skill in reaching inmates and in using rapport with them to maintain security or control. A modern maximum security institution represents the victory of external control over internal reform.

The prison invariably is surrounded by a masonry wall or double fence with manned towers. Electronic sensing devices and lights impose an unremitting surveillance and control. Inside the institution, the need for security has dictated that men live in windowless cells, not rooms. Doors, which would afford privacy, are replaced by grilles of tool-resistant steel. Toilets are unscreened. Showers are taken under supervision.

Control, so diligently sought in these facilities, is not limited to structural considerations. All activity is weighed in terms of its relationship to custody. Dining is no exception. Men often sit on fixed backless stools and eat without forks and knives at tables devoid of condiments.

Lest security be compromised by intrusions from outside, special devices are built to prevent physical contact with visitors. Relatives often communicate with inmates by telephone and see them through double layers of glass. Any contacts allowed are under the guard's watchful eyes. Body searches precede and follow such visits.

Internal movement is limited by strategic placement of bars and grilles defining precisely where an inmate may go. Areas of inmate concentration or possible illegal activity are monitored by correctional officers or by closed circuit television. "Blind spots" not capable of supervision are avoided in the design of the secure institution. Places for privacy or small-group activity are structurally, if not operationally, precluded.

Maximum security institutions, then, may be viewed as those facilities characterized by high perimeter security, high internal security, and operating regulations that curtail movement and maximize control.

In his masterful description of penitentiaries in the United States, Tocqueville wrote in 1833 that, aside from common interests, the several states "preserve their individual independence, and each of them is sovereign master to rule itself according to its own pleasure. . . . By the side of one State, the penitentiaries of which might serve as a model, we find another whose prisons present the example of everything which ought to be avoided."[4]

He was right in 1833. His words still ring true in 1975.

Medium Security Correctional Centers

Since the early twentieth century, means of housing the offender in other than maximum security prisons have been explored. Developments in the behavioral sciences, increasing importance of education, dominance of the work ethic, and changes in technology have led to modified treatment methods.

Simultaneously, field service—parole and probation—increased. Institutions were set up to handle special inmate populations, men and women, youths and adults. Classification was introduced by employing psychological and sociological knowledge and skill. Pretrial holding centers, or jails, were separated from those receiving convicted felons. Different levels of security were provided: maximum, medium, minimum, and open. Much of the major correctional construction in the last fifty years has been medium security. In fact, 51 of the existing 110 medium security correctional institutions were built after 1950. Today, over 57,000 offenders, 30 percent of all state inmates, are housed in such facilities (see Table 1-2).

Today medium security institutions probably embody most of the ideals and characteristics of the early attempts to reform offenders. It is in these facilities that the most intensive correctional or rehabilitation efforts are conducted. Here inmates are exposed to a variety of programs intended to help them become useful members of society. But the predominant consideration still is security.

These institutions are designed to confine individuals where they can be observed and controlled. All have perimeter security, in the form of masonry walls or double cyclone fences. In some cases electronic detecting devices are installed. Towers located on the perimeter are manned by armed guards and equipped with spotlights.

Internal security usually is maintained by locks, bars, and concrete walls; clear separation of activities; highly defined movement paths both indoors and outdoors; schedules and head counts; sightline supervision; and electronic devices.

Housing areas, medical and dental treatment rooms, schoolrooms, recreation and entertainment facilities, counseling offices, vocational training and industrial shops, administration offices, and maintenance facilities usually are clearly separated. Occasionally they are located in individual compounds complete with their own fences and sally ports. A complex series of barred gates and guard posts controls the flow of traffic from one area to another. Central control stations keep track of movement at all times. Circulation is restricted to specified corridors or outdoor walks, with certain spaces and movement paths out of bounds. Closed circuit television and alarm networks are used extensively. Locked steel doors predominate. Bars or concrete substitutes line corridors, surround control points, and cross all external windows and some internal ones.

Housing units in medium security institutions vary from crowded dormitories to private rooms with furniture. Dormitories may house as many as eighty persons or as few as sixteen. Some individual cells have grilled fronts and doors.

The variations found in maximum security institutions also are seen in medium security correctional facilities, but they are not so extreme, possibly because the latter were developed in a much shorter period.

Several heartening developments have occurred recently in the medium security field. Campus-type plants have been designed that largely eliminate the cramped oppressiveness of most confinement. Widely separated buildings are connected by meandering pathways, and modulated ground surfaces break monotony. Attractive residences house small groups of inmates in single rooms.

Schools, vocational education buildings, gymnasiums, and athletic fields compare favorably with those of the best community colleges. Yet external security provided by double cyclone fences and internal security enforced by excellent staff and unobtrusive building design protect the public from the inmates and the inmates from each other.

If confinement to institutions is to remain the principal sanction of our codes of criminal justice, medium security plants and programs such as these, not the traditional "minimum security" prison farms, should be the cornerstone of the system.

Minimum Security Correctional Centers

The facilities in this group are diverse, but generally have one feature in common: They are relatively open, and consequently custody is a function of classification rather than of prison hardware. The principal exceptions are huge prison plantations on which entire penal populations serve time. Minimum security institutions range from large drug rehabilitation centers to small farm, road, and forestry camps located throughout rural America.

Most, but not all, minimum security facilities have been created to serve the economic needs of society and only incidentally the correctional needs of the offenders. Cotton is picked, lumber is cut, livestock is raised, roads are built, forest fires are fought, and parks and state buildings are maintained. These are all legitimate tasks for prisoners, especially while our system still (1) receives large numbers of offenders who are a minimal threat to themselves and to the general public, and (2) holds men long after they are ready for freedom. Moreover, open facilities do serve therapeutic purposes, by removing men from the stifling prison environment, separating the young and unsophisticated from the predators, and substituting controls based upon trust rather than bars. All these aspects are laudable.

However, these remote facilities have important deficiencies. They seldom provide educational or service resources other than work. Moreover, the predominantly rural labor bears no relationship to the work skills required for urban life. Separation of the prisoner from his real world is almost as complete as it would have been in the penitentiary.

One remarkable minimum security correctional center was opened in 1972 at Vienna, Illinois, as a branch of the Illinois State Penitentiary. Although large, it approaches the quality of the nonpenal institution. Buildings resembling garden apartments are built around a "town square" complete with churches, schools, shops, and library. Paths lead off to "neighborhoods" where "homes" provide private rooms in small clusters. Extensive provision has been made for both indoor and outdoor recreation. Academic, commercial, and vocational education facilities equal or surpass those of many technical high schools.

This correctional center has been designed for eight hundred adult felons. Unfortunately, most of them will come from the state's major population centers many miles away. Today this open institution is enjoying the euphoria that often accompanies distinctive newness. One may speculate about the future, however, when community correctional programs siphon from the state's prison system many of its more stable and less dangerous offenders. Fortunately, this facility will not be rendered obsolete by such a development. The nonprisonlike design permits it to be adapted for a variety of educational, mental health, or other human service functions.

One generalization about the future of minimum security facilities seems warranted. As society finds still more noninstitutional and community-based solutions to its problems, the rural open institutions will become harder and harder to populate. Already they are operating farther below their rated capacities than any other type of correctional facility.

Institutions for Women

The new role of women may profoundly influence the future requirements of corrections. For whatever reasons, the treatment given to women by the criminal justice system has been different from that given men. Perhaps fewer commit crimes; certainly six men are arrested for every woman. The ratio is still higher for indictments and convictions, and thirty times more men than women are confined in state correctional institutions. Montana in 1971 incarcerated only eight women; West Virginia, 28; Nebraska, 44; Minnesota, 55. Even populous Pennsylvania incarcerated only 127 women.[5]

Tomorrow may be different. As women increasingly assume more roles previously seen as male, their involvement in crime may increase and their treatment at the hands of the agencies of justice change. A possible, if unfortunate, result could be an increase in the use of imprisonment for women.

Correctional institutions for women present a microcosm of American penal practice. In this miniature model, the absurdities and irrationalities of the entire system appear in all their ludicrousness. In one state, the few women offenders are seen to be so dangerous as to require confinement in a separate wing of the men's penitentiary. There they are shut up in cells and cell corridors without recreation, services, or meaningful activity. In other places, new but separate facilities for women have been built that perpetuate the philosophy, the operational methods, the hardware, and the repression of the state penitentiary. These facilities are surrounded by concertina fences, and the women's movements are monitored by closed circuit television. Inmates sit endlessly playing cards, sewing, or just vegetating. A woman superintendent has observed that these institutions should release exclusively to San Francisco or Las Vegas because the inmates have been prepared for homosexuality or card dealing. Everything about such places—their sally ports, control centers, narrow corridors, small cells, restrictive visiting rooms—spells PRISON in capital letters. Yet these institutions were not built in the nineteenth century. They are new.

Compared to women's institutions in other states, the prisons just described demonstrate the inconsistency of our thinking about criminals in general and women prisoners specifically. One center—the Women's Treatment Center at Purdy, Washington—vividly demonstrates that offenders can be viewed as civilized human beings. Built around multilevel and beautifully landscaped courtyards, the attractive buildings provide security without fences. Small housing units with pleasant living rooms provide space for normal interaction between presumably normal women. The expectation that the women will behave like human beings pervades the place. Education, recreation, and training areas are uncramped and well lighted with windows. Opportunity for interaction between staff and inmate is present everywhere.

About two hundred yards away from the other buildings are attractive apartments, each containing a living room, dining space, kitchen, two bedrooms, and a bath. Women approaching release live in them while working or attending school in the city. These apartments normally are out of bounds to staff except on invitation.

The contrasts among women's institutions demonstrate our confusion about what criminals are like and what correctional responses are appropriate. In six states maximum security prisons are the correctional solution to the female offenders. At least fifteen other states use open institutions exclusively.

This contrast raises questions about the nature of correctional planning. What is it really based upon? The propensities of the offender? The meanness or enlightenment of the general population? The niggardliness of the public? The broadness or narrowness of the administrator's vision? Whatever the reason, the architecture of these correctional institutions tells us either that women in State A are profoundly different from those in State B or that the correctional leadership holds vastly differing human values.

Youth Correction Centers

The reformatory movement started about a century ago. With the advent of the penitentiary, imprisonment had replaced corporal punishment. The reformatory concept was designed to replace punishment through incarceration with rehabilitation. This new movement was aimed at the young offender, aged sixteen to thirty. Its keystone was education and vocational training to make the offender more capable of living in the outside world. New concepts—parole and indeterminate sentences—were introduced. An inmate who progressed could reduce the length of his sentence. Hope was a new treatment dynamic.

The physical plant in the early reformatory era was highly secure. One explanation given is that the first one, at Elmira, New York, was designed as a maximum security prison and then converted into a reformatory. Other states that adopted the reformatory concept also copied the physical plant. Huge masonry walls, multitiered cell blocks, mass movements, "big house" mess halls, and dimly lit shops were all part of the model. Several of these places are still in operation. Later, in the 1920s, youth institutions adopted the telephone-pole-construction design developed for adults; housing and service units crisscross an elongated inner corridor. More recently campus-type plants, fenced and un-fenced, have been constructed. Some of these resemble the new colleges.

Most recently built reformatories, now called youth "correction" or "train-ing" centers, are built to provide only medium or minimum security. (However, the newest—Western Correctional Center, Morgantown, North Carolina—is a very secure seventeen-story facility.) These centers usually emphasize academic and vocational education and recreation. Some supplement these with counseling and therapy, including operant conditioning and behavior modification. The buildings themselves are central to the program in providing incentives. At the Morganton center, for example, as a youth's behavior modifies he is moved from the seventeenth floor to the more desirable sixteenth, or from an open ward to a single room, etc.

Overall plant, security, and housing, as well as education, vocational training, and recreation space, are similar in youth centers to those provided in adult centers of comparable custody classification. The only major difference is that some youth institutions provide more programs. The amount of space, therefore, often exceeds that of adult centers. Some youth centers have highly screened populations, and the center provides only one function—to increase educational levels and vocational skills. The effectiveness of such centers is highly dependent on inmate selection, placing a heavy responsibility on the classification process.

Facilities and programs in the youth correction centers vary widely from institution to institution and from state to state. While some provide a variety of positive programs, others emphasize the mere holding of the inmate. In the latter, few rehabilitative efforts are made; facilities are sparse and recreational space is inadequate. The general atmosphere is repressive, and the physical plant prohibits program improvement.

Youth institutions include at least two types of minimum security facilities, work camps and training centers, which present a series of dilemmas. In work camps, outdoor labors burn up youthful energies. But these camps are limited severely in their capacity to provide other important needs of youthful offenders. Moreover, they are located in rural America, which is usually white, while youthful offenders frequently are not. The other type of minimum security youth center has complete training facilities, fine buildings, attractively landscaped surroundings, and extensive programs. These, too, usually are remote from population centers. Though they probably represent our most enlightened form of imprisonment, quite possibly they soon will be obsolete.

Even today the various states are finding it difficult to select from their youthful inmate populations persons who are stable enough for such open facilities. Many, therefore, are operating far below normal capacity. Walkaways present such serious problems that insidious internal controls, more irksome than the visible wire fence, have been developed.

These open centers serve three important functions:

1. They bring the individual every day face to face with his impulse to escape life's frustrations by running away.

2. They remove youths temporarily from community pressures that have overwhelmed them.

3. They provide sophisticated program opportunities usually not available otherwise.

In the near future, it is to be hoped, these three purposes will be assumed by small and infinitely less expensive community correctional programs.

Institutions for Juveniles

Almost all human services in America have followed a similar course of development. When faced with a social problem we seek institutional solutions first. The problems presented by children have been no exception. Early in our national development we had to face the phenomenon of child dependency, and we built orphanages. Children would not stay put, and we established the "Home for Little Wanderers." When children stole we put them in jails, filthy places where the sight of them incensed pioneer prison reformers. They turned to a model already common in Europe where congregate facilities, often under the auspices of religious groups, cared for both dependent and delinquent children.

The first such facility in America was established in New York in 1825. Reflecting its purpose, it was called the "House of Refuge." Others followed, coinciding almost exactly with the first penitentiaries. The pioneering juvenile institutions were just about as oppressive and forbidding, emphasizing security and austerity. By today's standards they were basically punitive. In time they tended more toward benign custodial care along with providing the essentials of housing and food. They became characterized by large populations, with consequent regimentation, and by oversized buildings.

In the latter decades of the nineteenth century, attempts to minimize the massive institutional characteristics led to the adoption of the "cottage concept." Housing was provided in smaller buildings. "House parents" aimed at simulating a homelike atmosphere. This model has remained and today continues as a common, perhaps the predominant, type of institution for juvenile delinquents.

Institutions for the delinquent child usually have vastly different characteristics than those holding adults. Often they are located on a campus spreading over many acres. The housing units provide quarters for smaller groups, invariably fewer than sixty and frequently fewer than twenty. Often they also provide apartments for cottage staff. Dining is frequently a function of cottage life, eliminating the need for the large central dining rooms. Grilles seldom are found on the cottage doors and windows, although sometimes they are covered by detention screens. Security is not the staff's major preoccupation.

Play fields dot the usually ample acreage. Other resources for athletics, such as gymnasiums and swimming pools, are common. Additional recreational activity often is undertaken in nearby towns, parks, streams, and resorts. Teams from youth institutions usually play in public-school leagues and in community competition. The principal program emphasis at these children's centers quite naturally has been education, and many have fine, diversified school buildings, both academic and vocational.

Exterior security varies, but most juvenile centers have no artificial barriers separating them from the community at large. Space frequently provides such a barrier, however, as many juvenile centers are in rural settings. Fences do exist, especially where the institution borders a populated area. Usually they do not have towers. Walkaways are quite frequent and cause considerable annoyance to neighbors, who sometimes hold public subscriptions to raise money for fences.

At the risk of oversimplification, this section describes two predominant but conflicting philosophies about the care of delinquent children. This is done because they suggest profoundly different directions and consequently different facility requirements for the future.

One has its roots in the earliest precepts of both the penitentiary and reformatory systems. It holds that the primary cause of delinquent behavior is the child's environment, and the secondary cause is his inability to cope with that environment. The response is to provide institutions in the most remote areas, where the child is protected from adverse environmental influences and exposed to a wholesome life style predicated on traditional middle-class values. Compensatory education, often better than that available in the community, equips the child with tools necessary to face the world again, someday. This kind of correctional treatment requires expensive and extensive plants capable of providing for the total needs of children over prolonged periods.

The second philosophy similarly assumes that the child's problems are related to the environment, but it differs from the first model by holding that the youngster must learn to deal with those problems where they are—in the community. Institutions, if required at all, should be in or close to the city. They should not duplicate anything—school, recreation, entertainment, clinical services—that is available in the community. The child's entire experience should be one of testing himself in the very setting where he will one day live. The process demands that each child constantly examine the reality of his adjustment with his peers.

The first model clings to the traditional solution. Yet institutions that serve society's misfits have never experienced notable success. One by one, institutions have been abandoned by most of the other human services and replaced by community programs. The second model, still largely untested, moves corrections toward more adventurous and hopeful days.

Reception and Classification Centers

Reception and classification centers are relatively recent additions to the correctional scene. In earlier times there were no state systems, no central departments of correction. Each prison was a separate entity, usually managed by its own board, which reported directly to the governor. If the state had more than one institution, either geography or the judge determined the appropriate one for the offender. As the number and variety of institutions increased, classification systems and agencies for central control evolved. Still later, the need for reception and classification centers seemed apparent.

Not all such centers operating today are distinct and separate facilities. Quite the contrary. In most states, the reception and classification function is performed in a section of one of its institutions—usually a maximum security facility. Most new prisoners, therefore, start their correctional experience in the most confining, most severe, and most depressing part of the state's system. After a period of observation, testing, and interviewing, an assignment is made, supposedly reflecting the best marriage between the inmate's needs and the system's resources.

Today thirteen separate reception centers for adult felons (most of which are new) are in operation. Their designers have assigned priority to security on the premise that "a new fish is an unknown fish." Generally these institutions are the most depressing and regressive of all recently constructed correctional facilities in the United States, with the possible exception of county jails. Nowhere on the current correctional scene are there more bars, more barbed wire, more electronic surveillance devices, more clanging iron doors, and less activity and personal space. All this is justified on the grounds that the residents are still unknown and therefore untrustworthy. Moreover, their stay will be short.

A notable exception is worthy of brief description. Opened in 1967, the Reception and Medical Center at Lake Butler serves the State of Florida. The plant is campus style, with several widely separated buildings occupying fifty-two acres enclosed with a double cyclone fence with towers. There is a great deal of movement as inmates circulate between the classification building, gymnasium, dining room, clinic, canteen, craft shops, visiting area, and dormitories.

Housing is of two varieties. Three-quarters of the men are assigned to medium security units scattered around the campus. One maximum security building accommodates the rest.

Men not specifically occupied by the demands of the classification process are encouraged to take part in a variety of recreational and self-betterment activities conducted all over the campus. An open-air visiting patio supplements the indoor visiting facility that ordinarily is used only in inclement weather. Relationship between staff and inmates appears casual. Movement is not regimented. Morale appears high, and escapes are rare.

The contrast between this reception center and one in an adjacent state is vivid. In the Medical and Diagnostic Center at Montgomery, Alabama, the inmate spends the entire reception period in confinement except when he is being tested or interviewed. Closed circuit television replaces contact with correctional personnel—a contact especially needed during reception. In that center escapes and escape attempts are almost as common as suicide efforts. A visitor, observing the contrast between these two neighboring facilities, might speculate on the relative merits of the new correctional artifact vis-à-vis the responding human being, and be heartened that man is not yet obsolete in this technological age.

As physical plants contrast, so does the sophistication of the reception and classification process. Diagnostic processes in reception centers range from a medical examination and a single inmate-caseworker interview without privacy to a full battery of tests, interviews, and psychiatric and medical examinations, supplemented by an orientation program. The process takes from three to six weeks, but one competent warden feels that four or five days should be sufficient. It seems unlikely, considering the limitations of contemporary behavioral science, that the process warrants more than a week.

The Future of Institutions

For Adults

From the standpoint of rehabilitation and reintegration, the major adult institutions operated by the states represent the least promising component of corrections. This report takes the position that more offenders should be diverted from such adult institutions, that much of their present populations should be transferred to community-based programs, and that the construction of new major institutions should be postponed until such diversion and transfers have been achieved and the need for additional institutions is clearly established.

However, the need for some type of institution for adults cannot be denied. There will always be a hard core of intractable, possibly unsalvageable offenders who must be managed in secure facilities, of which there are already more than enough to meet the needs of the foreseeable future. These institutions have and will have a difficult task indeed. Nevertheless, the nature of imprisonment does not have to be as destructive in the future as it has been.

With growth of community-based corrections, emphasis on institutional programs should decline. However, the public has not yet fully supported the emerging community-oriented philosophy. An outdated philosophy continues to dominate the adult institution, thus perpetuating a number of contradictory assumptions and beliefs concerning institutional effectiveness.

One assumption is that the committed offender needs to change to become a functioning member of the larger law-abiding society. But it seems doubtful that such a change really can take place in the institution as it now exists.

Another assumption is that the correctional system wants to change. Even though research results have demonstrated the need for new approaches, traditional approaches have created inbred and self-perpetuating systems. Reintegration as an objective has become entangled with the desire for institutional order, security, and personal prestige. As long as the system exists chiefly to serve its own needs, any impending change represents a threat.

Correctional personnel who are assigned responsibility for the "treatment" of the committed offender traditionally have taken the attitude that they know what is best for him and are best qualified to prescribe solutions to his problem. Descriptions of offender problems compiled by personnel also have been traditional—lack of vocational skills, educational deficiencies, bad attitudes, etc.

Aside from the contradictory assumptions prevailing in the correctional field, adult institutions are plagued by physical shortcomings described previously in this chapter. Adult facilities generally are architecturally antiquated, overcrowded, inflexible, too large for effective management, and geographically isolated from metropolitan areas where resources are most readily available.

A major problem in adult institutions is the long sentence, often related more directly to the type of crime committed than to the offender. How can vocational training and other skill-oriented programs be oriented to a job market twenty years hence? What should be done with a man who is capable of returning to society but must spend many more years in an institution?

Conversely, individuals sentenced to a minimum term often need a great deal of assistance. Little can be accomplished at the institutional level except to make the offender aware of his needs and to provide a link with community resources. For these offenders, the real assistance should be performed by community resource agencies.

Correctional administrators of the future will face a different institutional population from today's. As a result of diversion and community-based programs, the committed offender can be expected to be older, more experienced in criminal activity, and more difficult to work with. The staff will have to be more skilled, and smaller caseload ratios will have to be maintained. Personnel standards will change because of new needs.

If a new type of institution is to be substituted for the prison, the legitimate needs of society, the system, and the committed offender must be considered.

For Juveniles and Youths

Use of state institutions for juveniles and youths should be discouraged. The emerging trend in treatment of young offenders is diversion from the criminal justice system. When diversion is not possible, the focus should be on community programs.

This emphasis reverses assumptions as to how youthful offenders should be treated. Previously there was a heavy emphasis on the use of institutional settings. Now it is believed that young offenders should be sent to an institution only when it can be demonstrated clearly that retaining them in the community would be a threat to the safety of others.

The nature of social institutions is such, however, that there is considerable delay between a change in philosophy and a change in practice. Despite major redirection of manpower and money toward both diversion and community programs, progress is slow. Use of major state institutions for juvenile delinquents is declining, but it seems likely that these facilities will continue to be used for some offenders for some time. Therefore, standards for their improvement and operation are required.

Arguments for diversion and alternatives to incarceration largely are negative, stemming from overwhelming disenchantment with the institution as a setting for reducing criminal behavior. Many arguments for community-based programs meet the test of common sense on their own merits, but are strengthened greatly by the failing record of "correctional" institutions. As long as institutional "treatment" is a dispositional alternative for the courts, there must be a continuing effort to minimize the inherently negative aspects and to support and maximize the positive features that distinguish community programs from institutionalization.

The failure of major juvenile and youth institutions to reduce crime is incontestable. Recidivism rates, imprecise as they may be, are notoriously high. The younger the person when entering an institution, the longer he is institutionalized, and the farther he progresses into the criminal justice system, the greater are his chances of failure. It is important to distinguish some basic reasons why institutional programs continuously have failed to reduce the commission of crime by those released.

Lack of clarity as to goals and objectives has had marked influence on institutional programs. Programs in youth institutions have reflected a variety of objectives, many of which are conflicting. Both society and the other components of the criminal justice system have contributed to this confusion.

A judge may order a juvenile committed as an example to others or because there are no effective alternatives. The police officer, whose function is to provide community protection, may demand incarceration for the temporary protection it provides for the public. The public may be fearful and incensed at the seriousness of an offense and react by seeking retribution and punishment. To the offender, commitment means he has been banished from society.

Institutions do succeed in punishing, but they do not deter. They protect the community temporarily, but that protection does not last. They relieve the community of responsibility by removing the young offender, but they make successful reintegration unlikely. They change the committed offender, but the change is more likely to be negative than positive.

While it is true that society's charges to the correctional institution have not always been clear or consistent, corrections cannot continue to try to be all things to all publics. Nor can the institution continue to deny responsibility for articulation of goals or objectives. The historical tendency of corrections to view itself as the passive arm of other state agents has resulted in almost total preoccupation with maintaining order and avoiding scandal.

Youth institutions have implicitly accepted the objectives of isolation, control, and punishment, as evidenced by their operations, policies, and programs. They must seek ways to become more attuned to their role of reducing criminal behavior. That the goal of youth institutions is reduction of criminal behavior and reintegration into society must be made explicit. This pronouncement is not sufficient to eliminate their negative aspects, but it is a necessary first step.

Another contributing factor to the failure of major youth institutions has been their closed nature. The geographic location of most institutions is incompatible with a mission of services delivery. Their remote locations make family visiting difficult and preclude the opportunity of utilizing the variety of community services available in metropolitan areas. They have been staffed largely with local residents, who, unlike the young offenders, are predominantly white, provincial, and institutionally oriented.

Most existing institutions were built before the concept of community programing gained acceptance. They were built to last; and most have outlasted the need for which they were established. For economic reasons, they were constructed to hold large numbers of people securely. Their structure has restricted the ability to change and strongly influenced the overall direction of institutional programing.

Many administrative policies and procedures in youth institutions also have contributed to their closed nature. The emphasis on security and control of so many people resulted in heavy restrictions on visiting, mail, phone calls, and participation with community residents in various activities and programs. For reasons that are now archaic, most institutions have been totally segregated by sex for both residents and staff.

All these factors have worked together to create an environment within the institution totally unlike that from which the population comes or to which it will return. The youths, often alienated already, who find themselves in such institutions experience feelings of abandonment, hostility, and despair. Because many residents come from delinquent backgrounds, a delinquent subculture flourishes in the closed institution. This in turn reinforces administrative preoccupation with security and control.

Large institutions are dehumanizing. They foster an increased degree of dependency that is contrary to behavior expected in the community. They force youths to participate in activities of little interest or use to them. They foster resident-staff relationships that are superficial, transient, and meaningless. They try to change the young offender without knowing how to effect that change or how to determine whether it occurs.

With the shift in emphasis to changing behavior and reintegration, the major institution's role in the total criminal-justice system must be reexamined. Changing that role from one of merely housing society's failure to one of sharing responsibility for their reintegration requires an attitude change by the corrections profession. The historical inclination to accept total responsibility for offenders and the resulting isolation clearly are counterproductive.

The public must be involved in the correctional process. Public officials, community groups, universities, and planning bodies must be involved in program development and execution. Such sharing of responsibility will be a new operational role for institutions. This refocus implies substantive changes in policy, program direction, and organization.

The institution should be operated as a resource to meet specific needs without removing responsibility for the offender from the community. Direct involvement of family, school, work, and other social institutions and organizations can have a marked positive impact on decreasing the flow of delinquents into corrections and on the correctional process.

Community responsibility for offenders implies more than institutional tours or occasional parties. It implies participation in programs with institutional residents both inside the institution and in the community. Educational, recreational, religious, civic, counseling, and vocational programs, regardless of where they are held, should have both institutional and community participants. Public acceptance of community-based programs is necessary, especially when they operate next door.

The institution always has existed in a changing world, but it has been slow to reflect change. Correctional administrators require the impetus of community development to respond and adapt to changing conditions and needs.

As diversionary and community programs expand, major institutions for juvenile and youthful offenders face an increasingly difficult task. These programs remove from the institution the most stable individuals, who previously had a moderating influence on others' behavior. The most hardened or habitual offender will represent an increasing proportion of those committed to institutions where adequate services can be provided by a professional staff, trained paraprofessionals, and volunteers. All staff and participants must be prepared to serve a "helping" role.

More committed offenders than ever before have drug-abuse problems. The ability to cope with this phenomenon in an environment isolated from the community has not been demonstrated. The aid of community residents must be enlisted in innovating, experimenting, and finding workable solutions.

Few treatment opportunities have been offered for the intractable offender. Common practice is to move such individuals from the general population and house them in segregation or adjustment centers. The concept of an ongoing treatment program for this group is recent but will become increasingly important as institutional populations change. The understanding and tolerance of the community will be crucial in working with these individuals.

It is no surprise that institutions have not been successful in reducing crime; the mystery is that they have not contributed even more to increasing it. Meaningful changes can take place only by attention to the factors discussed here. Concentrated effort should be devoted to long-range planning, based on research and evaluation. Correctional history has demonstrated clearly that tinkering with the system by changing individual program areas without attention to the larger problems can achieve only incidental and haphazard improvement.

The Correctional Dilemma

A major obstacle to the operation of an effective correctional program is that today's practitioners are forced to use the means of an older time. Dissatisfaction with correctional programs is related to the permanence of yesterday's institutions—both physical and ideological. We are saddled with the physical remains of last century's prisons, and with an ideological legacy that equates criminal offenses with either moral or psychological illness. This legacy leads inexorably to two conclusions: the sick person must be given "treatment," and "treatment" should be in an institution removed from the community.

It is time to question this ideological inheritance. If New York has thirty-one times as many armed robberies as London, if Philadelphia has forty-four times as many criminal homicides as Vienna, if Chicago has more burglaries than all of Japan, if Los Angeles has more drug addiction than all of Western Europe, then we must concentrate on the social and economic ills of New York, Philadelphia, Chicago, Los Angeles, and America.

This has not been our approach. We concentrate on "correcting" and "treating" the offender. This is a poor version of the "medical" model. What is needed is a good version of the "public health" model, an attempt to treat causes rather than symptoms.

If the war against crime is to be won, it will be won ultimately by correcting the conditions in our society that produce such an inordinate amount of criminal activity. These conditions include high unemployment, irrelevant education, racism, poor housing, family disintegration, and government corruption. These, among others, form the freshets that make the streams that form the rivers that flood our criminal-justice system and ultimately its correctional institutions.

Public policy during the coming decades should shift emphasis from the offender and concentrate on providing maximum protection to the public. A more just society, offering opportunity to all segments, would provide that protection. The prison, called by whatever name, will not. It is obsolete, cannot be reformed, should not be perpetuated through the false hope of forced "treatment"; it should be repudiated as useless for any purpose other than locking away persons who are too dangerous to be allowed at large in free society.

For the latter purpose we already have more prison space than we need or will need in the foreseeable future. Except where unusual justification can be proved, there is no need to build additional major institutions—reform schools, reformatories, prisons, or whatever euphemisms may be used to designate them—for at least ten years. Further, the use of major state institutions for confinement of juveniles should be totally discontinued in favor of local community-based programs and facilities.

In view of the dearth of valid data to substantiate the rehabilitative effectiveness of institutional programs, we have no basis for designing more effective physical facilities. Under these circumstances, new construction would represent merely a crystallization and perpetuation of the past with all its futility.

Under prevailing practices, institutional construction costs are excessive. They now run as high as $30,000 to $45,000 per inmate in some jurisdictions. Costs of operation vary widely, from $1000 per year per inmate to more than $12,000.[6] Construction of new major institutions should be deferred until effective correctional programs to govern planning and design can be identified, and until the growth of a more selected inmate population dictates. The potentially tremendous savings should be expended more productively in improving probation, parole, and community-based programs and facilities.

Planning New Institutions

Unusually convincing proof of need should certainly be required as a logical precedent to planning a new institution. Yet there are many impediments to recognizing this rationality in planning. One of them is fragmentation of the criminal-justice system.

The traditional division of the entire system into several parts—police, courts, institutions, and field services—and more fundamentally, the concept that the criminal-justice system exists apart from society and unto itself, have created an administrative and organizational climate that allows the construction of new institutions with little or no real consideration of other possible solutions.

The most fundamental question to be addressed in the planning of institutions is the reason for their existence. They obviously represent the harshest, most drastic end of the spectrum of possible correctional response.

Different states have different philosophies. Some rely heavily on incarceration, others do not (see Table 1-3). Some concentrate on size and security; others build more varied facilities.

This absence of correctional consistency poses a serious handicap to the administration of an equitable criminal-justice system.

Table 1-3
Comparative Use of State Correctional Institutions

Ratio of Prisoners in State Institutions to State Population	Number of States with Ratio
1 to 2501 and over	1
1 to 2001 - 2500	4
1 to 1501 - 2000	8
1 to 1001 - 1500	21
1 to 501 - 1000	16

Sources: Data from 1970 Census and ACA 1971 Directory.

If protection of society is seen as the purpose of the criminal-justice system, and if it is felt that this protection requires sequestration of some offenders, then institutions must exist to carry out this purpose. Immediately the planner is confronted with the question, "What kind of institutions?"

Of fundamental importance to any planning are the values and assumptions dictating the policies. Programs and structural responses are fixed by those policies. Their underlying values affect all subsequent planning and implementation. For nearly two centuries this nation has used the correctional institution as its primary response to illegal behavior. It is long past time for legislators, administrators, and planners to collect and examine the results of this vast institutional experience. Scholarly evaluation currently available suggests that our prisons have been deficient in at least three crucial areas—conception, design, and operation. These areas and two others—location and size—should be given serious consideration in all correctional planning.

Conception

The correctional institution has been poorly conceived, in that it is intended to hide rather than heal. It is the punitive, repressive arm whose function is to do the system's "dirty work."

Design

The designers of most correctional institutions generally have been preoccupied with security. The result is that they create demoralizing and dehumanizing environments. The facility design precludes any experience that could foster social growth or behavioral improvement. Indeed, institutions more often breed hostility and resentment and strip inmates of dignity, choice, and a sense of self-worth.

Operation

The punitive function and design of correctional institutions is reflected in their operation. Containment and control command a lion's share of resources. Activities aimed at modifying behavior and attitudes or at developing skills often are limited or absent altogether. The daily routine is dominated by frustration, idleness, and resentment, punctuated by the aggressive behavior such conditions breed.

Correctional institutions often are designed and constructed with little consideration of their place in the overall corrections system. Some system needs are duplicated, while others go unmet. Many administrators of maximum and medium security centers state that only 20 to 25 percent of their inmates need that level of security. Yet centers offering community programs are extremely scarce or nonexistent.

Improper design may prevent an institution from fulfilling its assigned function. Use of dormitories in maximum security prisons, for example, permits physical violence and exploitation to become a way of life. Conversely, inmates who are not considered a threat to others may be housed in single inside cells, with fixed furniture, security-type plumbing, and grilled fronts and doors.

Institutions intended as "correction centers" may have no more than two or three classrooms and a small number of poorly equipped shops to serve as many as a thousand inmates. This is token rehabilitation. Programs and facilities provided by "centers" that hold persons twenty-four hours a day from one year to many years may be totally inadequate for occupying the inmate's time. Here idleness is a way of life.

Lack of funds, haphazard planning, faulty construction, and inadequate programing and staffing all may account for failure to design and build institutions to serve their assigned functions adequately. Fund allocations may be insufficient because costs are unknown. Space may be programed without knowledge of the actual needs for a particular activity. Planners and programers may develop schemes without consulting architects and engineers. Architects may be engaged without being given adequate guidelines.

The architect often is inexperienced in design and construction of correctional facilities. To overcome this lack he may visit an institution serving an entirely different purpose. Errors are repeated and compounded because few institutions are worthy of emulation. New mistakes and inconsistencies are built on top of existing ones.

Location

Location has a strong influence on an institution's total operation. Most locations are chosen for reasons bearing no relationship to rationality or planning. Results of poor site selection include inaccessibility, staffing difficulty, and lack of community orientation.

In the early days of America's prison history, penitentiaries were built where the people were—Philadelphia, Pittsburgh, Columbus, Trenton, Baltimore, and Richmond. The urban location had nothing to do with the prevailing theory of penology. The idea was to isolate the prisoner—and he was isolated, even though his prison walls pressed tightly against the city streets.

During the last century, rural settings usually were chosen for new correctional institutions. This remoteness may have been relatively unimportant when America was predominantly a farm country. Life styles, rural and urban, had not yet hardened in their contrasting molds. At a time when the prison was viewed almost exclusively as a place of quarantine, where better than the remote reaches of a state?

These no longer are valid reasons, nor have they been for a quarter of a century. America has become increasingly urban. Life styles and values, born not only of population diversity but of ethnic differences, create gaps of understanding wider than the miles separating city dwellers from farmers.

The rhetoric, if not the purpose, of corrections also has changed. The ultimate objective now being expressed no longer is quarantine but reintegration—the adjustment of the offender in and to the real world.

But in 1975 correctional institutions still are being built in some of the most isolated parts of the states. Powerful political leaders may know little about "reintegration," but they know a pork barrel when they see one. Urbanites resist the location of prisons in the cities. They may agree on the need for "reintegration" of the ex-offender, but this objective is forgotten when city dwellers see a prison in their midst as increasing street crime and diminishing property values.

The serious disadvantages of continuing to construct correctional institutions in sparsely populated areas include:

1. The impossibility of using urban academic and social services or medical and psychiatric resources of the city.

2. The difficulty of recruiting professional staff members—teachers, psychologists, sociologists, social workers, researchers, nurses, dentists, and physicians—to work in rural areas.

3. The prolonged interruption of offenders' contacts with friends and relatives, which are important to the reintegration process.

4. The absence of meaningful work- and study-release programs.

5. Most important, the consignment of corrections to the status of a divided house dominated by rural white guards and administrators unable to understand or communicate with black, Chicano, Puerto Rican, and other urban minority inmates.

Other human services long since have moved away from dependence upon the congregate rural institution. Almshouses of old have been replaced with family assistance; workhouses, with employment insurance; orphanages, with foster homes and aid to dependent children; colonies for imbeciles, with day care and sheltered workshops. Drugs have made obsolete the dismal epileptic facilities and the tuberculosis sanitariums of yesteryear. Asylums are rapidly yielding to community mental-health approaches.

All of these human services changed because isolated institutions proved to be unsuccessful, expensive, and even counterproductive as responses to specific human problems. They also changed because better treatment methods were developed, making the isolated institutions largely obsolete and treatment in the natural community setting feasible and advisable.

And so it should be with corrections.

Size

Traditionally, institutions have been very large, often accommodating up to two and three thousand inmates. The inevitable consequence has been development of an organizational and operational monstrosity. Separation of large numbers of people from society and mass confinement have produced a management problem of staggering dimensions. The tensions and frustrations inherent in imprisonment are magnified by the herding together of troubled people. Merely "keeping the lid on" has become the real operational goal. The ideal of reform or rehabilitation has succumbed to that of sheer containment, a goal of limited benefit to society.

The usual response to bigness has been regimentation and uniformity. Individuals become subjugated to the needs generated by the institution. Uniformity is translated into depersonalization. A human being ceases to be identified by the usual points of reference, such as his name, his job, or family role. He becomes a number, identified by the cellblock where he sleeps. Such practices reflect maladaptation resulting from size.

Almost every warden and superintendent states that his institution is too big. This hugeness has been the product of many factors, including economics, land availability, population of the jurisdiction, the influence of Parkinson's Law, and an American fetish that equates bigness with quality. (A half century ago, one state built the "world's biggest wall," only to bow to another jurisdiction that gleefully surpassed it two years later.)

Any attempt to establish an optimum size is a meaningless exercise unless size is related directly to the institution's operation. The institution should be small enough to enable the superintendent to know every inmate's name and to relate personally to each person in his charge. Unless the inmate has contact with the person who has policy responsibility and who can assist him with his personal difficulties and requests, he will feel that the facility's prime purpose is to serve the system and not him. The reverse also is true: if the superintendent does not have contact with the inmates, his decisions will be determined by demands of the system and not by inmate needs.

The size of the inmate housing unit is of critical importance because it must satisfy several conditions: security, counseling, inmate social and informal activities, and formal program requirements. Although security conditions traditionally have been met with hardware and electronic equipment, these means contradict the purposes of corrections and should be deemphasized. Security is maintained better by providing small housing units where personal supervision and inmate-staff contact are possible and disturbances can be contained easily.

Informal counseling is easier in the small housing unit, because the inmate-counselor ratio is not as threatening as in the massive cellblock and negative group pressure on the inmate is minimized.

Many institutions are poorly cooled, heated, and ventilated. Lighting levels may be below acceptable limits. Bathroom facilities often are insanitary, too few, and too public. Privacy and personal space hardly ever are provided, because of overriding preoccupation with security. Without privacy and personal space, inmates become tense, and many begin to react with hostility. As tension and hostility grow, security requirements increase; and a negative cycle is put into play.

A Review of Correctional Standards

Correctional practice in the United States seems to defy standardization. Each state is virtually independent in its choice of correctional options. The U.S. Bureau of Prisons operates federal prisons, and has no mandate to regulate state institutions. The National Bureau of Standards has made studies for corrections but has no means of influencing change. The Law Enforcement Assistance Administration (LEAA), under the provisions of the Safe Streets Act, has provided the impetus for state and local governments to determine their own approaches to corrections and other criminal-justice problems. Consequently, the efforts of LEAA in large part have been directed to monitoring the fiscal and not the programmatic aspects of its grants.

In 1970 Congress created a new section of the Omnibus Crime Control and Safe Streets Act. This section (Part E) authorized LEAA to make grants to states that incorporated "advanced techniques" and "advanced practices" in a comprehensive state corrections plan. The standards in this report can serve as possible guideposts for the advanced techniques and practices. This promise of corrections reform will be met, and Part E funds can be used by states to implement the standards postulated in this chapter and this book.

The Constitution of the United States reserves to the states the power to promote the health, safety, morals, and general welfare of its citizens—by so-called police power—and in large part because of this power and the implications of federalism, the legislative and executive branches of the national government never have been authoritative in establishing or enforcing correctional standards. The judiciary is becoming so. The federal judiciary, however, is drawing upon the "due process" and "cruel and unusual punishment" amendments to the Constitution to define new standards for corrections, and, more important, is enforcing them. Judges see the Constitution as the ultimate source of certain correctional standards articulated in various court decisions. Thus in *Holt v. Sarver,* 309 F. Supp. 362 (E.D. Ark. 1970), aff'd., 442 F. 2d. 304 (8th Cir. 1971), the district court, with the ultimate concurrence of the Federal Court of Appeals, held that imprisonment in the Arkansas State Prison System constituted "cruel and unusual punishment," and gave the state two years to correct the situation or release all prisoners then incarcerated in the state facilities.

Some statutes also are a source of standards. Every jurisdiction has its own laws spelling out certain requirements for the correctional establishment. A few examples show they usually are explicit.

All prisoners who are suffering from any disease, shall be segregated from the prisoners who are in good physical condition.

All prisoners who are found or considered to be habitual criminals, evil-inclined, shall be segregated, and not allowed to be among or mingle with those of opposite inclination.

Every warden shall provide that such person shall have, at least two hours daily, physical exercise in the open.

No prisoner shall be confined in a cell occupied by more than one individual.[7]

These and other standard-setting statutes are honored most frequently in the breach. In April 1972, for example, the Court of Common Pleas in Philadelphia found in that city's prison system 161 violations of state statutes. Together, said the court, these transgressions added up to the violation of those provisions of both state and federal constitutions dealing with cruel and unusual punishment.[8]

The United Nations also has developed policy statements that attempt to set standards for correctional practices. Usually they are broad, idealistic, and ignored.

Private groups have contributed richly to the articulation of correctional standards. The objectives of these groups vary. An association of correctional professionals will have a different orientation than a group of civil libertarians or a manufacturer of security equipment. Each promotes those standards most in accord with its own objectives. The presence of so many interest groups, coupled with the lack of specific enforceable legislation at the state level, has resulted in an unorganized profusion of standards that sometimes are helpful but often are confusing. None provides the comfort of unquestioned authority or substantiated research.

Currently existing standards seem to be more oriented to administration than to goals or to offenders. This is quite natural because neither inmates nor philosophers usually serve on principal standard-writing committees. Individuals who do serve have careers and professional fortunes tied up in the operation of institutions. Results are colored by the limits of vision individuals bring to the task. Fundamental, essential changes at the goal level likely will come from a body not restricted by an operational orientation. Change, for a variety of reasons, seldom comes from within, and hardly ever without resistance.

In view of the foregoing it appears inappropriate to set forth formal standards applying to the creation of new major institutions. Despite such arguments, construction of additional institutions probably will continue to be considered by some jurisdictions. A standard applying to such planning, therefore, is suggested herein, but it can be no more than a statement of principles.

More appropriate is the standard for modification of existing institutions to provide a more humane environment for persons who must be confined. If proof cannot be offered that these institutions are serving a rehabilitative purpose, they must at least be operated to minimize the damage they do to those confined. If the institutions can even be neutralized in this respect, it will be an accomplishment far exceeding any that has occurred so far in American penology. It also will be an essential landmark in the quest for a solution of the correctional riddle.[9]

Planning New Correctional Institutions

Each correctional agency administering state institutions for juvenile or adult offenders should adopt immediately a policy of not building new major institutions for juveniles under any circumstances, and not building new institutions for adults unless an analysis of the total criminal justice and adult corrections systems produces a clear finding that no alternative is possible. If this effort proves conclusively that a new institution for adults is essential, these factors should characterize the planning and design process:

1. A collaborative planning effort should identify the purpose of the physical plant.

2. The size of the inmate population of the projected institution should be small enough to allow security without excessive regimentation, surveillance equipment, or repressive hardware.

3. The location of the institution should be selected on the basis of its proximity to:

    a. The communities from which the inmates come.

    b. Areas capable of providing or attracting adequate numbers of qualified line and professional staff members of racial and ethnic origin compatible with the inmate population, and capable of supporting staff life styles and community service requirements.

   c. Areas that have community services and activities to support the correctional goal, including social services, schools, hospitals, universities, and employment opportunities.

   d. The courts and auxiliary correctional agencies.

   e. Public transportation.

4. The physical environment of a new institution should be designed with consideration to:

   a. Provision of privacy and personal space.

   b. Minimization of noise.

   c. Reduction of sensory deprivation.

   d. Encouragement of constructive inmate-staff relationships.

   e. Provision of adequate utility services.

5. Provision also should be made for:

   a. Dignified facilities for inmate visiting.

   b. Individual and group counseling.

   c. Education, vocational training, and workshops designed to accommodate small numbers of inmates and to facilitate supervision.

   d. Recreation yards for each housing unit as well as larger recreational facilities accessible to the entire inmate population.

   e. Medical and hospital facilities.[10]

Commentary

The facts set forth earlier in this chapter lead logically to the conclusion that no new institutions for adults should be built, and existing institutions for juveniles should be closed. The primary purpose to be served in dealing with juveniles is their rehabilitation and reintegration, a purpose that cannot be served satisfactorily by state institutions. In fact, commitment to a major institution is more likely to confirm juveniles in delinquent and criminal patterns of behavior.

Similar considerations apply to adults, but it is recognized that for the safety of the public some offenders must be locked away. The Commission considers that sufficient security-type institutions already exist for this purpose. However, it is conceded that in rare instances a state may not have any institution that can be modified for satisfactory service, and further, may have its existing facilities condemned by court order.

The decision to build a new major institution for adults should be the result of a planning process that reviews the purposes of corrections, assesses the physical plants and operations of existing institutions and programs in light of these purposes, examines all possible alternatives, and identifies a clear and indispensable role for a new institution. The process should consider corrections as part of a broader human service network and as an integral system, rather than an aggregate of isolated entities.

The population of existing institutions and their operation should be examined to evaluate the appropriateness and effectiveness of programs with reference to inmate needs, particularly the need for custody. All inmates currently held in institutions who do not require confinement should be removed to community programs. This procedure may make it possible to close work camps and prison farms and to release substantial numbers of people from these facilities and medium security institutions. Inmates housed in maximum security prisons but not requiring high security should be transferred to medium security institutions or released to community facilities and programs if they do not constitute a threat to others.

If this process establishes a clearly identifiable need for a new physical plant, its planning and design should include the simultaneous participation of administrators, architects, planners, inmates, community representatives, and those involved in developing and operating inmate programs and activities.

This collaborative process should set forth the purpose of the new physical plant—in terms of its correctional role, type of inmate population, geographic area to be served, and its relationship to community-based transitional programs and to other elements of the correctional system. The design of the new institution should fit this purpose.

The projected institution should be small enough to enable the superintendent to develop a personal relationship with each inmate. It should facilitate the effective operation of its programs and the efficient use of its professional staff. It should also fit in with its environment with respect to the size of the buildings and the level of activity they generate. The number of inmates housed in a single spatially discrete unit should not exceed twenty-six, and for special program requirements, the maximum should be lower.

In states where it is feasible, a location for the institution not more than an hour's travel time from the homes of a majority of its inmates should be selected. The surrounding area should be able to support the community-program emphasis of the institution and offer services and a life style attractive to staff. The institution should not be located in small, closed communities with limited services and poor schools and recreational and cultural activities. It should be near enough to courts and auxiliary correctional agencies to facilitate the transfer of inmates to and from jails and courts and supporting programs. It should also be located on public transportation routes to facilitate visits to inmates by families and friends.

The design of the institution should provide for privacy and personal space by the use of single rooms with a floor area of at least 80 square feet per man, and a clear floor-to-ceiling height of 8 feet. Dormitories should not be used. All rooms should have solid fronts and solid doors with glazed observation panels. Toilets and showers should have modesty screens, The furnishings provided should enable the inmate to personalize his room.

Noise should be minimized by eliminating sources, placing sound barriers between activity spaces, decreasing size of spaces, and using noise-absorbing materials. Noise levels should be low enough not to interfere with normal human activities—sleeping, dining, thinking, conversing, and reading.

Sensory deprivation may be reduced by providing variety in terms of space, surface textures and colors, and both artificial and natural lighting. The institution should be spatially organized to offer a variety of movement options, both enclosed and outdoor. Lighting in individual rooms should be occupant-controlled as well as centrally controlled. All rooms should have outside windows with areas of 10 square feet or more. The setting should be "normal" and human, with spaces and materials as similar as possible to their noninstitution counterparts.

Constructive inmate-staff relationships may be encouraged by designing activity spaces to accommodate only the number of inmates that can be appropriately supervised. (For example, dining halls holding more than one hundred should be avoided.) Physical separation of staff and inmates should be minimized.

Utility services should furnish adequate heating, air conditioning, and ventilation for all areas including inmate housing. Temperatures should not exceed 80° at any time or 70° during normal sleeping hours. Adequate toilet facilities should be provided in all areas. Lighting levels should be 50-75 footcandles.

Program spaces should be designed to facilitate their special purposes. Visiting areas should be large enough to avoid undue restrictions on visiting hours and to provide dignified, private surroundings without undue emphasis on security. Separate areas should be provided for individual and group counseling. Education, vocational training, and work areas should be designed for small groups of inmates and furnished with modern equipment laid out to facilitate supervision. Outdoor recreation spaces should be provided for each housing unit, with larger spaces that will accommodate the entire inmate population. Medical and hospital facilities should meet American hospital accreditation standards, even though they may not be large enough for formal accreditation (usually requiring more than twenty-five beds).

**National Advisory Commission on
Criminal Justice Standards
and Goals**

Corrections Task Force

Judge Joe Frazier Brown
Attorney at Law
San Antonio, Texas

Fred Allenbrand
Sheriff, Johnson County
Olathe, Kansas

Norman A. Carlson
Director, U.S. Bureau of Prisons
Washington, D.C.

Hubert M. Clements
Assistant Director, South Carolina
Department of Corrections
Columbia, S.C.

Roberta Dorn
Program Specialist,
Law Enforcement Assistance Administration
Washington, D.C.

Edith Flynn
Associate Professor, University of Illinois
Urbana, Ill.

Eddie Harrison
Director, Pre-trial Intervention Project
Baltimore, Md.

Bruce Johnson
Chairman, Board of Prison Terms and Paroles
Olympia, Wash.

Lance Jones
District Attorney
Sheboygan County, Wis.

Oliver J. Keller, Jr.
Director, Division of Youth Services
Tallahassee, Fla.

George G. Killinger
Director, Institute of Contemporary Corrections
and Behavioral Sciences
Huntsville, Texas

William G. Nagel
Director, The American Foundation, Inc.
Philadelphia, Pa.

Rita O'Grady
Director, Family Court Center
Toledo, Ohio

Sanger B. Powers
Administrator, Division of
Corrections
Madison, Wis.

Peter Preiser
State Director of Probation
Albany, N.Y.

Rosemary C. Sarri
Professor, National Assessment Study
of Correctional Programs for Juvenile
and Youthful Offenders
Ann Arbor, Mich.

Saleem A. Shah
Chief, Center for Studies of Crime
and Delinquency,
National Institute of Mental Health
Rockville, Md.

John A. Wallace
Director, Office of Probation for the
Courts of New York City
New York, N.Y.

Martha Wheeler
President-Designate, American
Correctional Association
Ohio Reformatory for Women
Marysville, Ohio

References

1. For a history of these developments, see David Rothman, *The Discovery of the Institution: Social Order and Disorder in the New Republic* (Little, Brown, 1971), chs. 3 and 4.

2. Harry Elmer Barnes, *The Story of Punishment* (Patterson-Smith, 1972), ch. 6.

3. Data from American Correctional Association, *1971 Directory of Correctional Institutions and Agencies of the United States of America, Canada, and Great Britain* (College Park, Md.: ACA, 1971).

4. Gustave de Beaumont and Alexis de Tocqueville, *On the Penitentiary System in the United States and Its Application in France*, H.R. Lantz, ed. (Southern Illinois University Press, 1964), p. 48.

5. ACA, 1971 Directory.

6. Data derived from a two-year study of more than 100 institutions by the American Foundation Institute of Corrections.

7. Purdon's Penn. Stat. Ann., Title 61, ch. 1, secs. 2, 4, and 101.

8. Court of Common Pleas for the County of Philadelphia, Pennsylvania, February Term 1971 #71-2437, Complaint in Equity (Class Action), filed April 7, 1972.

9. Many of the standards that follow reflect the work of an intensive on-site study of over 100 of the newest correctional institutions made in 1971 by the American Foundation Institute of Corrections, Philadelphia. An extensive study with a multidisciplinary orientation, this project examined the relationship of correctional architecture and program. The experience and opinions of architects, psychologists, correctional administrators, officers, counselors, and inmates were used in the formulation of standards. A book based on the study is William G. Nagel, *The New Red Barn: A Critical Look at the Modern American Prison* (Walker, 1973).

10. Frederick Moyer and Edith Flynn, eds., *Correctional Environments* (Urbana: University of Illinois Department of Architecture, 1971).

2

Toward a New Criminology

Eugene Doleschal and Nora Klapmuts[a]

In *The Greening of America*, Charles Reich traces the historical development of three levels of consciousness in America.[1]

Consciousness I was characterized by a system of beliefs that held that success comes to those of moral character who work hard and practice self-denial. Its adherents today support political candidates who appear to possess moral virtues and who promise a return to the conditions of an earlier time, to law and order, lower taxes, reduction of government expenditures, and a general ethical revival among the people.

Consciousness II, often associated with liberalism, created the corporate state and an America in which the individual had to make his way in a world directed by others. It demanded sacrifices for a common good, the arrangement of things in a rational hierarchy of authority and responsibility, and the dedication of each individual to goals beyond himself. Its adherents today rely on social institutions to certify the meaning and value of their lives and subordinate private interests to the public interest. They are deeply committed to social reform and, above all, to the control of man and environment by technology, planning, administration, and rational ordering. Reich sees in Consciousness II a rejection of unfettered diversity and unresolved conflict.

Consciousness III maintains that the individual is the true reality, that it is a crime to become an instrument designed to accomplish an extrinsic end, to be alienated from oneself, to defer meaning to the future. It sees a society that is unjust to its poor and its minorities, run for the benefit of a privileged few, lacking in democracy and liberty, ugly and artificial. The central fact about Consciousness III is its assertion of the power to choose a way of life. Its adherents reject many of the laws, forms of authority, and assumptions that underlie our present political state and postulate respect for each individual, for his uniqueness and his privacy.

[a]Eugene Doleschal has been associated with the NCCD information office since its inception and assisted in organizing and developing a special staff responsible for abstracting and developing literature. He is responsible for *Crime and Delinquency Literature*, the only abstract journal of its kind in the United States. He has written numerous monographs and literature reviews on many crime and delinquency subjects.

Nora Klapmuts served as assistant director National Council on Crime and Delinquency information center from 1971 to 1973. She has written several monographs and literature reviews on various criminal justice subjects.

Stages of Criminology

The development of criminology and, with it, trends in the administration of criminal justice, parallel Reich's three levels of consciousness both historically and in basic assumptions. A distinct stage of criminology, in fact, can be found in each of Reich's levels, as a logical and integral part of each level. As in the case of Reich's consciousness levels, each stage of criminological development overlaps the other and there are individuals within each level who at least partly anticipate future levels.

Criminology I: The Classical School

The founding father of the first phase of modern criminology—the classical school—was Cesare Beccaria, whose *Treatise on Crimes and Punishments* established a standardized system of justice with a "tariff" to fit the severity of punishment to the gravity of the crime. Partly under his influence, eighteenth- and nineteenth-century criminal justice established "penitentiaries" and gave meaning and definition to such terms as penology, retribution, deterrence, and criminal responsibility, and to the criminal's ability to distinguish right from wrong. Criminology I, the classical school, was predominantly a servant and defender of society against its criminal predators, and placed the blame for crime (except in cases of criminal insanity) on the "moral turpitude" and lack of will power of the individual offender. Its method of crime control was punishment and incapacitation of the criminal, primarily through long periods of incarceration.

The classical school maintained that punishment is a deterrent and that it should cause enough fear, over and above the pleasure derived from the crime, to inhibit deviant behavior. Its proponents thought that punishment should be humane and reformative, and were responsible for the substitution of imprisonment for corporal punishment and torture. The classical school was a system of universal, abstract justice based on the assumption of free will.[2]

Those who still support the classical system of criminal justice believe that punishment should fit the crime and that criminals should be made to pay for their crimes. They demand a "crackdown" on criminals and protest their "mollycoddling" by courts and the penal system. They ignore the evidence that the most successful criminal predators are its cultural heroes (e.g., industrial robber barons), and that the mechanism of crime control often perpetrates the most harmful crimes.

Criminology II: The Positivist School

Criminology II began late in the nineteenth century as a reaction to the abstract justice of the classicists. The positivists challenged the idea of free will and maintained that the treatment must fit the criminal. The positivists view man and his behavior as determined and regard criminals as ill or deprived. The role of penology is to provide the offender with treatment and a cure for his deviance.[3]

Modern correction is experiencing the full impact of the positivist school in its efforts to "treat" and "rehabilitate" the criminal. Treatment approaches have taken myriad forms, including individual psychotherapy and counseling, group therapy, vocational training, and intensive community intervention and supervision. Some treaters recognize no limits to the extent they may go in attempting to rehabilitate the offender.[4] To the treatment spokesmen, whatever is wrong with correctional policies today could be corrected by expanding and intensifying treatment, by using more individualized treatment (finding exactly the "right" treatment for each offender), or by treating the offender in a more normal, noninstitutional environment. There are some who continue to assert, in reference to past efforts that have failed, that treatment has never really been given a fair chance. So strong is the faith in the potential of treatment that repeated efforts are made to find effective approaches to offender rehabilitation, even in the face of growing evidence that criminality and recidivism apparently cannot be "cured."

The primary underlying assumption of the treatment model is that criminal or delinquent behavior is merely a symptom of underlying maladjustment. Theories about the causes of such maladjustment changed over the years from a belief in the biological or psychological abnormality of deviants to a focus on the offender as a product of social dysfunctions, culture conflict, unavailable opportunities, or poverty and slum living. But while the implications for correction of offenders changed (from attempting to alter the criminal personality to trying to compensate for lacks in his social situation), the focus of attention remained the offender, and correction still worked to change him or his life situation to prevent repetition of his criminal behavior.

Criminology III: The Interactionist School

Still largely unknown to the majority of correctional practitioners today, a new criminological and correctional philosophy is slowly gaining acceptance both in the United States and abroad. Originating in Scandinavia, the new philosophy rejects the treatment ideology on several grounds, including the practical grounds of ineffectiveness: the magic pill to cure recidivism cannot be found because the "ailment" does not exist. True successes in rehabilitation have been virtually nonexistent. A survey of all studies of correctional treatment published between 1945 and 1967 found that the present array of correctional treatment efforts has no appreciable effect—either positive or negative—on the recidivism rates of convicted offenders.[5] In another review of numerous correctional programs, Robison and Smith concluded that there is no evidence to support claims of superior rehabilitative efficacy of any correctional alternative over another.[6] This conclusion is supported by the most sophisticated research studies: generally, the more rigorously scientific the methodology the less likely is success to be reported.

The treatment ideology is rejected on legal grounds, as enforced treatment has led to the disregard of civil liberties, and as it has come to be viewed as often more punitive than punishment under the classical system. The treatment philosophy clearly has not resulted in more humanitarian handling of the offender.[7]

Most important, the ideology of treatment to fit the offender is being rejected because studies of "hidden" or undetected crime of the past decade have challenged the traditional distinction between criminals and noncriminals, showing that those who become officially known as criminals are merely a small biased sample of the universe of persons who commit crimes selected to fulfill a scapegoat function. In a report to the directors of criminological research institutes of the Council of Europe, B. Kutchinsky sums it up as follows: "What makes a person "criminal" is not the fact that he has committed a crime (because non-criminals have done that also) but the fact that he was caught, tried, convicted, and punished."[8]

Hidden Crime Studies

A larger number of self-report studies of crime have concluded that close to 100 percent of all persons have committed some kind of offense, although a few have been arrested.[9] In a substantial portion of the offenses revealed by these studies, the crime was so serious that it could have resulted in a sentence of imprisonment if the offender had been arrested.

Most of the studies examined the relationship of social class to crime and delinquency. While the evidence is contradictory, most recent studies come to the conclusion that persons of all classes commit crimes, and that no social class is responsible for a disproportionate share of crimes committed.

Among the most significant recent studies is a national survey of youth in the United States.[10] Based on a national probability sample of persons thirteen to sixteen years old, the findings are representative of this age group as a whole. Data were drawn from interviews with and records of 847 boys and girls who comprised the sample, and the frequency and seriousness of self-reported delinquent behavior were analyzed for differences by sex, age, race, and socioeconomic status. The data were then compared with self-reported police contacts and with data from police and court records.

Of the total sample, 88 percent confessed to committing at least one offense for which they could have been adjudicated delinquent. Only 9 percent were detected by police; only 4 percent received police records; and less than 2 percent were adjudicated delinquent. The acts of the 9 percent caught represent less than 3 percent of the total chargeable acts of delinquency.

In support of recent studies, this research found that the relationship between social status and delinquent behavior was weak, except that higher-status white boys were more delinquent than lower-status white boys. The greater seriousness of the higher-status boys' delinquent behavior stemmed from their committing proportionally more thefts, joy riding, and (surprisingly) assaults. The frequency much more than the seriousness of delinquent behavior was positively associated with getting caught. Getting caught was thus to a large extent a chance occurrence.

A study of risk ratios in juvenile delinquency, or factors associated with detection by police and court action, found that while frequency of delinquent behavior was positively associated with getting caught, neither frequency nor seriousness of behavior was related to social class.[11] In other words, despite the preponderance of lower-class persons in official records, the lower classes neither commit offenses more often nor commit more serious offenses. Studies in Sweden, Norway, and Finland discovered a similar discrepancy a decade ago.[12] Edmund Vos in English Canada and Marc LeBlanc in French Canada also found this to be true.[13] It appears that while persons of all social classes commit crimes, those who are caught up in the criminal-justice system are primarily lower class. Kutchinsky observes that "it is becoming increasingly clear that most criminals are created through a process of discriminatory selection, ostracizing stigmatization, and dehumanizing punishment."[14]

The discovery that crime and delinquency do not vary significantly from one social group to another while the vast majority of inmates of correctional institutions are lower class had led criminologists to take a closer look at the way in which offenders are selected for arrest, prosecution, and punishment.

Selection of Offenders for Punishment

It is common knowledge among most students of crime and delinquency that the officially designated criminal is the final product of a long process of selection. Studies of this selection process support hidden-crime studies in consistently demonstrating that certain groups and certain classes of persons are overrepresented while others are underrepresented in the criminal-justice system. Those caught up in the system are overwhelmingly poor, the lower class, members of minority groups, immigrants, foreigners, persons of low intelligence, and others who are in some way at a disadvantage. Those who have a good chance of escaping the system are the affluent criminals, corporate criminals, white-collar criminals, professional criminals, organized criminals, and intelligent criminals. In general, the most successful criminals (i.e., those realizing the greatest economic gain) escape the system, while the less successful are caught.

If, as hidden-crime studies have indicated, only a small proportion of persons who commit crimes are eventually caught and punished, and if these are usually the least successful, then the criminal-justice system expends most of its resources on a small group of individuals whose offenses are relatively less significant.

Using examples drawn from criminal statistics and from reports of court proceedings, Dennis Chapman demonstrates how society, through the legal system, selects for punishment a scapegoat group drawn from a much wider population of antisocial individuals. This group, composed of working-class men lacking education, influence, and resources, is liable to penalties of imprisonment and desocialization from which members of the middle and upper classes are relatively immune, even though they may engage in behavior that, defined in operational terms, is identical in its social effects. This very selective bias in the legal system means that most studies of crime and the offender take as their starting point a stereotype of the "criminal" that is a social and legal artifact.[15]

Throughout the world one of the main determinants in the process of selection for punishment is socioeconomic status. A study of white-collar offenders known to police in Helsinki in 1955 examined the relationship between the socioeconomic status of the suspect and the decisions of the police, the prosecutor, and the judge.[16] Like many American studies of this relationship, this study found that a person of higher socioeconomic status had a significantly greater chance of having his case adjusted informally by the police, of avoiding prosecution even if referred to court, and of not being sentenced. Only 26 percent of offenders from the higher socioeconomic group were sentenced by the courts, while 57 percent of the lower-status offenders were involved in judicial processing to the final stage of sentencing.

In the United States and a few other countries the social class factor is complicated by race. An American study of the effect of race on sentencing analyzed the disparities between the sentences of whites and those of blacks in the South. Utilizing 1205 cases drawn from the prison and parole records of seven southern states, it arrived at this simple conclusion:

There is a significant absolute disparity between the sentences received by black offenders and those received by white offenders. . . . Careful analysis of the data failed to reveal any general factor which would account for the disparity other than race.[17]

Typical of American studies is one of 3475 Philadelphia delinquents, which found that blacks and members of lower socioeconomic groups were likely to receive more severe dispositions than whites and the more affluent, even when the appropriate legal variables were held constant.[18]

The process of selection for punishment is arbitrary but apparently not random. Many of the numerous studies on this subject point out the influence of the police, the prosecutor, and the judge upon the selection process. Studies of discretionary decision-making on the part of criminal justice officials have shown that some of the factors that affect the selection process are quite subtle. A rather revealing study, by Nathan Goldman, of police discretion in Pennsylvania indicates that systematic selective biases influence the decision to process an alleged juvenile offender through the court. Goldman found that, in addition to the policeman's own private attitudes and experience and his concern for status and prestige in the community, the attitudes of the community toward the offense, the offender, and his family also affect the decision of the officer in his reporting of juvenile offenses. The availability of a juvenile offender for official recording, and for research on delinquency, thus depends on the responsiveness of the police officer to a series of collective social pressures and personal attitudes. The policeman's interpretation of these pressures will determine the composition of that sample of juvenile offenders who will become officially recognized from among all those known to him.[19]

Numerous studies of the process of selection in specific types of offenses have also been made with similar results. A study of drunken driving, for instance, demonstrated that minority-group members, the lower class, males, and youth are consistently more likely to be convicted of driving while intoxicated than are whites, the upper class, and older persons.[20] A study of the corporate and judicial disposition of employees involved in embezzlement found that when the amount stolen was held constant, more lower-status employees than higher-status employees were prosecuted, indicating that offenders with whom the enforcers could more easily identify were treated sympathetically.[21] A German study of selection for prosecution and punishment of shoplifters found that only 2 percent of shoplifters are eventually subjected to a legal sanction, and these 2 percent are not representative of the total sample. Of one hundred shoplifters, fewer than five are detected. Of every one hundred detected, fewer than fifty are reported to authorities. Of one hundred reported, eighty are punished. At all stages of the selection process from detection to punishment, certain groups were consistently more likely to be processed to the next stage: foreigners, adults, and members of the working class. For example, while 8 percent of thefts were committed by foreign workers, 15 percent of those reported to the authorities were foreign workers.[22] Another study of public reactions to shoplifting consisted of a field experiment in which rigged shoplifting events were enacted in the presence of store customers who were in a position to observe and react to the shoplifting incidents. It was found that while sex of shoplifter or of store customer had little effect on reporting level, appearance of shoplifter exerted a major independent effect on reporting levels. A highly significant relationship was found between "hippie" appearance of the person acting as shoplifter and willingness on the part of store customers to report the incident. The study concludes that the imputation of deviance not only resides in the fact of deviance itself but also depends heavily on the meanings that the observer attaches to the behavior and the actor. Willingness to report deviant acts can be assumed to depend on the "deviate's" other social identities, a significant clue to identity being provided by appearance.[23]

Studies of the types of offenders who escape punishment and how they are selected are also numerous. It is well known that organized criminals are among the economically most successful. How they escape detection and punishment through bribery, threats, loopholes in the law, and society's apathy and ambivalence has been aptly described by Donald Cressey in *Theft of the Nation.*[24]

Similar in his success is the professional criminal. A British study notes that offenders who make a full-time job of crime and who establish relationships and networks in the pursuance of their common occupational interests operate at an economic cost to the community that is disproportionately high relative to their numbers. On the basis of two pilot studies it was estimated that there is one full-time professional criminal for every ten thousand inhabitants in Britain.[25] In a city of one million, 102 full-time offenders were analyzed. A very large proportion was found to be both able and successful in their criminal occupation—i.e., making a lot more money than they would have made in such legal occupations as are open to them and successful in avoiding court appearance, conviction, and imprisonment. This study makes the important point that the major skill of the professional criminal, avoiding detection and imprisonment, suggests a serious distortion in criminological research, which consistently studies those offenders who are caught and punished. The offenders most available for study are the persistent criminal failures who have little in common with the able and successful professional criminal.

No sociological studies of corporate criminals are reported in the literature, but the selective, discriminatory system of justice in favor of the rich is amply documented. U.S. Senator Philip Hart observes from his questioning of corporate criminals that, for the affluent and influential, loopholes in the law are so abundant that it takes determination to avoid them. Corporate criminals are availed of a host of quiet settlement procedures that the government never employs to keep a burglar out of prison. Discriminatory justice in favor of the rich occurs at all stages of criminal justice. Upper-class crimes generally result in civil damage suits, cease-and-desist orders, license revocations, and fines. The upper classes, simply because they have access to government decision-makers, can also influence the development of the very statutes that regulate upper-class behavior.[26]

A review of studies of juvenile offenders of high intelligence concludes that the comparative rarity of known bright delinquents is the result of differential immunity accorded them by reason of their higher intelligence. It is suggested that they are more skillful in escaping detection and that their high intelligence may influence the police in deciding not to arrest. Intelligent delinquents share largely the same criminological, educational, and general social characteristics as the majority of other delinquents, but they differ in important respects: they are rarely encountered, they are treated differently by the courts, and they are more often presented as emotionally disturbed. These delinquents are more readily adjudged psychiatrically disturbed, because of their greater verbal fluency and ability to communicate with psychiatrists.[27]

These studies, and many others like them, have suggested that any approach to crime that concentrates on the characteristics of the convicted criminal, the "causes" of his behavior, or his treatment aimed at preventing further convictions is likely to be unproductive. If the population of officially labeled criminals is as unrepresentative of the crime problem as these studies indicate, a very large portion of criminological literature is leading us up a dead-end street.

Toward A New Criminology

While most criminologists today are preoccupied with such traditional concerns as the offender, his characteristics, and his classification and treatment, a few have begun to move in a totally different direction which, if it proves productive, may radically change both criminology and correction. The new criminology has drawn on the findings of hidden crime studies of the selection of offenders for punishment. The most recent (and most sophisticated) of these have found that, while the vast majority of persons who are caught and punished are lower class, the commission of crime does not vary significantly from one social group to another. In effect, it is primarily the poor and the powerless who are caught.

The work of several criminologists serves to illustrate the direction that criminology has taken. What these criminologists have in common is a deemphasis of the importance of the individaul offender as an object of study, and a focus on the role of society in creating and maintaining crime and criminals for a necessary function. A crucial implication of these theories is that society is currently operating at cross-purposes: society apparently has a need to designate certain individuals as criminal and certain behaviors as crime at the same time that it tries to prevent such behavior and to punish or "treat" persons who engage in it.

Patrik Törnudd believes that the low utility of criminological research is attributable to the failure of traditional criminologists to view crime as a necessary social function.[28] He believes that society *needs* crime, or at least a certain amount of behavior that is publicly defined as deviant. Crime serves three major functions: social integration, norm reinforcement, and innovation. (1) The identification of acts as criminal allows a harmless channeling of aggressions, while at the same time reinforcing group solidarity and other social values. The quotation, "Nothing unites a nation as much as its murderers," describes this mechanism. (2) Norms are needed to uphold social organization. To maintain norm conformity, continuous reinforcement must take place. Each public denunciation of an identified act is a reminder of the norm's existence and importance. (3) Fundamental moral innovations call for deviance manifested in action, with the attendant conflict (crime) a necessary element of the process. Crime, according to Törnudd, also fulfills a number of lesser functions, including self-regulating deviance for instrumental purposes: e.g., theft of bread by a hungry person.

With respect to prevention of crime, Törnudd suggests that the range of permissible crime can be viewed as a dynamic equilibrium in which society can settle for differing levels of crime at the cost of, among other things, production, the speed of social change, and solidarity. If crime is necessary and normal, then any measure of crime must take into account the degree of necessity.

Törnudd recommends that, instead of searching for the "causes" of crime, criminologists should formulate their research strategies and communicate their results with respect to (a) fluctuations in the level of crime or (b) the process that determines the selection of offenses and offenders for punishment.

Inkeri Anttila views crime as the visible expression of a balance among conflicting social pressures,[29] and points out that treating the offender will never solve the crime problem, since criminals serve a useful purpose as scapegoats of the social system.[30] Although the treatment approach to correction was a breakthrough in its time, the undesirable aspects of the approach have become evident as the concept of treatment of offenders has come to dominate the correctional system. Equating offenders with the sick, Anttila argues, is a fallacy when the "sick" and the "doctor" are in conflict and when the treatment does not bring about a cure. This fallacy has led to an acute problem of legal rights and safeguards, because of the absence of treatment predictability and a frequent disproportion between the seriousness of a crime and the intensity of treatment. Preoccupation with the individual offender blinds the treaters to the existence of social evils that are much more urgent targets for society's crime control efforts. The treatment system, says Anttila, must not be used to camouflage social injustices and delay vital reforms. It is more urgent to repeal obsolete laws and to eliminate arbitrary decision-making and discrimination against the socially powerless.

While the elimination of crime is not a realistic goal, Anttila believes that we can strive for social balance and influence the structure and gravity of crime. This has important policy implications: For every crime problem it becomes as important to examine the possibilities of changing society's control of crime (to the point of decriminalization) as it is to change the offender. This social balance, Anttila says, has an inner logic of its own that does not permit decriminalization of previously proscribed behavior to go too far, and does not permit the number of criminal laws, crimes, and criminals to fall below a certain level.

Projecting into the future, Anttila suggests that alternatives to traditional punishment and treatment will perhaps include efforts to affect the standard of living of the offender or to express, in some subtle way, society's disapproval of certain types of harmful behavior. This prediction appears reasonable if one accepts the hypothesis that the proportion of persons sentenced for traditional crimes will decrease while the proportion of persons sentenced for tax and business fraud, polluting the environment, and misuse of public office will increase.[31] A systems-change model of crime control is already operative in traffic insurance legislation: Insurance eases the suffering inflicted on the victim and satisfies society with an economic sanction in the form of raised insurance premiums, even in cases of criminal negligence. Such financial charges and other economic sanctions can, in many cases, take the place of traditional punishment.[32]

Another criminologist, Raimo Lahti, points out that Scandinavian criminology no longer searches for the causes of crime in the characteristics of criminals or their environment. The question asked is not why some individuals become criminal but why they are identified as criminals in a selective process. Mere reduction of crime can no longer be accepted as an objective. Crime reduction must be sought at the lowest possible cost and with due regard to equity and justice. Society, as owner of the largest resources, must accept primary responsibility for the reduction of the costs of crime.

For the future, Lahti predicts that a value- and cost-conscious school of thinking will probably gain influence in the decision-making process concerning crime. This means that when several alternatives are available, the costs of these solutions and their applicability will be compared with different values, and the decision will be based on this comparison. It will frequently be more expedient to develop measures to prevent opportunities for crime than to deal with offenders.[33]

Applied criminology, according to Marc LeBlanc, runs the risk of becoming an instrument of control, especially as criminology is transformed into a technological science. This danger is compounded by the fact that crime is a political concept: Since each political regime defines its own criminality, criminology can easily become a political tool. The distinction between crime and deviance, between concern and control, between punishment and treatment, between criminology and repression, is always politically defined.[34]

Dennis Chapman has presented what is perhaps the most systematic statement of a new theory of crime, incorporating many of the research findings on hidden crime and the selection of offenders for punishment. The main theses of his theory can be summarized as follows:

1. Apart from the fact of conviction there are no differences between criminals and noncriminals. Criminal behavior is general, but the incidence of conviction is controlled in part by chance and in part by social processes that divide society into criminal and noncriminal classes, the former corresponding roughly to the poor and underprivileged.

2. The social system operates to select individuals from a larger universe of individuals with identical behaviors.

3. Behavior that has a disapproved form (crime) also has objectively identical forms that are neutral or approved. The choice among disapproved, tolerated, and approved forms of behavior may depend on chance, knowledge, learning, or training. The designation of certain actions as permitted, tolerated, or condemned in different circumstances is arbitrary.

4. Different social groups are treated differently for behaviors that are objectively identical. Certain persons and groups are immune from selection as criminals, primarily because of the protective institutional environments in which they live.

5. Crime is a functional part of the social system. Identification of the criminal class and its social ostracism permits the guilt of others to be symbolically discharged and reduces social class hostility by deflecting aggression that might otherwise be directed toward those in power. A special part of the official ideology functions to prevent the designated criminal from escaping from his sacrificial role, and institutional record-keeping maintains his identity.

6. The legal system is a crime-creating institution: once created, an institution develops a dynamic of its own and becomes involved in the behavior with which it is concerned as a participant, and in special circumstances as an instigator. It may do this in response to social pressures.[35]

These statements raise many complex issues, including the plurality of the moral and legal order, the conflict between society's belief system and its goal system, and the conflict between groups with power and groups without power. Unlike other crime theories, this "theory of the stereotype," as Chapman calls it, begins not with the person and his characteristics or behaviors but with the moral order and the law. It sees society, not the criminal, as the main problem. It asks why a legislature decides that an action must be punished. While much law is in the public interest, it still reflects the distribution of power in society, and much legislation (or the absence of it) serves the interests of particular classes, groups, or organizations. These laws are then selectively administered by the police and the courts. The differential distribution of privacy is one of the crucial variables in this process: The affluent are immune, since most of their behavior occurs in private. Poor urban areas, on the other hand, are heavily policed, thus producing high arrest rates—a classic example of the self-fulfilling prophecy. Defense against a legal charge depends not on innocence but on power, social connections, knowledge of the law, and financial resources, all of which are unequally distributed. Following conviction the discriminatory process continues along class lines, with the rich more likely to escape imprisonment and more likely than the poor to appeal the conviction and the sentence. Finally, the theory is concerned with removing the stigma. The first step in this direction, says Chapman, is to rid ourselves of all we have been led to believe on the subject. It calls for better understanding of the range of behavior we have designated criminal, and the futility of punishment for most types of behavior.

Even a brief review of the thinking of these criminologists indicates that the new criminology is more than just another theory of the labeling process. Labeling theory has contributed to the knowledge on which the new criminology is based. Studies of the labeling process have pointed out that criminal labels are dispensed in such a manner that persons who are expected to be the most criminal (i.e., the poorly educated, indigents, blacks) are given the greatest opportunity to develop a criminal identity or career. Labeling theorists have helped to turn attention away from the deviant acts of individuals and the causes of their deviance toward the criminogenic effects of negative societal responses to deviance. They have suggested that official action (imposition of a criminal label) may lock the person so stigmatized into a criminal career, thus creating more crime in the effort to prevent or deter it. They have also pointed out that the processes of labeling fulfill a social function: The identification of deviant "outsiders" functions to bring the labelers closer together.

The new criminology builds on the work of the labeling theorists, but it goes further. Labeling theorists still concentrate on the effects of labeling on the persons stigmatized, the impact of social processes on the individual. Labeling theory makes assumptions about the predisposing characteristics that lead an individual to commit his first offense and the changes in him resulting from his stigmatization. In other words, there is an implicit assumption of the existence of a group of criminals and delinquents or "predelinquents," some of whom are caught and labeled officially while others escape such labeling. The new criminology does not consider these concerns to be of critical importance, claiming that the concept of a criminal or criminally predisposed group is a social and legal artifact. The new criminologists consider a "criminal" to be anyone who is convicted of a crime, whether or not he has actually committed it, and include among "noncriminals" anyone who breaks the law but avoids detection.[36] It is processing by the criminal-justice system that distinguishes the criminal from the noncriminal. This approach is concerned not only with the social rejection of some forms of behavior and the ostracism of some persons who engage in it, but also with the acceptance by society of other forms of the same behavior engaged in by other persons. It considers not only stigmatization and destigmatization but *non*stigmatization, showing us that while people of all classes and groups engage in some form of "appropriation of property of others without their consent" (theft), only certain forms of this conduct are wholly disapproved and only some kinds of persons are subject to penalties for it.

Conclusion

Current public and official views of crime and criminals, and the "solutions" to the crime problem that derive from them, appear obsolete from the perspective of those who have begun to take criminology into new territory. The tenets of Criminology III are not entirely new: In the early part of this century Emile

Durkheim wrote that criminality is a normal element of every society, that society needs criminals to reinforce social norms, and that even a society of saints would have its social norms and its norm-breakers.[37] In the 1950s Aubert explained that each society organizes itself for the protection of the ruling classes against the socially inferior.[38] Criminologists today are rediscovering and expanding on these views, fortifying their arguments with the research evidence of the intervening years. Their theories point up the weaknesses and limitations of traditional conceptions of the crime problem which present crime as an aberration and criminals as a minority of ill, immoral, misguided, or improperly socialized persons who are somehow different from the average citizen. The orthodox view encourages the belief that if we could just find out what is wrong with people who offend against society these people could be rehabilitated to become useful and productive citizens like the rest of us.

The new criminologists view the crime problem from a wholly different perspective. They consider the search for the "causes" of crime and a "cure" for the criminal a waste of time, since official crime and the detected criminal are produced and maintained by social forces that have little or nothing to do with the harmfulness of actual behavior.

The most successful criminals (those realizing the greatest economic gain) are rarely caught, rarely prosecuted, and rarely punished. When punished, they are punished less severely. These are persons with power or access to power, the rich, and the intelligent. The less successful criminals are more likely to be caught, prosecuted, and punished. When punished, they are punished more severely. They are the powerless, the poor, and the unintelligent.

The new criminology concentrates not on the officially designated criminal but on (1) the definition of crime—the decision to make, for instance, intoxication by marijuana or other drugs criminal while intoxication by alcohol (the drug of those who make the laws) is noncriminal; and (2) the selection of certain lawbreakers for identification as criminals—for example, the decision to arrest, prosecute, and imprison the lower-class man who steals a hundred dollars, and to deal informally with the upper-class embezzler of thousands of dollars by quiet settlement to avoid damaging his reputation.

The new criminology views crime as an integral part of society—a normal, not a pathological, kind of human behavior. It assumes that crime cannot be eliminated—although its structure and form might be affected by changes in crime control policy[39]—and that crime in some form serves useful purposes in integrating what is known as law-abiding society and in defining its boundaries. Most of all, it points out that deviance is a relative concept, that what we call "crime" and "criminals" are more or less arbitrarily defined classes of acts and actors rather than the clear-cut distinctions implied by the labels "criminal" and "noncriminal." Although people and behaviors are viewed as one or the other, in reality the classifications of criminal and noncriminal shade into each other with no sharp lines of demarcation. The distinctions made between them are arbitrary but apparently not random; criminal labels are usually dispensed in ways that uphold the established order and do not threaten the lives and life styles of the classes or groups with power and influence.

That crime and delinquency are political concepts has frequently been noted. Edwin Schur, in his book on labeling deviant behavior, discusses the value-laden nature of deviance and its control, and concludes that deviance is essentially political.[40] Richard Quinney writes that crime has become a political weapon that is used to the advantage of those who control the processes of government. The state, he observes, has used its power through the law to define as criminal what it regards as a threat to the social and political order.[41] This has always been true—there are few acts, no matter how heinous, that have not at one time or under some circumstances been tolerated or approved; and there are few acts, no matter how petty, that have not at some time been considered punishable offenses. Quinney claims that in recent times the theme of law and order has shaped the official conception of crime; in many ways, the war on crime has become a substitute for the earlier war on internal communism.[42] The influence of official conceptions of the crime problem is evident in the recent focus on "crime in the streets." This type of crime having been officially identified as *the* major crime problem, both public concern and the bulk of governmental crime control resources are directed against the perpetrators of street crimes. In another time or place, the crime problem might just as well be identified as environmental pollution, misuse of public money, or large-scale embezzlement, fraud, or other actions that adversely affect large numbers of people.

The political nature of crime control policies is most obvious with respect to juveniles and the laws of juvenile delinquency. Children and young people represent a class of persons who, despite their large numbers, have little or no power in society. Most of them cannot vote and cannot make or change the laws that affect them. Their own norms and values, to the extent that they differ from those of the adult world, are not embodied in the law. For example, while leaving his parents' home may be quite legitimate from a juvenile's point of view and that of his peers, in the statutes it is called "running away" and is punishable by measures that are often quite severe. A wide range of other activities and behaviors, relatively harmless or completely justified from a youthful point of view, can lead to a lengthy period of incarceration for the juvenile unfortunate enough to be caught. Consideration of the juvenile justice system in operation has led Langley, Graves, and Norris to propose that juvenile delinquency be viewed as "a community-enacted, legally based political procedure for controlling and altering youthful behavior that is disruptive to an orderly adult way of life." They suggest that juvenile delinquency be defined as "behavior that the state deems necessary to control and to alter through the political structure of the community."[43]

Adult crime could easily be defined in the same way. Our prisons are full of people whose particular offenses are disruptive to an orderly middle- or upper-class way of life. Theirs are the crude offenses, less socially acceptable than the more subtle white-collar crimes, even though the white-collar criminal may inflict more social harm or monetary loss. The "real" criminals, according to official ideology, are in prison or under some form of correctional supervision. The vast majority of them lack the power to influence the law-making process in their own favor and, without skill, knowledge, or social influence, they are easily caught and punished. They are the criminal failures and society's scapegoats. They have, of course, committed real crimes for which their punishment is authorized by statute. But so have the great many who go free.

While these facts are acknowledged by a growing number of modern criminologists, traditional views of crime and criminals are still predominant in both correctional practice and criminological research, especially in the United States. Because of this, much criminological thinking and research is handicapped and is falling behind. The prestigious President's Crime Commission stated what was then (1967) and still is widely accepted as fact: "Delinquency is a *lower-class* phenomenon." And standard reference works on criminal procedure suggest that prosecutors refrain from prosecuting in cases where the offender comes from a "respectable" background[44]—implying that prosecution for a crime may be harmful to middle-class lives. Most crime and delinquency research deals with that small proportion of criminals who have failed at crime and are caught.[45] The causes of criminal behavior are thus assumed to lie somewhere in the psyche or the social and family background of the criminal failure. Yet the biased nature of the official criminal population suggests that the study of this group may be productive only to the extent that it indicates what it is about its members that leads to their selection for criminal justice processing.

In addition to the important implications for criminology theory and research—that the focus of attention should shift from the stigmatized to the stigmatizers and that more attention be directed toward crime and deviance as part of the normal functioning of society—the new criminology raises issues for criminal justice that suggest the need for a dramatic reordering of priorities. It appears that society has been bearing down heavily on a hapless group of secondary offenders who have been unsuccessful in escaping justice, while tolerating or helplessly watching the depredations of the more successful criminals.

One approach to reform of our system of crime control, consistent with the new criminology and geared toward providing equal justice, might be first to redefine crimes operationally, and then to decide which kinds of operationally defined kinds of behavior are widely believed to be the most harmful. If, as seems to be the case, there is a general consensus that violence against persons (e.g., murder, assault, etc.) is the kind of behavior that society most abhors, then crime control efforts should be directed not against "street crime" (which by circumstance is almost exclusively the domain of the lower classes), but against personal violence in whatever form it takes. Upper-class and official violence should not be disguised by euphemism, nor should its perpetrators be excused because their credentials imply that violence was either justifiable or merely an aberration from a normally "respectable" life style. Conversely, if upper-class economic crimes (e.g., embezzlement, fraud, tax evasion, etc.) are fairly well tolerated and absorbed by society and the economy, then surely it is both unnecessary and unfair to punish so severely the economic crimes (theft, larceny, robbery without violence, burglary, etc.) of the less advantaged.

Any society concerned not only with law and order but with justice for all must first decide which are the serious crimes, which crimes cause the greatest social harm, and then commit itself to the equal distribution of punishment for all kinds and classes of persons who engage in such behaviors. Until we can achieve such a just redirection of crime control and correctional efforts, we should at least be aware that our present system, upheld by our most cherished notions of what is a criminal and what is a crime, is set up and operated in ways that work to the distinct advantage of certain social groups and classes and to the clear disadvantage of others. The research and theory of Criminology III can help us to understand why this is so, what functions are served by this arrangement and by alternative ones, and what can reasonably be expected in the way of productive change.

References

1. Charles A. Reich, *The Greening of America* (New York: Random House, 1970).

2. Herbert Gloch and Gilbert Geis, *Man, Crime, and Society* (New York: Random House, 1962), pp. 84-87.

3. Ibid., pp. 87-90.

4. Inkeri Anttila, "Punishment versus Treatment—Is There a Third Alternative?" *Abstracts on Criminology and Penology*, 12(7):287-90, 1972.

5. Douglas S. Lipton, Robert Martinson, and Judith Wilks, *Effectiveness of Correctional Treatment: A Survey of Treatment Evaluations* (New York: State Office of Crime Control Planning, 1970).

6. James Robison and Gerald Smith, "The Effectiveness of Correctional Programs," *Crime and Delinquency*, 17(1):67-80, 1971.

7. Anttila, op. cit.

8. Council of Europe, Ninth Conference of Directors of Criminological Research Institutes, *Perception of Deviance and Criminality* (Strasbourg: 1971), pp. 75-79.

9. Eugene Doleschal, "Hidden Crime," *Crime and Delinquency Literature*, 2(5):546-72, 1970.

10. Jay R. Williams and Martin Gold, "From Delinquent Behavior to Official Delinquency," *Social Problems*, 20(2):209-29, 1972.

11. Nanci Koser Wilson, *Risk Ratios in Juvenile Delinquency* (Ann Arbor, Mich.: University Microfilms, 1972).

12. Doleschal, op. cit.

13. Ibid.

14. Ninth Conference of Directors of Criminological Research Institutes, op. cit.

15. Dennis Chapman, "The Stereotype of the Criminal and the Social Consequences," *International Journal of Criminology and Penology*, 1(1):15-30, 1973.

16. "White Collar Crimes and Status Selectivity in the Law Enforcement System" (Research Report No. 120), Institute of Sociology, University of Helsinki, 1969.

17. "Races Makes the Difference," Southern Regional Council, Atlanta, Ga., 1969.

18. Terence Patrick Thornberry, *Punishment and Crime: The Effect of Legal Dispositions on Subsequent Criminal Behavior* (Ann Arbor, Mich.: University Microfilms, 1972).

19. Nathan Goldman, *The Differential Selection of Juvenile Offenders for Court Appearance* (New York: National Council on Crime and Delinquency, 1963).

20. Ross L. Purdy, *Factors in the Conviction of Law Violators: The Drinking Driver* (Ann Arbor, Mich.: University Microfilms, 1971).

21. Gerald Robin, "The Corporate and Judicial Disposition of Employee Thieves," *Wisconsin Law Review*, (3):685-702, 1967.

22. Erhard Blankenburg, "Die Selektivität rechtlicher Sanktionen: eine empirische Untersuchung von Ladendiebstählen," *Kolner Zeitschrift fur Soziologie und Sozialpsychologie*, 21(4):805-29, 1969.

23. Darrell J. Steffensmeier and Robert M. Terry, "Deviance and Respectability: An Observational Study of Reactions to Shoplifting," *Social Forces*, 51(4):417-26, 1973.

24. Donald R. Cressey, *Theft of the Nation* (New York: Harper & Row, 1969).

25. J.A. Mack, "The Able Criminal," *British Journal of Criminology*, 12(1):44-54, 1972.

26. Philip A. Hart, "Swindling and Knavery, Inc." *Playboy*, August 1972, pp. 155-62.

27. Dennis Gath and Gavin Tennent, "High Intelligence and Delinquency—a Review," *British Journal of Criminology*, 12(2):174-81, 1972.

28. Patrik Törnudd, "The Futility of Searching for Causes of Crime," *Scandinavian Studies in Criminology*, Vol. 3, Oslo, Universitetsforlaget, 1971, pp. 23-33.

29. Inkeri Anttila, "Conservative and Radical Criminal Policy in the Nordic Countries," *Scandinavian Studies in Criminology*, Vol. 3, Oslo, Universitetsforlaget, 1971, pp. 9-21.

30. Anttila, "Punishment versus Treatment—Is There a Third Alternative?"

31. Ibid.

32. Anttila, "Conservative and Radical Criminal Policy in the Nordic Countries."

33. Raimo Lahti, "On the Reduction and Distribution of the Costs of Crime: Observations on the Objectives and the Means of Criminal Policy," *Jurisprudentia*, no vol. (1):298-313, 1972.

34. Marc LeBlanc, "Theorie-Recherche-Pratique: Une Interaction à Developper," *Canadian Journal of Criminology and Correction*, 15(1):13-24, 1973.

35. Chapman, op. cit.

36. Ibid.

37. Emile Durkheim, *Rules of Sociological Method* (Glencoe, Ill.: Free Press, 1950), pp. 65-73.

38. V. Aubert, *On Straffens sosiale funksjon* (Oslo: 1954).

39. Anttila, "Punishment versus Treatment—Is There a Third Alternative?"

40. Edwin Schur, *Labeling Deviant Behavior: Its Sociological Implications* (New York: Harper & Row, 1971).

41. Richard Quinney, *The Social Reality of Crime* (Boston: Little, Brown, 1970).

42. Ibid.

43. M.H. Langley, H.R. Graves, and B. Norris, "The Juvenile Court and Individualized Treatment," *Crime and Delinquency*, 18(1):79-92, 1972.

44. *Struggle for Justice: A Report on Crime and Punishment in America*, prepared for American Friends Service Committee (New York: Hill and Wang, 1971), p. 107.

45. There is evidence to suggest that the emphasis of American researchers on the individual offender and their use of official sources of data have been heavily influenced by the concerns of those who fund research, particularly the government, and some evidence that this may change. John F. Galliher and James L. McCartney, "The Influence of Funding Agencies on Juvenile Delinquency Research," *Social Problems*, 2(1):77-90, 1973.

3

The Dissolution of the Training Schools in Massachusetts[a]

Andrew Rutherford[b]

Introduction

In 1969 provisions for young offenders in Massachusetts were not in any marked respect different from those which exist today throughout most of the United States and Western Europe. They were characterized by the reformatory heritage of the nineteenth century, and by a very limited array of alternatives for the court. The institutions tended to brutalize both staff and youngsters, and the few community programs that did exist offered nothing more than a mediocre level of supervision. The dramatic changes that occurred during the next three years comprise one of the most significant and hopeful events in the bleak history of corrections. By rejecting rather than reforming the old system, Massachusetts developed a very wide range of services for youngsters in trouble. It was the abrupt closing of the training schools that caught the attention of people throughout the United States and beyond. This event has taken on a symbolic significance, and perhaps because of this there has not often been a close scrutiny of what has actually taken place in Massachusetts. This chapter is an attempt to provide a concise and up-to-date account of the Massachusetts Department of Youth Services.

The study represents part of a larger comparative description and analysis of correctional change in several states.

The 1969 Legislation and The Mandate for Change

During the 1960s youth corrections in Massachusetts had been characterized by continued scandal and mismanagement. There were a series of inquiries into the

[a]This article published originally by The Academy For Contemporary Problems, March 1974.

[b]Andrew Rutherford is a Fellow in the Crime and Justice programs at the Academy for Contemporary Problems. After study at Durham and Cambridge Universities, he joined the English Prison Department in 1962. He was an assistant governor at Hewell Grange and Pollington Borstals. From 1968 to 1970 he was a Harkness Fellow of the Commonwealth Fund of New York at the University of California (Santa Barbara) and at the Yale Law School. On returning to England he became deputy governor of Everthorpe Borstal. He resigned from that post in May 1973 to take up his appointment at the Academy.

operations of the Division for Youth Services and the Youth Services Board. Following a number of critical state investigations came the most devastating of all, the report by the Children's Bureau of the Department of Health, Education and Welfare in August 1966. A further study was conducted during 1967 by the Massachusetts Committee on Children and Youth and by a special committee of the Senate, which reported in June of that year. Most of the reports were in agreement as to the general direction of the changes required. There was considerable comment in the press, and a growing demand for a more humane approach to children in trouble. On becoming governor in early 1969, Francis Sargent strongly identified himself with this demand. He stated, "Simply caging children is not the way of an enlightened society." Following the growing public outcry against the Division's leadership, pressure was brought to bear on the director, Dr. John Coughlin, to resign, in March 1969. Two months later a committee set up by the Massachusetts Conference on Social Welfare called for further resignations and for institutional closures. Sargent gave his backing to legislative moves to bring about important administrative changes. With support from the governor and some key legislators, and with the constant urging of the media, especially the *Boston Globe*, the legislation, which had been debated for two years, moved easily through the House and Senate.

The legislation, expressed in Chapter 838 of the 1969 Acts, was signed into law by Governor Sargent in August 1969. It contained several important features:

1. The division for Youth Services and Youth Services Board were transformed into a Department of Youth Services, which was placed under a commissioner within a newly created super agency, the Department for Human Services.

2. The commission was empowered to select four assistant commissioners.

3. The Department's spending flexibility was greatly increased, including the authority to purchase services from outside sources.

4. The Department was empowered "to establish necessary facilities for detention, diagnosis, treatment, and training of its charges including post-release care." It was given full control over the juvenile institutions, which had formerly been somewhat autonomous.

5. The Department was given the authority to place children in any institution or program.

A blue-ribbon search panel was set up to find a commissioner. After Coughlin's departure in May 1969, Frank Maloney, formerly of the Boston University School of Social Work, was appointed as acting commissioner. Governor Sargent would have been prepared to confirm Maloney, who had managed to calm the institutions down by giving strong support to staff. To some extent the political heat had been lifted from the agency, but Sargent had agreed to accept the choice of the committee. Dr. Jerome Miller, an associate professor of social work at Ohio State University, had seen the job advertised and was one of eighty applicants. At the interview he made it clear he had a bias against institutions. Prior to his teaching work he had had several years' experience developing services for the children of Air Force personnel stationed in England. Following the committee's recommendation, Miller was appointed commissioner on October 28, 1969.

The Moral Crusade for Children, 1969-72

The humanizing of the institutions was an obvious goal, given Miller's stance as the advocate for the children committed to the Department. The decision to close the training schools was preceded by an attempt to make them a better place for children to live. Miller had a number of advantages. He was from out of state and was more easily able to present himself as the agent of change. He arrived on the scene in the wake of considerable public disquiet as to the manner in which youth institutions were run, and a solid legislative framework had been created. Miller possessed considerable ability in dealing with the media, and was able to clearly and dramatically present his message. He built upon the active commitment already established the *Boston Globe*, and made good use of whatever television coverage came his way. He had the ability to quickly grasp the political complexities of Massachusetts. He made a point of establishing some firm allies from the start. These included Tom Winship, editor of the *Globe*; David Bartley, Speaker of the House of Representatives; Maurice Donahue, then president of the Senate; Mrs. Jessie Sargent, wife of the governor; and John McGlynn, chairman of the Joint Legislative Committee on State Administration and of several other legislative committees. Although Miller had a number of persistent political enemies, he was able to use their opposition to magnify the polarization of the issues in such a way as to gain support from various groups. A great deal of his time was spent either on television or radio, or speaking to groups, large and small, throughout the state. On many of these occasions he was accompanied by youngsters who echoed his dismay at the system as it existed and stated the need for immediate change. The presence of these youngsters, often articulate and persuasive, dramatically strengthened Miller's basic message that the issue was not one of young hoodlums and offenders, but of kids who had been battered by an inefficient and corrupt system for too long.

This may well have been one of Miller's greatest achievements. He significantly modified the public image of the young offender throughout the state. He demonstrated the havoc and destruction caused by institutions on the lives of countless youngsters over the years. Throughout his crusade, he had the vocal encouragement of such varied groups as the Lifers' Group of Walpole Prison and the League of Women Voters. It should be noted that it was the groups composed of lay people, such as the League of Women Voters, which were to provide consistent support to the agency throughout the fundamental changes. A similar level of support was not generally forthcoming from professional social-work and established penal-reform organizations, which maintained a somewhat ambiguous position during the period of change. Miller was very aware that there would be considerable resistance to meaningful change, some of it from those groups with a vested interest in arrangements as they existed. This resistance, which took a number of forms, was countered by a solid base of informed public support for reform.

Miller set out to humanize the training schools in a forceful and direct manner. He developed open lines of communication with youngsters, by talking with them on his visits to the institutions, and encouraging them to write or call him. There were, in fact, occasions when youngsters left the training school and made their way to his office. He was aware that there were considerable difficulties in upgrading the quality of staff. Although superintendents could be replaced, the state civil-service regulations made it virtually impossible to remove line staff, even if they were highly unsuited for work with young people. Attempts were made to train staff in new techniques and in a broader understanding of the needs of youngsters. Consultants used for such training sessions included Dr. Maxwell Jones, one of the originators of the therapeutic community concept, and Dr. Harry Vorath, who had developed group techniques with young offenders in Minnesota. Miller's attempts to improve institutional settings were not pursued for long at the segregation unit which the agency maintained at the Bridgewater Correctional Institution. He was appalled by the conditions that existed at this eighty-bed unit, known as the Institute for Juvenile Guidance. He had on one occasion visited the facility with the governor's wife, and they had together witnessed staff assaulting some youngsters who had attempted to abscond. The difficulties that followed in attempting to discipline the staff involved in this incident and the persistently punitive character of the Bridgewater unit convinced Miller that the only appropriate action was to close it down completely, and this was accomplished by September 1970. A little over a year later Miller was to apply much the same reasoning to the training schools themselves.

During his first year in office Miller was joined by a number of former associates from Ohio and from the United States Air Force. They were not, on the whole, people with experience in working with youngsters who had been before the courts. They came to Massachusetts to be a part of Miller's crusade for children in trouble. Expertise in penology and experience in working within correctional bureaucracies were less valuable qualifications than a high degree of commitment to change. Miller and his associates were very conscious of the high level of staff sabotage of the attempts to humanize the institutions, including the creation of incidents in the schools to undermine the credibility of the new administration. Apart from coping with active staff opposition, they also attempted to confront the tendency of any institutional program, even the most carefully designed, to slide back into a deadening routine. Miller and his colleagues, however, became increasingly impressed that there was no way of maintaining the impetus for change and growth within the institutional setting. By the time he had been in office for a year Miller was convinced that humanizing the institutions could be no more than a short-term solution. It simultaneously became clear that some of the more effective programs that Miller had developed would be still more appropriate in a community setting. As a result of reducing the length of time youngsters remained in the training schools Miller had already brought about a drop in the institutional population. In 1971 there was a daily average of 465 youngsters in training schools.

By the end of 1971 he was convinced that it would be politically feasible to move all the youngsters out of the four training schools. He possessed the administrative authority to transfer youngsters to any program, but did not have the authority to totally close the schools. The training school buildings and many of the staff, for the time being at least, had to remain. Miller was certain the best strategy would be a rapid rather than gradual approach, which would have produced heavy resistance. Attempts to gradually phase out the Shirley Industrial School during 1971 had been thwarted by staff resistance, which included the encouragement of runaways. He established task forces within the agency to develop plans, and it was clear the regional structure which had already been established would play an increasingly significant role. The seven regional offices, however, lacked the experience and resources to fully develop the potential that Miller was convinced existed in the community for a wide array of programs. Given the political context, the process had to be swift if it was to succeed, and the main thrust had to come from the central office. Time did not permit the full preparation of the regional offices for the rapid deinstitutionalization that took place.

The main effort to empty the institutions took place in January 1972. The population had been reduced at the Shirley Industrial School; those boys remaining were transferred to the Lyman School. An original and effective device was used to de-institutionalize the residual group at Lyman, which became known as the University of Massachusetts Conference. The boys remaining at Lyman moved to the campus at Amherst, where they participated in a one-month National Conference on Juvenile Delinquency Prevention and Treatment Program. About one hundred youngsters, including girls from Lancaster School, were involved, and they were joined by a similar number of college students. Joint student-youth groups were established with guidance from agency staff to develop community placements for the youth involved. The idea of using a university in this novel manner was conceived only a month or so before, and the final decision to go ahead was made on very short notice. The decision to remove the youngsters from the training schools was made completely within the agency, and there were no consultations with either the secretary of Human Services or the governor. Miller, however, was correct in his calculation that he would receive support from these two offices, and Governor Sargent visited Amherst to participate in some of the proceedings. It was a good time to move. The period between semesters was convenient to the university and the legislature was in recess. Because of the short notice, there were some difficulties of coordination between central office, the regional offices, and the conferees at Amherst, but despite these problems the device proved to be effective. The conference was run in a rather less formal manner than had originally been intended, and a study by the Harvard Center for Criminal Justice noted: "Advocates and 'their kids' did their own thing and for the most part this appeared to work out rather well."[1] Two-thirds of the youngsters were placed at their own homes, foster, or group homes, and the remaining twenty (eleven ran away from the conference) were held by the agency pending a placement decision. The Harvard paper indicates some of the points of learning that arose from the experience. There is considerable promise in its replication with a number of possible variations.

The agency was able to develop a wide range of new programs, which included arranging services for youngsters who resided at home. Many of these services were purchased rather than directly provided, and it was soon very clear that the process of de-institutionalization had radically altered the whole character of the agency. There was a movement of decision-making from the central to the regional offices, and many of the staff found that they were less involved in direct contact with youngsters and were instead involved in the tasks of selecting and monitoring services provided by groups outside the agency.

Consolidation 1973-74

Dr. Miller left Massachusetts in January, 1973, his moral crusade completed. (He is now an assistant and advisor on child welfare to the Governor of Illinois.) He considered that his essential work was accomplished and that the task of consolidation was better in the hands of someone else. The new commissioner did not have to carry the full weight of all the opposition that Miller had generated. Although Joseph Leavey was seen as one of Miller's people, having been deputy commissioner with responsibility for the development of the regional structure, he was from Massachusetts and would be more able than Miller to improve agency relations with such groups as the juvenile court judges.

During his first year in office, Leavey was concerned with strengthening the regional offices which now have complete responsibility for placement within the community. It is planned that the regional offices will have responsibility for detention placements and, probably in the long run, intensive treatment placements. The other crucial task facing Leavey was to develop an administrative and budgeting structure that would support the massive move in the direction of purchased services. For much of 1973 the agency faced a series of financial crises, but considerable progress was made in developing sound procedures both within the agency itself and with related parts of the government machinery. During the 1973 fiscal year one-third of the agency's budget was used for the purchases of services, with plans to increase this to half the budget in 1974. By the fall of 1973, the worst of the financial crisis was over. More effective administrative methods had been developed by the agency and within other government departments to accelerate payments to programs. The changed financial situation has greatly improved the relationship between the Department and the various groups with which it does business.

Staff salaries are still being paid and other costs borne by the agency at the former training schools which continue to be part of the Department's responsibility. There are indications that this double cost, borne by the agency since its transition from institutions to community programs, will not continue much longer. Increasing attention is being given to contract-making with the private groups that provide services for youngsters. At the same time, more attention is being given to evaluation of programs, both by regional staff who have responsibility for placements and by evaluation teams which are based within the central office and visit each program periodically. This process will be refined as evaluation procedures become more sophisticated and the standard setting develops greater precision.

It is not surprising that some of the staff who felt closely identified with Miller and the crusading phase have left. Some of these in fact have joined Miller in Illinois, where he is presently director of Children and Family Services. Leavey has assembled his own team of senior staff, and has recognized that the phase of consolidation requires a different style of administration. The main political battles appear to be over; substantial work remains to be done on developing and refining procedures, and there is considerably less staff contact with the youngsters themselves. Some staff failed to recognize that the agency faced new tasks, and misinterpreted structural changes within the agency as regressive developments. The phase of consolidation is likely to be a search for consensus rather than a further polarization of the issues. The change in relationship with youngsters also poses problems for staff. Now that agency staff is essentially concerned with initiating, facilitating, coordinating, and evaluating programs, they are perceived by youngsters in programs as playing a controlling rather than a helping role, as compared with program staff, who receive a more positive rating.[2] This change of role for many agency staff may be just as difficult as that which faced institutional staff three or four years ago. Given these changes in the agency task and structure, it can still be said that the central office of the Department must be one of the most informal headquarters of a corrections agency in the world. It has an exceptionally young staff, who tend to be casually attired and who work with an unusual degree of open communication between the different sections. A small number of youngsters, committed or referred to the agency, work at central office on a part-time basis. The headquarters is characterized by its ease and informality, and a visitor is left in no doubt that the staff's basic concern is the youngsters served by the agency.

Facts and Fantasies Concerning
Developments in Massachusetts

There has been widespread circulation of rumor throughout the United States concerning the consequences of the removal of youngsters from training schools in Massachusetts. There is no doubt that it was a very threatening event to many correctional administrators across the country. They and others have been only too anxious to hear some of the rumors. Fifty-eight of the sixty participants at the 1973 Annual National Conference of Superintendents of Training Schools and Reformatories, it seems, intended that their endorsement of the so-called Manwell Report be regarded as a censure of Miller. This report (compiled by a former training-school superintendent from Ohio) presents a fairly straight-forward account of the agency. The closest, however, that Manwell came to a criticism of the agency was his conclusion that: "Granted that in the Massachu-setts program there is much that is innovative, creative, and progressive, this preliminary survey indicates also many flaws and weaknesses, due in part to the haste in which the program was constituted."[3] The forthcoming findings of the Harvard team, and of the comparative study by the University of Michigan's National Assessment of Juvenile Corrections (Massachusetts is one of the sixteen states in the sample receiving intensive study), will greatly assist the serious consideration of what has taken place.

The most prominent of the rumors are:

1. The training schools have been quietly reopened. With the exception of Lancaster (the former girls' school), it can be categorically stated that there are no agency youngsters at any of the former training schools. The situation is as follows:

Bridgewater Institute for Juvenile Guidance—closed September 1970 and not used by the Department since.

Shirley Industrial School—closed January 1972. The facility houses some drug programs operated by the Department of Correction. It has also been used by a private agency that has a drug program, but not involving agency youngsters. It was officially handed over to the Department of Correction in January 1974.

The Lyman School—closed January 1972 and has held no agency youngsters since. It currently houses computers for the Department of Public Welfare.

Oakdale—closed June 1972 and now used as an administration office.

Lancaster School for Girls—closed August 1972. Cottages at this facility are used for several purposes. Up to ten girls are held there for placement in community programs; a cottage is used as a regional girls detention center. Other cottages are used by private groups for their own programs.

There is certainly no intention by Leavey and his colleagues to reopen the training schools. He is anxious to transfer total administrative responsibility for them to other government agencies as soon as he can, both on economic grounds and to reduce the chance that facilities may revert to their former use. (It should be noted that the three county training schools were closed during the winter of 1972-73, following the failure of the legislature to appropriate the required funding. Miller and others in the agency had campaigned actively for their closure. For an excellent account of a county training school and its political environment see the novel by John Hough, Jr., *A Two-Car Funeral* (Boston: Little, Brown and Company, 1973).

2. An increasing number of youngsters are being sent to adult state and county facilities. This is the stated belief of a number of people in and beyond Massachusetts. It is a view commonly expressed, for example, by some juvenile court judges, who believe that this is the case because they are aware of an increase in the number of youngsters bound over by their court to the adult court. It is difficult to form a conclusion as to an increase in bindovers, because figures on a statewide basis do not exist. It is clear, however, that not all such bindovers result in the imposition of a custodial sentence. In perhaps the majority of cases, the youngster is placed on adult probation. Other cases are passed back to the juvenile court for a disposition. The important point here is that a bindover is not synonomous with committal to an adult facility.

The latest published figures on youngsters in adult facilities appeared in an information bulletin issued by the Department of Correction on May 30, 1973. These figures exclude committals to the psychiatric prison at Bridgewater. It should be noted that the cut-off age for the analysis is seventeen, whereas courts currently have power to commit youngsters to the Department of Youth Services who are sixteen or younger. The maximum age of commitment to the Department was raised from sixteen to seventeen in 1974.

Between January 1972 and March 1973, 56 (4.2 percent) of the 1326 persons sentenced to state adult institutions were seventeen or younger, compared with a percentage of 4.3 percent for the previous six years. As of August 1 there were one sixteen-year-old and fourteen seventeen-year-olds in adult state institutions.[4] While there was no increase in number of youngsters going to state institutions, there was a slight increase in the percentage going to county facilities. The actual number of committals has not increased, but the rate for youngsters has not followed the declining pattern that has characterized committals as a whole. There are no figures available for 1973. On the basis of these figures, there is no evidence to support the contention of certain judges and others that more youngsters are now being committed to adult institutions because of the closing of the training schools.

3. The Department places many youngsters out of state. The suggestion has

Table 3-1

Number and Percentage of Persons Committed to State Prisons and County Jails by Year and Age

	Adult State Institutions				County Jails		
Year	Total Committed	Age 17 and Under		Year	Total Committed	Age 17 and Under	
1966	826	39	(4.7%)	1966	8990	275	(3.1%)
1967	739	32	(4.3%)	1967	8550	263	(3.1%)
1968	855	42	(4.9%)	1968	8467	263	(3.1%)
1969	875	30	(3.4%)	1969	8108	247	(3.0%)
1970	859	38	(4.4%)	1970	8119	287	(3.5%)
1971	1091	47	(4.3%)	1971	6474	240	(3.7%)
1972	1127	50	(4.4%)	1972	5449	252	(4.6%)
1973[a]	199	6	(3.0%)	1973	No figures available		
Total	6571	284	(4.5%)	Total	54207	1847	(3.4%)

[a]First three months only.

been made that the agency has simply rid itself of difficulties by moving large numbers of children to institutions or programs in other states. Selective use is made of some particularly good programs, such as an outward bound camp in Maine. The allegation that large numbers of youngsters are simply moved out of state is without any basis. Of some 2600 active cases during 1973, a daily average of 65 were placed in programs outside Massachusetts.

4. Dr. Miller was forced to resign. There is no evidence for this rumor; in fact both the governor and the secretary of Human Services attempted to persuade Miller to remain in Massachusetts. Miller made the decision to go to Illinois as director of Children and Family Services with some reluctance, as he felt that he was needed in Massachusetts for several more months. He was, however, convinced that in the long run his deputy, Joseph Leavey, would be more able to take the agency through the period of consolidation.

Some Contemporary Issues

The Number of Youngsters in Secure Facilities

The question as to how many agency youngsters are held within secure facilities is complicated by program definitions. Intensive treatment might mean confinement to a program characterized by tight security, or one where there is a high staff-youth ratio and an intensive program is in operation. There are a small number of youngsters confined to psychiatric hospitals, where the services purchased are considerably more expensive than those provided once by the training school. (On December 1, 1973, there were twelve youngsters who had been placed by the agency in psychiatric hospitals.) The main provision for fairly close security at present is the Andros program, which is a purchased service in a part of the Judge Connolly Youth Center in Roslindale, Boston. This program usually accommodates about thirty-five boys, with an average stay of nine months. There is general consensus within the Department that the number of intensive treatment placements will have to be increased. Current planning is to increase the number available from 35 to 109; this reflects the difficulty in placing certain youngsters in the existing range of services. These new intensive treatment programs will probably develop within the detention facilities at Worcester and Westfield. Considerable thought is being given, within the agency, to their program content. It is unlikely that they will rely on total physical security; instead they will place more reliance upon sound relationships with staff and a purposeful program. During 1974 a priority in the allocation of federal funds was the development of these units, with particular attention to the provision of a wider range of services for girls.

Unlike the practice in most states, the state agency, rather than county authorities, has the responsibility for those youngsters detained pending their court hearing. The regional director has the responsibility to decide the form of detention. The Department has been able to reduce the number of youngsters held in secure detention by developing some creative alternatives. On December 1, 1973, the Department was responsible for 219 youngsters in detention. Of these, 70 were in secure facilities, 118 in shelter-care detention, and 31 in temporary foster-home detention. Secure detention is provided within a purchased program at the Roslindale facility and at the Worcester and Westfield detention centers. The agency would like to completely abandon Roslindale, which is a bleak and barren place, and it is hopeful that further reductions can be made in the number of youngsters held in secure detention. There are seven shelter-detention programs throughout the state, consisting of a short-term residence without physical security for about ten youngsters. They are purchased programs, and two of them are located within YMCA buildings. Temporary placement in foster homes while in detention status is the least used of the options. The agency is planning to extend its strategy of purchasing rather than directly providing services for detained youngsters.

The Budget for the Department
of Youth Services

The agency's budget has increased from $7.2 million in 1969 to $16.3 million for the fiscal year 1974. The agency is still meeting the cost of maintaining the training schools and paying the salaries of about two hundred institutional staff positions. These items, for which the agency hopes soon to lose responsibility, amount to $2.7 million. In addition there are 150 positions that the agency would like to abolish, but the very strict civil service laws in the state have so far prevented this. It is also necessary to take into account the impact of inflation and the large increase in the agency's caseload. The new pattern of services has resulted in some additional costs, such as the establishment of regional offices and evaluation teams. The agency has also firmly resolved to provide a comprehensive range of services, and in some cases these are very expensive. Leavey would like to see a greater emphasis on the use of foster homes and on nonresidential services. One consequence of this would be a reduction in the overall cost of purchased services. Because the agency has had to bear the double cost of the old and new systems it is not yet possible to conclude, in the context of the total budget, that the expenditure for each youngster has decreased since 1969. Within the next two or three years some or most of the unwanted line items on the budget are likely to be removed. (Budget details are provided in the Annual Report of the Department of Youth Services, 1973.) The agency's budget and staff complement should then match its new tasks. Evaluative research data will also be available by then to enable the assessment of comparative costs to take into account data on recidivism.

The Purchase of Services

The agency either purchases individual placements or makes a contract for the entire program. During 1973 many of the groups that provided services, and in particular foster parents, were put to very severe financial strain, with the agency being on many occasions unable to pay for the services it had purchased. This occurred, in the main, because the financial mechanisms had not developed at the same pace as the other major structural changes in the agency. The Department was still bearing much of the cost involved in the upkeep of the training schools, while at the same time greatly increasing its expenditure on purchased services. Neither the agency nor the other parts of state government (such as the Rate Setting Board, which sets the rate for each program) had adjusted to the new and increasing demands resulting from this dramatic organizational change. Furthermore, federal funding was extensively used in the early stages of service purchasing, but as the procedures became routinized state finances were increasingly required.

The level of strain on individual programs caused by these financial difficulties was in part determined by the resources of the program or its parent organization. There did, however, appear to be certain differences in response to the crisis that were not simply a function of financial reserves. A visit to eight community programs in August 1973, just after the worst of the financial crisis, suggested that there might be three broad responses:

1. An exclamation of shocked outrage at the way in which change had occurred in the state. A number of statements such as "The real victims are the kids" and "No one was in favor of the old training institutions" were accompanied by protestations about the lack of professionalism of agency staff. The financial situation was seen as evidence that the agency did not know what it was about and as proof that it failed in its mission to provide an alternative system. Those who took this position tended to come from the more established agencies, and were mainly outraged at the challenge to their prescriptive approach to the offender and at the apparent removal of sanctions that had in the past made their job seem easier. As professional social workers they had developed a particular perspective on the offender and operated comfortably within a system that had shaped offenders to respond to its needs. They were now, however, being asked to make difficult adjustments at both a personal and organizational level. With the easing of the financial situation, such conflicts are likely to become more visible.

2. A response of strained tolerance. Most programs were concerned with providing a good service, but remained very anxious as to whether the program could continue to operate effectively at a high level of frustration and uncertainty.

3. A determined commitment to overcome the challenges of a new situation. The people involved in these programs were less likely to see themselves in professional social work terms and were more closely identified with the youngsters. Financial security, although welcome, was not an essential part of their lives. The program staff was likely to share the problem with the youngsters and to work out a joint method of tackling it. This was seen as part of the process of being involved in the program, and on one occasion staff members and youngsters took part in a sleep-in at the agency headquarters to focus attention on their situation. Although such confrontation tactics were used, the staff expressed a great deal of sympathy for the agency and placed the blame on factors beyond its control.

Philosophy and Content of Services

The purchase of services approach has allowed the agency to place youngsters in wide variety of programs. As of December 1, 1973, the agency was responsible for 2602 youngsters in over 200 programs (not including 219 detention cases).[5] They were to be found within the broad categories indicated in Table 3-2.

Specialized services that were not part of the residential situation were also provided to 71 youngsters placed in residential programs. There were also 837 youngsters with an inactive parole status.

The residential programs include a variety of types of group homes, placement in boarding schools, and very exceptionally in a psychiatric hospital.

Table 3-2
Placement of Delinquents in Residential Services in Massachusetts, 1973

	Committals	Referrals
Residential Services		
Group homes		
Boarding schools, etc.	379	199
Foster care	136	63
Nonresidential services		
Street programs,		
Day care, etc.	368	294
Parole	1163	–

The agency itself is responsible for a small forestry camp at Cape Cod. Most youths can expect to stay at a group home for three to four months. Placement in other residential programs, and in foster care, is likely to be for longer periods. Some interesting research is being collected by the Harvard team, which indicates that youth placed in group homes have a considerably higher regard for the staff of these programs than did the youngsters for staff in training schools three years ago. There are two particularly pertinent issues concerning programs:

1. Alternatives to the medical model. Miller hoped that it would be possible to develop programs that would avoid moving from penal to medical definitions. In relation to the emerging changes in Massachusetts, he wrote:

In terms of ideology, the question of correctional reform is not whether we can break out of previous definitions to more up-to-date definitions. It is rather whether we can 1) effectively break the vicious circle of definitions calling for institutional arrangements which, in turn, revalidate the definitions and 2) build into new definitions (since they will come) enough categories that show the social and psychological strengths and life-span of those defined as delinquent or criminal.[6]

Many of the programs, however, still operate within a prescriptive frame of reference, with assumptions about personal pathology very much to the fore. There is considerable room both to extend the choice that youngsters have as to the program they enter and to allow youngsters more opportunity to shape program design and operation. Leavey and his staff intend to give more time to the development of standards that would prompt program design to experiment with alternatives to the medical model.

2. The meaning of "community corrections." Deinstitutionalization did not mean that all youngsters went home. A number of the residential programs are situated a considerable distance from the youngsters' homes. The need to link

the residential program with the youngster's own community to which he will be returning is as critical as it was in the training school.

Some of the residential and all the nonresidential programs are situated within the youngster's own community, and continued attention is being given to program design that has immediate relevance to young persons' needs. A related and key question concerns whether decisions about such crucial issues as placement should be made by a state agency or the court. It can be argued that the court is closer to the local scene than the regional office of a state agency. One result of this, however, might be considerable discrepancies in the qualities of services provided across the state. Without careful safeguards, a further consequence might be the reappearance of youth institutions in Massachusetts. Leavey is very conscious of the role that the agency plays both in maintaining the level of services and in offsetting pressures toward reinstitutionalization.

The Implications of Referrals
to the Department

One of the factors that contributed to the agency's budgetary problems was the increase in the number of youths served. This was partly the result of an unanticipated increase in the number of youngsters referred by the courts to the agency. In December 1973 referrals represented a little over 21 percent of the total of the agency's active caseload, excluding detention. The purpose of referral is to avoid the stigma of commitment, and to ensure that the youngster receives adequate services. A referral requires the voluntary agreement of the youngster, his attorney, his parents, and the judge. A key role is usually played by the agency's court liaison officer. (It should be noted that court liaison officers, who are employees of the Department, have played a key role in improving the relationship with the courts.) One reason for the increase in referrals during 1973, which is interesting given the critical stance of many judges toward the agency, is that the courts have been more impressed by the quality of services that youth receives through the agency than with services arranged by the Department of Public Welfare. The agency, however, does refuse to accept a large number of referrals, and by the end of 1973 was taking active steps to reduce the referral rate. The acceptance of referrals by the agency raises important issues quite apart from additional financial strain that results. A central concern is the possibility that the process widens the correctional net to include youngsters who might not otherwise have penetrated so far into the criminal-justice system. How this issue is resolved will depend a great deal on the way in which the agency is perceived by youth and the public in general. Given a widespread reduction in the stigma attached to the agency, and continued provision of high quality services, the referral method of intake can be justified. It is clearly a matter that requires careful research and continual review.

An associated issue is the agency's policy to retain youngsters on an inactive parole status after the provision of services has been terminated. (The Department can retain responsibility up to the age of twenty-one.) This is done so that the agency can be an advocate for the youngster if occasion arises, and a strong defense of the practice can be made. If, however, the agency were less benign, it would be under considerable pressure to make a clear parole termination. This points to some central issues that the agency must face concerning the rights of all youngsters, whether committed or referred. These include the opportunity for the youngster to protest a program placement at any time, and to be given a hearing as to parole termination should he request one. During the crusading phase, when the task was to get the youngsters out of the institutions, such issues did not arise. The grievance was seen as the old system and the agency as the advocate of change. This advocacy role will continue to be important, but it should not be allowed to obscure the development of procedures that provide the young person with the means of redress concerning decisions made about him by the agency, however benign in intent they might be.

Evaluation

Mention has been made of the teams sent out from central office to evaluate programs. This process is growing in sophistication, and plays an important part in the establishment of standards. Four programs have been terminated and others modified as a result of these inspections. The agency has undertaken a small research program, and its organization of data requires considerable refinement. It is particularly fortunate that a major research study commenced in 1969 under the direction of Professor Lloyd Ohlin of the Center for Criminal Justice at the Harvard Law School. The Harvard study, which is financed by the Law Enforcement Assistance Administration, and by the Governor's Committee on Law Enforcement and Administration of Criminal Justice, has five main components:

1. An organizational study of the agency during this period of radical change in shape and function.

2. A study of the political arena within which the changes occurred.

3. Subculture studies within institutions and group homes.

4. Program evaluation. The focus here is on general strategies rather than particular programs. This is the closest that the Harvard study comes to action research.

5. The cohort study. Successive admissions are being followed through the system, within two regions at any one time. The data that is generated by the cohort study will answer the question as to the recidivism of those youngsters who went through the institutional system as compared with those who went through the system after the training schools were closed.

A number of papers have already been prepared and many others will appear during the next few years, including two or three major publications.[7] The Harvard research is important in a number of respects. In particular, it will provide an objective account and analysis of a significant landmark in correctional change. The Harvard study started before the training schools were closed, and its findings will throw significant light on a development that no part of the United States has been able to ignore. In the meantime, the quarterly and other reports from the Harvard study should enable the Department to avoid becoming trapped with new panaceas. This regular flow of information and the constant stream of visitors to the agency should encourage staff to think through the implications of the considerable feedback material that is available. Youth served by the system should also have input into these deliberations. David Rothman in his book, *The Discovery of the Asylum*, has clearly expressed the required note of warning:

Proposals that promise the most grandiose consequences often legitimate the most unsatisfactory developments. . . . [But] we need not remain trapped in inherited answers. An awareness of the causes and implications of past choices should encourage us to greater experimentation with our own solutions.[8]

The Political Context of Correctional Change in Massachusetts

When Miller arrived in Massachusetts, there was little political support for the status quo, and the legislation enacted in 1969 was clearly a mandate for meaningful change. Such change had the very strong backing of the governor, a number of influential legislators, and a large number of groups across the state. Much of the media had played an important part in drawing attention to the inequities of the old system, and the press continued to provide Miller with considerable support. His crusading style allowed the issues at stake to be dramatically polarized and neatly articulated by the press and television; people were either for or against kids. The removal of children from the training schools took place within this context, and although Miller was to face considerable opposition from some legislative committee members and certain segments of the media, he was never in deep trouble. By the beginning of 1973, the closing of the training schools had ceased to be a political issue. None of the opponents whom Sargent may face in the 1974 gubernatorial election is likely to use youth corrections as an issue. During 1973 some judges expressed concern about the limited options they had for the more serious offender. In September a number of them gave testimony to a Commission on Children in which they went on record as calling for legislation that would give courts the power to determine the length of institutional sentences. Leavey and his staff have had a number of meetings with judges, and there is little likelihood of such regressive legislation being enacted. Much of the criticism of the Department of Youth Services during 1973 arose from the budgetary situation, and this in part reflected the very real concern of many personnel in the programs affected. A Post-Audit Committee of the Legislature undertook a very detailed investigation of the administration of the agency but the committee's report is not expected to create much of a furor. Given the improvement in the agency's financial position, the report will probably seem out of date.

In January 1972 John Boone was appointed commissioner of the Department of Correction, and a continuing series of controversies deflected some of the political heat away from the youth corrections. This was particularly so in the case of certain legislators and a daily newspaper, the *Boston Herald American.* Boone had arrived in the state with apparently bipartisan support for an overhaul of the adult prison system. Some important prison reform legislation, in the main developed before his appointment, was enacted in July 1972, pointing adult corrections in the direction of the community. Boone, however, was to find himself involved in upsets and crises involving one prison after another, each of which was used by some legislators and segments of the media as justification for demanding his resignation. The adult corrections scene was to a large degree shaped by correctional officers' unions, which together with the increasing organization of prisoners, created a highly volatile situation. There is little doubt that Sargent backed meaningful change in adult corrections for longer than narrow political considerations suggested was wise. It was with considerable reluctance that Sargent decided, in June 1973, that Boone had to go. The presence in Massachusetts of this liberal Republican governor (both Houses are controlled by the Democrats) in part explains why during 1972-73 Massachusetts was the most interesting state to watch in relation to both youth and adult corrections. Governor Sargent was defeated in his re-election bid in November 1974.

The changes that have taken place in youth corrections in Massachusetts have implications for every state in the Union and beyond. No agency for young offenders can ignore the fact that Massachusetts has now existed without training schools for two years. The process of deinstitutionalization is, throughout the Western world, taking place over a wide range of areas of social concern. It implies not the ready solution of problems, but the creation of opportunities to face them more realistically. The Massachusetts experience, one of the major correctional events of our time, has enhanced our ability and confidence to take the creative leap forward that is needed in the development of more humane and effective approaches to social problems.

References

1. R.B. Coates, A.D. Miller, and L.E. Ohlin, "Strategic Innovation in the Process of De-institutionalization: The University of Massachusetts Conference,"

in Closing Correctional Institutions, edited by Yitzhak Bakal (Lexington, Mass.: Lexington Books, D.C. Heath, 1973).

2. Lloyd E. Ohlin, Robert B. Coates, Alden D. Miller, "Radical Correctional Reform: A Case Study of the Massachusetts Youth Correctional System," Harvard Educational Review, 44(1) 1974.

3. Manwell's report is reprinted in *Impact*, Raleigh, N.C., Vol. 1, 6, 1973.

4. Massachusetts Department of Corrections, Research and Planning Division.

5. It is interesting to compare the 1970 and 1973 situation. In 1970 the agency was responsible for 932 youngsters (average daily count). They were distributed as follows:

Institutions:	507	Group care:	125
Detention:	238	Foster care:	30
Forestry:	25	Nonresidential:	7

Exact parole figures are not available for 1970. It is estimated that there were approximately 1200 youngsters on parole status, but most of these were receiving minimal services.

6. Jerome Miller, "The Politics of Change: Correctional Reform," in Closing Correctional Institutions, edited by Yitzhak Bakal (Lexington, Mass.: Lexington Books, D.C. Heath, 1973).

7. Ohlin, op. cit.

8. David Rothman, *The Discovery of the Asylum* (Boston: Little, Brown, 1971), p. 295.

Part II: Alternatives

4

Prison Without Walls Summary Report on New York Parole Citizens' Inquiry on Parole and Criminal Justice, Inc.[a]

Introduction

Parole is an idealistic concept. It seeks simultaneously to protect the public and to give the criminal offender a new chance. But these noble purposes have not been realized. Parole is a tragic failure. Conspiring with other elements of the criminal justice system—unnecessary pretrial detention, overlong sentences, oppressive prison conditions—it renders American treatment of those who break society's rules irrational and arbitrary.

This chapter summarizes a three hundred-page study of the New York State parole system conducted by the Citizens' Inquiry on Parole and Criminal Justice. Research for this study included observing two hundred parole release hearings, interviewing thirty parole officials and over one hundred parolees, reviewing all the statutes relating to parole since 1877, reading all the annual reports of the Division of Parole since 1930, checking all *New York Times* references to parole in the last forty years, and studying the relevant legal and sociological scholarship. But that does not mean that the viewpoint is value-free. While the report strives for objectivity in reporting its findings, it is also informed by a set of strongly held beliefs about the use of the criminal sanction in a free society.

The Citizens' Inquiry study was premised, in part, on the following values:

1. Individual freedom is an axiom of a democratic society, and should be preserved unless there is incontrovertible evidence that the actions of one person include the use or threat of violence against another.

2. Prisons create crime, rather than correcting criminals.

3. When some sort of confinement appears necessary to accomplish the aims of the criminal sanction, the offender should not be removed farther than is absolutely necessary from his peers and his community.

4. Coercion that extends beyond basic confinement should be avoided as much as possible, since it further antagonizes offenders and reduces their ability to solve their own problems.

[a]The Citizen's Inquiry on Parole and Criminal Justice is a private, nonprofit corporation engaged in research and public education on problems of the postconviction criminal justice system. Its chairman is former Attorney General Ramsey Clark, and its director for the period of the parole study was David Rudenstine. This summary report was prepared by Diana R. Gordon and David Rudenstine. A similar version appeared in the November 1974 *Criminal Law Bulletin.* The full report, *Prison Without Walls: Report on New York Parole*, will be published by Praeger Publishers in 1975. This chapter reprinted by permission of the copyright authors.

A list of the names of the members of the Citizens' Inquiry and Investigation staff follows this chapter.

5. Parolees should have all of the civil and individual rights of other citizens. Inmates should be deprived of their rights only to the extent made necessary by the fact of their incarceration. Neither group should have to submit to authorities trying to shape them into a single, middle-class model of good citizenship.

A call for change generally challenges the practices of the institution under fire, but accepts its theory. The Citizens' Inquiry study repudiates both the theory and the practice of parole. It finds that the parole board and the parole service do not live up to their own standards, and that even if they did, the invalidity of basic parole theory would prevent the realization of its goals. It would surely be desirable to have a well-prepared parole board conducting careful release interviews based on full information about inmates; but such an achievement would not result in rational decision-making. Parole boards would still act arbitrarily if they applied legally prescribed release criteria, because, for the time being at least, future human conduct cannot be predicted and even basic changes in personality and character cannot usually be assessed. Without standards against which to measure the fact-finding of the parole board, due process protections are meaningless. Since the theory of rehabilitation includes vague and subjective notions of moral character and future conduct, there is no way that the parole board can measure the degree of an inmate's rehabilitation.

It is important to note that parole is part of a process that begins with arrest, proceeds through the pretrial stage (where a defendant may be held in detention or released), through the trial to sentencing and the period of imprisonment. Both long-range and interim recommendations for parole depend on the future direction of pretrial detention, of sentencing, and of prisons. To abolish parole because of its demonstrated irrationality and harm and leave the rest of the process as it presently exists would cause even more harm. With all its faults, parole is not as destructive as imprisonment, and the possibility of release is preferable to the certainty of confinement.

Although the Citizens' Inquiry has not focused on the related institutions that would have to change if parole were to be abolished, the study involved some examination of them, and a number of the Task Force members have direct professional experience with them. Those changes which are most intimately related to parole and which must be coordinated with the abolition of parole are outlined in the recommendations section at the end of this summary. Other criminal justice reforms are also necessary, like the decriminalization of victimless crimes; the elimination of most pretrial detention; abolition of large, remote prisons; and the development of small neighborhood facilities. Continuing careful study should precede and accompany the institution and use of these reforms.

This chapter describes the theory of parole in New York, shows how current practice diverges from this theory, demonstrates the invalidity of the theory itself, and sets forth long-term and transitional recommendations. It reaches the following general findings and conclusions:

1. Both elements of the New York State parole system—the decision-making function and the community supervision program—have failed dramatically and are beyond reform. But parole is part of the present indeterminate and reformatory sentencing structure, and could be abolished only with simultaneous, extensive changes in that structure.

2. Parole in New York rests on faulty theory and has unrealistic goals. The humanitarian goal of treatment and rehabilitation of the offender has been used to justify unnecessarily lengthy incarceration and parole supervision. Since there is no agreement on the meaning of rehabilitation, and no one now knows what rehabilitates or who is rehabilitated, decisions as to length of sentence and timing of release based on an assessment of an inmate's rehabilitation are irrational and cruel.

3. The parole system is often unnecessarily abusive and unfair; offenders have many serious and legitimate grievances. Much of the daily oppressiveness of parole flows from the enormous amount of unstructured and invisible discretion exercised by the parole board and the parole service.

4. Parole allows many actors in the criminal justice system to hide the real nature of their actions and thereby escape responsibility for them. District attorneys may call for and judges may impose excessively long sentences in the name of law and order, knowing that the deferred sentencing process of parole will mitigate their harshness. The parole board's extensive and invisible discretion makes it possible for these officials to mislead the public.

5. A wide gap separates what the New York parole system professes to do and what it actually does. One indication that parole has not lived up to its aims is its failure to consider or adopt widely accepted reforms proposed by responsible professional groups.

A general note about racism and parole is appropriate here. The racial consequences of our society's use of the criminal sanction are evident in the disproportionately high percentage of black prisoners and the imbalance of racial backgrounds between the jailers and the jailed. National commission reports and scholarly studies alike have pointed out the pervasiveness of racism in virtually all operations of the criminal-justice system. In order to wipe out discrimination, both independent groups and the institutions of the system must understand its nature and causes. Only sensitivity to the problem, combined with careful data collection and interpretation at every step of the process, can ensure that understanding.

The Citizens' Inquiry, in conducting its study, requested information about racial matters from state officials. The Division of Parole, however, as a matter of policy, does not collate statistical data that would reveal the extent to which parole operates in a racially discriminatory manner. As a result, an informed judgment as to the practices and effect of racism in the parole system is not possible. We know that inmates and parolees are largely poor minority-group men and women, while parole board members are generally comparatively affluent and well-educated white males. Informal inquiries reveal that the proportion of black and Puerto Rican parole officers is considerably lower than that of inmates and parolees. Racial differences between the parole officials and the parolee population manifest the presence of considerable racial bias in fact and appearance. Parole officials are derelict in not documenting racial facts and maintaining a vigilance over any discrimination they may reveal. Not until blacks and other minorities participate equally with whites in shaping the criminal justice system—as corrections officers, parole officers, administrators, judges—will our society provide equal justice to its citizens.

The Image of Parole

Parole was conceived as a liberal, humane way to mitigate the agonies of incarceration. Those who administer it see it in this light today; New York parole officials are proud of what they believe to be a fair and effective institution. This section sets forth a brief history of parole, a description of its place in New York's criminal-justice system, and a picture of the way in which the parole system sees itself—its goals, policies and practices.

Background

Until the nineteenth century, prisons were used mainly to house detainees, who awaited trials at which they were sentenced to such punishments as whipping, maiming, or execution. Long-term incarceration became the practice when institutionalization was seen as a means whereby deviants could be reformed into productive citizens. Even within the first half-century of the existence of prisons as we know them, their defects became apparent. They did not rehabilitate their inmates. An 1867 report to the New York State legislature said of state prisons around the country, "There is not one, we feel convinced . . . which seeks the reformation of its subjects as a primary object." The late 1800s saw the birth of parole, an attempt to extend the theoretically rehabilitative benefits of prison life into the community while simultaneously reducing the likelihood that prison would have detrimental effects.

New York adopted parole at the Elmira Reformatory nearly one hundred years ago, the first state to do so. In 1899 it spread to some adult institutions, and during the early years of the twentieth century, sentencing laws were changed to make a larger number of inmates eligible for parole. Since the framework of the present parole system was established in 1930, parole has grown from an obscure agency with a three-member board and a budget of less than $350,000 into a substantial bureaucracy (617 professionals in 1969, the last year for which figures were available) with a twelve-member parole board, a budget of over $12 million, and several offices around the state. In 1972 4412 inmates were released from state institutions on parole, and at the end of the year there were approximately 10,000 people under parole supervision in the state.

Parole Today

The basic structure of parole is the same now as it was a century ago. Parole is granted to inmates after they have served a portion of their sentence, but before completion of the maximum term. Parolees in theory are supervised while in the community by parole officers and are expected to abide by special rules, on penalty of parole revocation.

All states and the federal government now have parole systems. Parole is crucial to many parts of the criminal-justice system: sentencing schemes are built around it, prosecutors take it into account in charging defendants and participating in plea bargaining, judges' roles in sentencing have been diminished as parole boards' jurisdiction over release has grown. Parole is also important in the operation of prisons. In New York nearly two-thirds of all inmates leaving state prisons annually are released by the parole board; another one-fifth, released through a mechanism other than parole, are subject, like parolees, to community supervision. Prison programs may be well or poorly attended depending on whether inmates believe that their participation will improve their chances for parole. While parole is often viewed by prison officials as a way of maintaining prison order and discipline, it may also be a cause of a catastrophic prison uprising. After a thorough investigation of the uprising at Attica prison in September 1971, in which forty-three inmates and guards died, the official report of the New York State Special Commission on Attica concluded:

Inmates' criticisms were echoed by many parole officers and corrections personnel, who agreed that the operation of the parole system was a primary source of tension and bitterness within the walls.

Parole in New York has become a more and more important part of the postconviction criminal-justice system. Yet, like all parole systems, it continues to function under a veil of secrecy. The New York board is the largest, best salaried state parole board in the country, yet few people could name or identify a single member. The public has only the slightest notion of parole's functions, goals, modes of operation, and degree of success or failure. As a quasi-judicial, autonomous body, the board is uniquely removed from the scrutiny of the courts, legislature, media, or public.

How Parole Is Supposed to Work

Parole is seen by corrections officials, legislators, judges, and the general public as the best way to ease the inmate's difficult transition from incarceration to freedom. It is intended to shorten sentences and to provide individual consideration of offenders' problems. To this end, the parole board theoretically tries to release an inmate when he has reached that optimal moment when he can lead a crime-free life "on the street." Then the community supervision program claims to aid his reintegration into society by offering him services and guidance beyond the prison walls.

For the past hundred years, corrections professionals have embraced an undefined goal of rehabilitation of offenders as the aim of incarceration. The theory of rehabilitation, as commonly espoused by parole officials, is set forth in the "Preliminary Report of the Governor's Special Committee on Criminal Offenders" of June 1968 (p. 55):

1. There are certain personal characteristics that impede an individual's ability to function at a generally acceptable level in one or more basic social areas.
2. The difficulty of performing at a generally acceptable level in such areas significantly contributes to criminal conduct.
3. Treatment should be directed at overcoming the aforesaid personal characteristics.

Thus, the aim of rehabilitation is to treat those characteristics of the offender which are inconsistent with the basic characteristics needed to function acceptably. It is felt that, if the treatment has a positive impact, the offender will be more likely to satisfy his needs through socially acceptable conduct and the likelihood of his return to crime will be reduced.

Neither the parole board nor the parole service attempts to enumerate the "certain personal characteristics that impede an individual's ability to function at a generally acceptable level."

Parole officials see the parole decision-making process as expert, fair, and guided only by determinations of an inmate's degree of rehabilitation. The parole board is supposed to be an independent body of exemplary citizens with a range of experience to insure their impartiality. They are theoretically enabled to make highly individualized decisions because they are supposed to receive careful, official reports on each inmate and conduct an interview with him designed to reveal the likelihood that he will be a successful parolee. Preparation for parole is to be started in the prison with the skilled assistance of institutional parole officers.

All aspects of parole supervision are intended to further its two principal aims: the protection of the public and the assistance of the parolee in becoming reintegrated into nonprison life. The community supervision parole officer is to be a well-educated, sensitive man or woman able to maintain a helping relationship with the parolee, while at the same time enforcing the terms of the parole agreement. Parole officers are to be equally concerned about finding jobs for parolees and checking up to make sure that parolees live and work where they say they do. The parole service considers it important to leave these officers broad discretion in enforcing the less important parole conditions, but it also aims to provide effective guidance and regulation through a detailed manual. A good parole officer is able to anticipate when a parolee is beginning to stray and return him to prison, through initiating revocation proceedings, before a new offense is committed. The parole service considers that it treats the parolee equitably throughout.

The Reality of Parole

New York corrections officials believe that the goals of parole are sound, and that its operation reflects professional competence and even-handed performance. The Citizens' Inquiry study found a great gap between what the parole system professes to do and what it actually does. This section will elaborate on the ways in which parole in New York does not live up to its declared aims, policies, and practices.

Decision-Making—Parole Release

The New York Board of Parole is an autonomous body within the State Department of Correctional Services, whose twelve members serve full time and are appointed to six-year renewable terms by the governor. The autonomy of the board does not guarantee its independence, for board memberships are often given out as political reward or favors. The range of experience among board members is not wide; most are white males over fifty from outside New York City. Many have come to the board from corrections and law enforcement. People who have made careers of confining and arresting are now asked to wield the power of release. By contrast, the current state prison population is mostly under thirty, nonwhite, and from New York City.

The parole board's jurisdiction is very broad. It decides when most inmates will become eligible for parole; who shall or shall not be paroled; what conditions parolees must obey while in the community; who shall or shall not have his parole revoked; who shall or shall not be discharged from community supervision prior to completing the normal term; and who shall or shall not be granted a certificate partially restoring his civil and employment rights. Its jurisdiction extends to all inmates serving sentences of more than ninety days—a total well in excess of 20,000—and to all former inmates under parole officer supervision. As a result the board's work load is enormous; for example, in 1971, the board reported that it was responsible for 17,628 hearings or decisions.

Parole panels are, as a theoretical matter, supposed to let the parole eligibility date largely reflect their judgment as to when an inmate might be sufficiently rehabilitated so that he could seriously be considered for parole. As a result the board is endowed with broad discretion in establishing the date. In practice, however, parole eligibility dates are reflections of rules of thumb rather than judgments about the individual characters of each inmate. For most inmates serving an indeterminate sentence parole eligibility will be set as a matter of course at one-third of the maximum term or three years, whichever is less. This practice not only ignores the board's stated objectives, but abrogates its responsibilities under New York law.

Institutional parole officers prepare for parole board members a case file on each inmate. But this file does not ensure a truly individualized decision-making process. Although crammed with reports from prison officials (warden, chaplain, disciplinarian, and psychiatrist), the inmate's presentence report, juvenile and criminal-justice attorney, the file is not very useful. The board members receive it only at the moment they are ready to hold an inmate's release interview, and there is no opportunity to examine the reports closely. Except for the "parole summary," which is prepared by an institutional parole officer usually a few months before an inmate's hearing, only one board member actually sees the case file; duplicates are not provided to other members. In addition, even though the case files were not available for examination, their quality and method of use is not good enough to be very helpful to parole board members. With only one officer for every 241 inmates, contacts with inmates are necessarily infrequent and superficial. Also inmates and institutional parole officers do not meet in circumstances likely to elicit candid information for reports. In 1967 a National Council on Crime and Delinquency study found that New York case files contained inadequate depth as to the causes and manifestations of inmates' problems.

The parole board makes its release decisions in panels of three during monthly visits to each state prison. The conduct of release interviews makes a mockery of the board's claim that it considers each individual inmate's case carefully. Because of the board's work load, the interviews are generally very short. Those observed by the Citizens' Inquiry generally lasted less than twelve minutes, with some as short as five minutes; the longest release interview observed lasted twenty-five minutes. Although New York law requires that the release interview be conducted by three members of the parole board, in practice only the member who reads the file usually questions an inmate, while the other two panel members are examining the files of the inmates who will come next. Most of the questions asked are, of necessity, predictable and general. Inmates are tense and usually try to say what they think will most favorably impress the parole board members.

The release process is unfair. The inmate is not permitted to have an attorney or other respresentative appear with him at his interview. He is permitted neither to present his own witnesses, nor to confront those against him. He may not see any of his case file. New York officials claim that to provide the inmate with

Table 4-1
Released and Returned as Violator–Same Year, by Method of Release[a]

	1968		1969		1970		1971	
	Parole Release	Conditional Release	Parole Release	Conditional Release	Parole Release	Conditional Release	Parole Release	Conditional Release
Released to community supervision	4623	1703	4086	1633	3860	1795	4051	1793
Returned as violators	475	191	414	189	393	250	325	194
%	10.3	11.2	10.1	11.6	10.2	13.9	8.0	10.8

[a]This chart does not purport to reflect general recidivism rates, even for a one-year period, because it shows only the return rates of inmates released and returned within the same year. Inmates released in November or December of one year are included, as well as those released in January or February, although their return rate will clearly be much lower.

Prisoners released by the parole board and on conditional release are subject to the same community supervision program.

There is one unmeasured factor that might affect the validity of this comparison. A parole violator has his sentence credited by the time he spent in the community, whereas a conditional release violator does not.

Source: Annual Report of the Division of Parole 1968-1971, Tables 25, 25A, 28, 28A.

material problems are staggering when he first comes out of prison. Nevertheless, he is given only a suit, forty dollars, the name and address of a community supervision parole officer to whom he must report within twenty-four hours, and a list of rules that he must follow, on pain of losing his freedom. He is generally qualified only for unskilled or semi-skilled work, and he faces other major problems in getting and keeping a job. Although the parole service recognizes employment as a major goal of each parolee, the parole officers provide little assistance in finding jobs. In 1970 New York parole officers helped obtain only 506 jobs, although over 16,000 people were on parole at some time during the year, 5,680 of them employed full-time. Similarly, the Department of Correctional Services does next to nothing to help the penniless parolee with financial problems. "Gate money" of forty dollars is inadequate, the parole service has no loan fund, and New York parolees are not eligible for unemployment benefits. Furthermore, that recourse is at odds with the system's goal of leading a person into self-sufficiency and dignity in the nonprison world. The parole service also does not provide adequate housing assistance; the parole service, in fact, often impedes a parolee's attempts to get settled, because every proposed residence must be approved by the parole officer. The parolee's housing problems are further complicated by his ineligibility for public housing, at least in New York City.

The law-enforcement aim of the community supervision program is at least honored by a genuine effort at realization. Community supervision officers are urged to expend the greater part of their time and energy on trying to enforce the parole rules as embodied in the list which every parolee signs. This list is an agreement between the parolee and the parole board that the former will abide by restrictions on his life imposed by the latter. The Correction Law specifies a number of conditions that may be imposed. The parole agreement currently goes well beyond the minimal statutory provision, regulating virtually every aspect of a parolee's life.

Some of the more controversial conditions are the prohibition from leaving the area of the state to which the parolee is released without the parole officer's permission; the requirement that a parolee must allow his parole officer to search him, or to visit him at home or at work, without prior notice; the limitation that a parolee may not associate with people who have a criminal record; the requirement that a parolee must consult with his parole officer before applying for a marriage license or changing his job or residence; and the requirement that a parolee must get permission from his parole officer to drive or own a car.

Parolees interviewed by the Citizens' Inquiry felt that these restrictions often unnecessarily inhibited their reintegration into society. The prohibition against driving and traveling interstate reduces a parolee's employment opportunities. The agreement in general denies the parolee usual constitutional guarantees to the right of privacy at home, on the job, and with respect to personal relations. Furthermore, the conditions are so comprehensive that it is practically impossible for a parolee not to violate one of them occasionally. The parole conditions are too numerous, coercive, and intrusive. Their imposition seems more likely to hinder a parolee's integration into society than to help it.

After release, a parolee's principal contact with the parole system is through the community supervision parole officer. A college graduate with experience in social work, law enforcement, or law, the parole officer has a difficult role. He has two responsibilities: to assist parolees in adjusting to the outside world, and to prevent or punish parole violations and criminal activities. This means that the parole officer is both social worker and policeman. He cannot fill either role very well.

As policeman, the parole officer is armed, authorized to search the parolee and his property, given power to restrict many aspects of his life, and charged with enforcing parole rules and initiating revocation proceedings if the rules are violated. He is statutorily classified, along with police and prison guards, as a "peace officer." As social worker, he is supposed to counsel the parolee on basic social and financial problems. He may assist in finding a job or housing or drug therapy. He may mediate between the parolee and the agencies or organizations that he deals with. The two roles of the parole officer regularly conflict. He often must decide between an action that protects the community and one that aids the parolee. When such a situation arises, he is expected to choose the solution that he believes will protect the public. The conflict is apparent to parolees, and precludes the development of a relationship of mutual trust.

New York's parole system emphasizes more than in many jurisdictions the role of law enforcement in community supervision. This emphasis is misplaced, for several reasons. For one thing, it is ineffective. Most parolees are apprehended for a new offense before their parole officer has initiated parole revocation proceedings. Studies have shown that community supervision does not significantly decrease the recidivism rates of releasees, and that criminal violations leading to parole revocation are usually uncovered by law-enforcement officials, rarely by parole officers. The law-enforcement aspects of community supervision also deny the parolee fundamental freedoms enjoyed by other citizens. Finally, the surveillance and the ever-present possibility that even minor conditions may be enforced to send a parolee back to prison can frustrate him in such a way to increase his general alienation.

Community supervision, in summary, does not assist the parolee and does not protect the public. Scarce resources are spent on inept social services and ineffective enforcement of the parole agreement. The parole regulations became an albatross around the neck of most parolees, actually impeding their reentry into society.

Revocation

The basic coercive power of the community supervision program is the revocation of parole, followed by the parolee's return to prison for all or part of his sentence. Although the parole service maintains that this power is exercised fairly, parolees are often treated as having none of the rights of ordinary citizens.

Revocation cuts across both the decision-making and community supervision aspects of parole. Parole board members are ultimately responsible for deciding whether parole should be revoked in particular cases, and community supervision officers usually initiate and recommend a parolee's revocation. Because revocation leads back to prison, parolees live in terror of it.

The parole officer has enormous discretion in enforcing the parole agreement. The relevant statute provides that if the parole officer has "reasonable cause to believe that such [parolee] has lapsed, or is probably about to lapse, into criminal ways or company, or has violated the conditions of his parole in an important respect," he is to report that to the parole board or its representative, who may then apprehend the parolee, or he may retake the parolee himself. Under the provisions of this statute a parole officer may choose to overlook violations, and where a parolee has shown a generally good adjustment to the community, he often does so. When a violation of parole rules (often called a "technical violation") leads an officer to initiate revocation proceedings, it is often because he suspects that a parolee is "slipping," moving from a life that he thinks is fairly stable to one that seems to the officer more likely to bring about the commission of a crime. Other situations which parole officers deem appropriate for revocation proceedings are cases where a parolee is arrested, has absconded, or is convicted of a new felony. When a parolee is taken into custody, he is held without any possibility of release, often for two or three months, pending his revocation hearing.

In general, a parole officer prizes his wide discretion, and a certain amount of it is necessary to maintain the present system. Since the parole agreement contains so many technical rules, nearly every parolee violates one of them at some time. If a parole officer were obligated to recommend revocation every time he was aware of a rule violation, most parolees would be returned to prison for only minor infractions.

The New York statute does not provide any due-process safeguards for a parolee faced with revocation proceedings. But during the past few years, constitutional rulings of the United States Supreme Court and the New York Court of Appeals have begun to carve out some protection. Taken together, these rulings have established, among other things, a two-step hearing process whereby the parole board determines whether or not the parole agreement has been violated. Recent decisions have also given the parolee the right to representation, the right to present witnesses, the right to be confronted by witnesses against him, and the right to partial disclosure of information in the case file. While New York has complied in most respects with these rulings, it has refused to allow parolees to confront witnesses against them. In addition to providing parolees with procedural due-process rights once revocation proceedings have begun, the judicial developments have also restrained parole officers somewhat in their decisions to recommend revocation.

The new due-process rights are primarily important to the revocation process at its fact-finding state. Once a parole violation is verified, parole board members must decide whether to retain a parolee in prison or return him to the community. They must make a prediction very similar to that made at the release stage, with no more secure justification.

The Defects of Parole Theory

Parole grows out of a set of assumptions popularly known as the treatment or rehabilitation theory. This theory, which gained wide currency in the nineteenth century and became the basic goal of both sentencing and imprisonment, assumed that the cause of criminality was primarily the result of a personality defect or disorder within the offender. This defect, it was reasoned, could be diagnosed and treated within a penal setting. The offender's response to treatment could be evaluated so that he could be released at the optimum moment of his rehabilitation (i.e., when he was least likely to commit another crime).

Under this theory, sentences had to provide for a flexible period of imprisonment, since the amount of time necessary for the offender's rehabilitation could not be predicted at the time of trial, and prisons had to provide treatment programs. In addition, a mechanism was needed to provide for evaluating an offender's rehabilitation, releasing him from prison, and supervising him in the community. This mechanism is parole.

The goals of community supervision are: (1) to continue the treatment of the offender that was begun in prison by assisting him in his adjustment to the community; and (2) to protect the public from criminal activity by returning the offender to prison for violation of parole rules prior to the committing of a crime. To fulfill the latter goal parole officers must identify parolees who are about to commit a crime; and the parole board, which possesses the final revocation authority, must agree with the parole officer's prediction.

Previous sections of this chapter have discussed the gap between the reality of parole and its image. Instead of making carefully reasoned decisions based on an inmate's rehabilitation, the parole board uses a rule of thumb in setting the parole eligibility date, and speeds through release interviews making decisions often not based on its assessment of the likelihood of an inmate's recidivism. The similarity between defendants granted parole and those denied is striking enough to suggest that, despite its attempts at professionalism and competence, the parole board is unable to distinguish the rehabilitated from the nonrehabilitated. The community supervision program, instead of helping parolees adjust to nonprison society, is usually irrelevant and sometimes harmful. The parole service has not been able to fulfill its crime prevention function because of its inability to identify which releasees are about to endanger the public safety.

The usual response to the gap between the image and reality of parole is to assume the validity of the theory and to recommend reforms in the practice. Typically these reforms urge: (1) improving parole board decisions, through acquiring high qualifications for membership; (2) reducing the work load of the parole board to permit its members more time to consider each case; (3) improving the comprehensiveness and accuracy of the information in each case file; (4) imposing some form of due-process and review procedures to protect inmates against arbitrary and abusive action by board members; (5) developing specific written criteria to guide board members in making prediction decisions; (6) expanding the parole service and reducing the officers' caseloads; (7) de-emphasizing law enforcement activity by parole officers and (8) increasing social services for parolees.

The practice of parole in New York diverges so widely from what is considered ideal that conceivably there is room for reform of the sort outlined above. Merely to implement these measures, however, would be to reform parole without changing it. If a system rests on invalid assumptions and has unrealistic goals, changes in its practice will not remedy those defects. Granted—and important—those changes could make it generally fairer, but the system would not be any more effective in carrying out its intentions. That is the problem with parole.

The parole system rests on the assumption that recidivism can be measurably reduced by exposing the offender, while in prison, to social programs such as education or vocational training or group therapy, or by giving him assistance in the community once he gets out. But the overwhelming evidence is that these programs and services are ineffective in reducing recidivism. A survey by Robert Martinson, NYU sociologist and former consultant to the New York State Office of Crime Control Planning, of all studies of rehabilitation programs undertaken around the country between 1945 and 1967 found that "the present array of correctional treatments has no appreciable effect—positive or negative—on the rates of recidivism of convicted offenders." A survey of studies of the California correctional system—which has instituted more sophisticated rehabilitation programs than in New York State—goes even further:

It is difficult to escape the conclusions that the act of incarcerating a person at all will impair whatever potential he has for a crime-free future adjustment and that, regardless of which "treatments" are administered while he is in prison, the longer he is kept there the more he will deteriorate and the more likely it is that he will recidivate.

Finally, even the "Preliminary Report to the Governor [of New York] on Criminal Offenders"—a report that completely endorsed the treatment model—admitted that "We are unable to state at the present time [June 1968] with demonstrable certainty whether any particular treatment method is effective in preventing recidivism."

Parole theory is further weakened by the fact that neither the parole board nor the parole officer seems able to predict the nature and likelihood of recidivism for inmates in general. High parole revocation rates—which indicate about 80 percent of the time that a new criminal offense has been committed—cast doubt on the efficacy of the parole board's predictions. The very small number of parolees for whom revocation proceedings are initiated before apprehension for a new offense suggests that the parole officers are equally unsure in their predictions. The state of the art of prediction is still too primitive to be used as justification for substantially restricting human freedom.

Even though the parole system is ineffective in meeting its stated goals, its continuation might be justified if parole fulfilled important alternative objectives. It does not. The granting of parole is not necessary to maintain prison discipline. Prison officials have many devices which they can use as rewards and punishment for that purpose. It is also commonly believed that the parole board reduces sentence disparities by paroling similar offenders after they have served comparable amounts of time. While this function may be important in some jurisdictions, the New York parole board has no procedures to ensure its effective performance here. Even if it did we would not regard the mitigation of sentence disparities as a sufficient justification for an entire parole system, especially since that function could be performed in other ways.

In addition to failing to fulfill its own goals or to fulfill an important alternative function, parole is oppressive and wasteful in its operation. Because parole is presently the inmate's best exit from prison, its procedures have a great impact on inmate morale and behavior. Inmates are aware that the irrationality of parole decision-making keeps some of them in prison for reasons that do not promote any justifiable public policy. Parolees feel hindered in their adjustment to the community by parole restrictions, and some know they have been returned to prison even though they were not a danger to the public and would not have become so. Last, the parole system costs money to operate. And while it is usually thought that the system actually saves the state money, that is only true if the alternative is imprisonment. If inmates were absolutely discharged from prison at a time when they otherwise would have been paroled, the state could save the funds now expended to support the parole system.

Long-term Recommendations

The Citizens' Inquiry report concludes that parole in New York is oppressive and arbitrary, cannot fulfill its stated goals, and is a corrupting influence within the penal system. It should therefore be abolished. But abolition of the present system cannot occur within a vacuum. The following recommendations reflect the conclusion that parole is only one segment of an integrated process. Changing parole must also mean changing the other elements of the postconviction criminal justice system, if the outcome is to make our use of the criminal sanction more humane and more effective.

1. The goals of rehabilitation as it has been described in this summary are unrealistic and should not shape sentencing and release decisions. At present this society is not able to measurably reduce recidivism by exposing the offender to treatment or rehabilitation programs either in prison or in the community. Discretionary release and compulsory community supervision that rely on the rehabilitation theory should therefore be discontinued.

2. Sentences should be shorter and have a narrower range of indeterminacy. The criteria used to determine the length of terms and the justifications for indeterminacy must await further research. But certainly a sentence structure founded on the rehabilitation theory is baseless.

3. The discretion in parole decision-making has been abused. In the light of past experience, the likelihood of basing the exercise of this discretion on rational criteria seems so low that it is tempting to suggest the elimination of all discretion from release procedures. At least until sentences are short and definite, some limited discretion over release will be necessary. There is need for the study of the appropriate overall sentencing and release process, but some of its qualities can be specified. Its operations must be open to scrutiny to avoid the corrupting tendencies of discretionary power. It should favor the earliest possible release for the largest possible number of inmates, perhaps by requiring corrections officials to show cause why, at a certain point, an inmate should not be released. The present parole board should be dissolved, and release decisions should be made by citizens who are not part of the penal system, but are related to it by virtue of their contacts with inmates in out-of-prison situations, such as work-release or adult education programs. Those who decide should have varying race, class, and occupational backgrounds, and should include an inmate's peers. The decision-making process should provide customary due-process protections. The release criteria should be matters of fact demonstrably related to a legitimate public purpose. Judicial review should be available for release decisions.

4. New and extended alternatives to incarceration should be developed and used. Confinement, when necessary, should be in small neighborhood facilities as little isolated from normal community activities as possible.

5. Prison administration, release decisions, and postrelease services must be open to public scrutiny. General public ignorance of prison life, release decision-making, and parole supervision have made it difficult to develop understanding of the penal system and press for change. Only with greater public accountability will new and better programs and practices gain support.

6. A wide range of programs should be offered to offenders before, during, and after incarceration. Participation in the programs should be voluntary at all times; presumably, one test of their effectiveness will then be evidence that many offenders use them. They should be paid for by the penal system but administered by people who provide similar kinds of service to ordinary citizens.

The programs should not be justified by a vague, condescending, and unmeasurable standard of rehabilitative value. They should be supported instead because our society believes that the opportunities they present to live as comfortably and productively as possible are worthwhile in and of themselves and should be shared equally by all citizens, whether they are criminal offenders or not.

a. The ex-offender's most immediate need is for cash. He should receive financial aid, set at the minimum standard of living for his family size, for a period of several months after release from prison when employment is not readily available and need exists. He should have access to low-interest loans for a lengthy period after direct aid is discontinued.

b. Decent emergency housing should be available at no cost for the ex-offender's first days or weeks outside of prison. A sophisticated referral service should help him locate permanent housing, deal with housing agencies and management companies, and finance home purchases.

c. Job training, with living wages, should be available, as well as employment counseling and referral. Where decent jobs are not available in the private sector, government should provide them. Current policies in both public and private job sectors restricting ex-offenders from jobs should generally be abandoned.

d. Educational opportunities should be available to inmates and ex-offenders on the same basis as students. Tutoring, aptitude testing, and financial aid will be necessary to help inmates and ex-offenders prepare for school, college, and vocational programs.

e. Low-cost medical services should be offered to inmates and ex-offenders—both inside and outside the penal institutions. The services should include dental and psychiatric care, as well as programs for alcoholics and drug users.

f. Both public and private legal services should be available to the offender free or at low cost from the moment of arrest until some time after release. Legal help should include representation of the client before agencies from which he may be eligible for benefits, such as welfare or workmen's disability.

One way to enlist an individual in whichever of the service programs are appropriate is to offer him, immediately after arrest or the issuance of a summons, the help of a community services advisor. This person should come from a socioeconomic background similar to that of the offender, and should be fully prepared to act as his advocate in seeking help from the range of programs available. The advisor should have no enforcement role. If requested to do so by the offender, the advisor would keep in touch during incarceration and would assist with arrangements for family visits, out-of-prison activities, and preparations for the return home. When inmates are confined in neighborhood facilities, the advisor would work there and canvass the surrounding community for programs that the inmate can use. He would help the ex-offender with postrelease problems for as long a period as requested. He would be supervised by an organization with the power to inspect prisons, and report to the public on the problems of the penal system (perhaps an ombudsman organization based on the structure of the present New York State Commission of Correction). Present members of the parole service would have first priority for consideration as community service advisors.

Transitional Recommendations

The long-term recommendations just enumerated will necessitate a lengthy period of change. It seems worthwhile to try to articulate some of the desirable transitional steps, reforms that are easily grafted on to the present parole system. They are not offered as substitutes for the changes discussed above, for they do not alter basic inadequacies of theory or practice. They are offered in the hope that they will insure fairness for inmates and tend to expose and educate. It is crucial that the interim recommendations lead to further change and do not themselves come to symbolize an entrenched and inflexible system.

Our short-term recommendations for the decision-making aspect of the parole system are:

1. At the setting of the minimum period of imprisonment by the parole board and at parole release interviews, an inmate should have the right:

a. to be represented by retained or assigned counsel;

b. to present witnesses on his own behalf;

c. to examine personally or through counsel the entire case file prior to the release interview;

d. to receive a statement of findings of fact and reasons for the decision within a short time of the interview;

e. to receive a decision based on information disclosed to the inmate during the interview;

f. to receive a written statement of the detailed and specific criteria which the parole board uses in deciding cases;

g. to have judicial review of the substantive and procedural aspects of the decision.

2. The burden of proof should be shifted so that it rests with the parole board to show why an inmate should not be released.

3. Parole board hearings, records, and regular reports should be open and available to the press and public, subject only to the right of privacy of the individual involved to request secrecy as to details personal to him.

Short-term recommendations for the community supervision aspect of the parole system include:

1. The length of time under community supervision should not exceed one year.

2. The parole rules should be substantially reduced in number and simplified,

so that they are not coercive and do not permit a parole officer any more right to invade the privacy of one's person, home, or property than those of ordinary citizens. One set of simple parole rules might include requirements that the parolee

    a. seek and hold a job, or demonstrate another legal means of livelihood;

    b. abide by the law; and

    c. report to the parole service regularly.

3. All law-enforcement activities and authority of parole officers should be abolished.

4. Parole should be revoked only when the parolee has committed and been convicted of a new criminal offense of a magnitude that would ordinarily lead to incarceration.

5. The law should provide each parolee with direct financial assistance comparable to unemployment or welfare benefits. These benefits should extend from release until another means of livelihood is established.

6. Extensive social services, of the sort outlined as a long-term recommendation, should be provided on a voluntary basis to all parolees. Other government agencies, such as public housing authorities, civil-service examiners, and welfare departments, should be prohibited from maintaining discriminatory bars against parolees.

7. Inmates who are conditionally released should have their sentences credited with the time they spend in the community in the event that they have their conditional release revoked and are returned to prison.

Members of the Citizens' Inquiry

CHAIRMAN
Ramsey Clark

EXECUTIVE VICE-CHAIRMAN
Herman Schwartz

VICE-CHAIRMEN
Felicia Bernstein
Coretta Scott King
Victor Marrero
Jean Vanden Heuvel

EXECUTIVE COMMITTEE
Haywood Burns
Fred Cohen
Shirley Fingerhood
Moe Foner
Ira Glasser
William E. Hellerstein
Jack Himmelstein
Stanley Levison
David Rothman
Dorothy Teryl
Julius Topol
William J. Vanden Heuvel

COMMITTEE MEMBERS

Amyas Ames
Herman Badillo
Carol Bellamy
Kenneth J. Bialkin
Lenore Cahn
George Carson
Schuyler G. Chapin
Kenneth B. Clark
Leroy Clark
Richard Cloward
Constance E. Cook
Charles S. Desmond
Norman Dorsen
Jules Feiffer
David Fogel
Caleb Foote
Betty Friedlander
Thomas E. Gaddis
Betty Gaylin
Willard Gaylin
Ronald Goldfarb
Charles Goodell
Victor Gotbaum
Marilyn G. Haft
D. John Heyman

Tom Johnston
William Josephson
May Kraus
Arthur L. Liman
Donal E.J. MacNamara
Vincent McGee
Michael Meltsner
George R. Metcalf
Arthur Miller
Victor Navasky
Basil Paterson
David Rothenberg
Anne Rudenstine
Bayard Rustin
Edgar Scherick
Alan U. Schwartz
Jeanette Spencer
Hope R. Stevens
Harry Wachtel
Gillian Walker
Tom Wicker
Roger Wilkins
Edward Bennett Williams
Federick Wiseman

Staff for the Investigation[c]

David Rudenstine
Sander M. Bieber
Kathryn Haapala

Director
Researcher
Administrative Assistant

Part-time Staff

Stanley Adelman
Linda Cleveland
Nancy Lee
Sally Mendola
James Weill

---

[c]Diana R. Gordon, the Present Director of the Citizens' Inquiry, worked full time during the last several months of the investigation. At that time she was incoming director.

5 Community Alternatives to Prison

Nora Klapmuts

Incarceration in closed, security-oriented institutions is rapidly losing popularity as a rehabilitative or control measure for most offenders. The movement toward the expanded use and development of alternatives to the institutionalization of juvenile and adult offenders is spurred by observations that the traditional prison or training school is both excessively costly and ineffective as a rehabilitative tool. Not only has it been shown that imprisonment does not effectively rehabilitate or deter, but the actively destructive potential of most correctional institutions has frequently been emphasized.

It is not that prisons have suddenly become inhumane or destructive to individual lives, or even necessarily that society has become more sensitive to the plight of those imprisoned. Prisons have never been less than terrible places, and the history of prison reform is as long as imprisonment itself. The distinctive characteristic of the current reform effort is its emphasis on abolishing rather than improving the prison: it is no longer popular to hold that imprisonment can be transformed into an effective vehicle of rehabilitation through a massive infusion of manpower or treatment resources. In the light of criminological theory of the past decade, which views crime and delinquency as symptoms of disorganization of the community as much as of individual personalities—or even as a product of an inadequate mesh between the two—imprisonment is coming to be viewed as hopelessly anachronistic. It is now widely believed that reintegration of the offender with the law-abiding community—the primary goal of the "new" correction—cannot be accomplished by isolating the offender in an artificial, custodial setting.

Reintegration of offender and community was accorded legitimacy as the new direction in correction by the President's Crime Commission, which described the earlier orientation toward treating supposed defects in the individual offender as "a fundamental deficiency in approach." The Commission clearly stated its position that, since institutions tend to isolate offenders from society, "the goal of reintegration is likely to be furthered much more readily by working with offenders in the community than by incarceration."[1]

Since the Commission's report was issued in 1967, the goal of reintegration and the conviction that correction is best undertaken in the community setting

aReprinted from Crime and Delinquency Literature, June 1973. Copyright 1973, National Council on Crime and Delinquency; by permission.

101

have been restated by numerous official planning and policy-making bodies. The Wisconsin Council on Criminal Justice, in its report to the governor, unequivocally established as its study committee's fundamental priority the replacement by 1975 of Wisconsin's existing institutional correction system with a community-based noninstitutional system. The committee stated that all available resources, especially those previously expended for maintaining large correctional institutions, should be devoted to developing offenders' community ties.[2] The President's Task Force on Prisoner Rehabilitation concluded from its study of existing and alternate forms of prisoner rehabilitation that "any offender who can safely be diverted from incarceration . . . should be."[3] The single most important recommendation emerging from the California Board of Corrections' study was that the bulk of the correctional effort, its programs and resources, be moved to the community level.[4] The National Council on Crime and Delinquency has issued a policy statement calling for a halt in institutional construction until maximum development and utilization of noninstitutional correction have been achieved.[5] The New Jersey Coalition for Penal Reform has recommended that the state abandon plans for future construction of large-scale custodial prisons while phasing out existing massive institutions.[6] The long-range master plan developed by the John Howard Association for Maryland's Department of Juvenile Services envisions a 50 percent reduction in rates of institutionalization and a tripling of community services.[7] And in Massachusetts a series of bold steps has led to the closing of juvenile institutions and efforts to rapidly develop alternate programs for juvenile offenders.[8]

Disillusionment with the traditional correctional institution as a rehabilitative tool appears justified. Research evaluating institutional treatment has shown that incarceration, and especially lengthy incarceration, does not deter crime or recidivism.[9] The National Advisory Commission on Criminal Justice Standards and Goals notes in its task force report on corrections that treatment program tests have been conducted in a wide variety of incarcerative settings without establishing the rehabilitative value of any. Comments the task force: "The consistency of this record indicates that incarcerative treatment is incompatible with rehabilitative objectives."[10]

An interesting explanation of the counterproductive nature of imprisonment is offered by Robert Martinson in a series of articles on prison reform.[11] In documenting the disintegration of the correctional treatment approach (the offender-oriented medical model of individualized treatment), Martinson observes that efforts over the last 150 years to upgrade the prison environment and to improve and intensify the rehabilitation of inmates have not reduced recidivism rates. He suggests that recidivism rates are not affected by the prison regime itself; that instead they simply reflect the interruption of normal occupational or life-cycle progress. In today's highly technological society removal from the community for a period of years, especially at the ages when crime peaks (fifteen to twenty-five), interferes with the exacting series of moves required to "make it" socioeconomically, and produces perhaps irreparable "life-cycle damage." While admittedly speculative, Martinson's view has explanatory potential: It suggests why prison reform and the introduction of a range of treatment approaches have not reduced the number of repeaters; it offers an explanation for the observed similarity in recidivism rates among systems with varying correctional practices;[1 2] it suggests why longer prison sentences (for the same offense) are associated with greater recidivism.[1 3] Prison, Martinson claims, even as it is enriched and improved, produces the paradoxical result of increasing recidivism—not directly by doing or not doing anything to the offender, but simply by removing him from society. He concludes, "Society has outgrown the prison, and deprivation of liberty has come to be a self-defeating measure in a modern industrial economy."[1 4]

Repeated evidence of the ineffectiveness of imprisonment has led to the radical redistribution of offenders from institutional to community programs in a few jurisdictions. In many others a new interest in community-based correction and a willingness to consider alternatives to incarceration are accompanied by confusion over where and how to reallocate correctional resources. State correction departments and planning groups, conscious of the failure of traditional correctional practices and of the possibilities for greater cost-effectiveness associated with a reorientation toward community-based correction, frequently do not know how to begin. What is meant by community correction? Who should be eligible for community management? What kinds of programs and resources must be developed to absorb the correctional population displaced by the phasing out of prisons and training schools? What programs have been tried and which have been successful? What should be the guiding principles for the use of community resources in lieu of confinement?

The range of programs and resources that should be developed by correctional systems as alternatives to jail, prison, and training school is outlined by the National Advisory Commission on Criminal Justice Standards and Goals in the working papers of its National Conference on Criminal Justice.[1 5] Its Task Force on Corrections has recommended that each correctional system begin immediately to develop a systematic plan with timetable and scheme for implementing a range of alternatives to institutionalization. Minimum alternatives to be included in the plan are specified: (1) pretrial and presentence diversion programs; (2) nonresidential supervision programs in addition to probation and parole; (3) residential alternatives to incarceration; (4) community resources open to confined populations and institutional resources available to the entire community; (5) prerelease programs; and (6) community facilities for release offenders in the critical reentry phase, with provision for short-term return as needed.[1 6] The Commission stresses the need to systematize on a state level the orderly development of community correction, with full consideration of specific local needs. The guiding principles stated by the Commission are supported by others who advocate the most limited possible use of institutionalization: (1) No individual who does not absolutely require institutionalization for the protection of others should be confined. (2) No individual should be subjected to more supervision or control than he requires.

The trend toward deinstitutionalization begins before trial, with alternatives to jailing, or even before arrest, with diversion of noncriminal or marginally criminal cases to social, medical, or other nonjudicial resources. It extends to postinstitutional services for parolees and includes a range of partial-imprison-ment measures designed to maximize, or at least expand, the community involvement of incarcerated offenders. The principle that no person should be kept in a more secure condition or status than his potential risk dictates or receive more surveillance or "help" than he requires clearly demands the creation of alternatives to institutional handling at every stage of judicial and correctional processing. It implies a special emphasis on the development and use of alternatives at the initial stages of criminal justice, and the diversion of more offenders to lower levels of correctional intervention at the earliest feasible opportunity.

Efforts to divert some classes of offenders from the criminal-justice system entirely and the use of noninstitutional measures (suspended sentences, fines, probation) for potential jail inmates have been described elsewhere,[17] as have the programs of partial or graduated release (work release, furlough, halfway houses) for prison inmates and parolees.[18] This chapter deals with community-based alternatives for serious (but not dangerous) offenders who would other-wise be candidates for incarceration in prison or training school. It is an attempt to respond to the questions that arise in connection with recommendations, currently coming from many sources, that the traditional prison or training school be abolished, phased out, or drastically reduced in population, and that a large proportion of offenders now sentenced to such institutions be managed in community-based programs.

Recommendations that prisons and training schools be phased out or abolished generally recognize that a relatively small proportion of offenders—those who are genuinely dangerous to the public, and those whose crimes are so repulsive that public opinion demands retribution—will have to be incarcerated even under a reorganized correctional system. But, while the proportion of felony offenders incarcerated varies widely from one jurisdiction to another, probably nowhere are community alternatives being maximally utilized. Esti-mates of the percentage of offenders who must be imprisoned vary, largely because criteria of "dangerousness" have yet to be stated definitively[19]; but the consensus is that imprisonment is often greatly overused and institutional populations could be significantly reduced without additional risk to the community. Some of the ways in which institutional populations can be or have been reduced include the expanded use of probation, diversion to "intensive" or specialized probation or other nonresidential treatment programs, immediate release to special parole services, referral to halfway house, group-home, or other residential programs, and, where such centers are a real alternative to prison, placement in a community-based correctional center.

Probation Programs

A considerable proportion of offenders incarcerated in prison or training school probably are no more dangerous than many of those retained in the community on probation.[20] This would imply that the use of probation could be expanded to include many persons now sentenced to an institutional term. There is evidence that this could be accomplished without an increase in probation violation rates. The California Assembly Office of Research examined probation usage and violation data for eighty-eight U.S. district courts, for California superior courts, and for eight California counties. The findings indicated that violation rates are unaffected by the percentage of offenders granted probation. An examination of changes in probation usage in the eight counties showed no pattern of relationship between the granting of probation and removal from probation for violation. In the federal district courts, probation usage ranged from 37 percent to 66 percent, with no significant variation in violation rates. There was no support for the assumption that greater reliance on probation as a sentencing disposition is associated with an increase in violations.[21]

These data contradict the belief that offenders now incarcerated could be released to probation in the community only under greatly intensified supervision. Widely divergent rates of probation usage indicate that offenders who are incarcerated in one jurisdiction are retained on probation in another, apparently without adversely affecting crime or other violation rates. And probation appears to do fairly well with those offenders it handles, even under the supposedly adverse conditions of unmanageably large caseloads and little officer time for supervision. Studies of offenders under normal probation supervision have indicated a relatively high success rate. A study of 943 male probationers sixteen to eighteen years old revealed that about 72 percent were successfully discharged.[22] In a summary analysis of fifteen probation studies in various jurisdictions, Ralph England found reported success rates ranging between 60 and 90 percent; and a survey of probation effectiveness in Massachusetts, California, New York, and a number of foreign countries reports similar results, with the modal success rate at about 75 percent.[23]

England explains that many offenders are "self-correcting" and are not likely to recidivate, while others would be dissuaded from further offending merely through exposure to the limited surveillance of the suspended sentence. Empey has suggested that, since the majority of offenders now placed on probation can succeed without much supervision, many of those offenders now incarcerated might succeed under intensified community supervision.[24] Many, apparently, also can succeed under normal or minimal supervision. Certainly no assumption should be made that the candidates for institutionalization necessarily require more intensive supervision or "treatment."

Efforts to reduce the use of imprisonment by placing more offenders on probation have often assumed that more officers and smaller caseloads would be prerequisite. The Saginaw Project of the Michigan Council on Crime and Delinquency successfully reduced the percentage of felony offenders imprisoned during the three-year (1957-60) experiment from 36.6 percent to 19.3 percent by increasing the use of probation and other dispositions.[25] The number of probation officers was increased and caseloads were reduced to the "ideal" maximum of fifty units per officer. This project demonstrated that prison dispositions could be cut in half with no additional risk to the community. However, it is far from clear that small caseloads alone were responsible for the success of this project. Research on the impact of reduced caseloads in probation and parole has not supported the assumption that more intensive supervision in small caseloads would reduce violation and offense rates among those supervised.

Caseload Research

Despite the appeal of reducing caseloads to improve supervision, research during the 1960s clearly indicated that merely reducing caseload size does not reduce recidivism. A parole research project in Oakland, California, began in 1959 to test whether reducing caseloads of parolees would improve parole performance. Additional agents were employed and ten experimental thirty-six-unit caseloads were established, with five seventy-two caseloads as controls. When the project was terminated in 1961 no overall difference was found in parole performance for reduced and full-size caseloads.[26]

California's Special Intensive Parole Unit (SIPU) studies,[27] conducted in four segments from 1953 through 1963, obtained similar results. Adult parolees were randomly assigned to caseloads of fifteen, thirty, thirty-five, seventy-two, and ninety men (the last two serving as controls), and comparisons were made between experimentals and controls and among experimentals. These studies involved several thousand men and follow-ups of at least two years. No significant differences were found in the performances of conventional and any of the three experimental caseloads, when offenders were randomly assigned. In the third phase, parolees were classified and assigned according to "risk" categories on base expectancy scores. The results of this experiment were equivocal but there was evidence that, regardless of caseload size, high-risk parolees violated extensively and low-risk parolees seldom violated, while the middle-risk cases performed distinctly better in smaller caseloads. The low-risk cases did as well in very large caseloads as in regular caseloads.

The University of California's San Francisco Project focused on federal probation and parole and the effects of different caseload sizes.[28] Individuals placed on probation or parole were randomly assigned to caseloads receiving one of four types of supervision: minimum, intensive, "ideal," and normal. Persons in minimum or "crisis" caseloads were required only to submit a monthly written report to the probation office; no routine contacts occurred unless requested by the offender. Intensive caseloads consisted of twenty units each and contact occurred at least weekly. Ideal caseloads were composed of fifty units, and normal caseloads consisted of one hundred units per month. The results of this experiment indicated that offenders in minimum caseloads performed as well as would be expected had they been receiving normal supervision. The minimum and the ideal caseloads had almost identical violation rates. In intensive caseloads, despite fourteen times the attention provided the minimum cases, the violation rate not only failed to decline but increased with respect to technical violations. Caseload groupings did not differ with respect to nontechnical violations; thus the small caseload was not demonstrated to be more effective in reducing recidivism. The results were interpreted as suggesting (1) that some offenders will succeed under supervision regardless of the type of service, while others will violate no matter how much attention they receive; and (2) that with identification of these offender groups, officer time could be allocated to give most attention to those (middle-risk) offenders whose success depends on the presence of certain types of supervision.

These and other studies indicated that reduced caseloads in themselves are of relatively little importance. In both the SIPU studies and the San Francisco Project it was found that good risks could be managed safely in very large, minimally supervised caseloads. Both also found that small caseloads were associated with higher rates of technical violation, a fact that has been attributed to the increased supervision made possible by reduced caseloads.[29] Attention has since shifted away from the study of numbers and toward an emphasis on differential caseload management—that is, toward offender classification and assignment to specialized caseloads identified as appropriate for specific offender (risk-level) types. Experience with differential management in "work-unit" caseloads has suggested that it is feasible to place the more serious offender or the poorer risk on probation without increasing the danger to the community.

Differential Caseload Management

In California the work-unit concept has been operative since 1965, when the Work Unit Program was experimentally introduced into parole.[30] This was an experiment in parole programing that provided differential levels of supervision for parolees through a reduction in the size of certain caseloads. The program was designed to provide intensive supervision for selected parolees (such as high violence-potential cases) and less intensive supervision for parolees whose behavior indicated a potential for favorable adjustment. Three levels of supervision were designated, with different weights assigned to cases at each level. The sum of weights assigned to the cases supervised by an agent was set at 120 (an average caseload of thirty-five). The Work Unit Program was expected to result in greater use of community resources and in reductions in both parole violation rates and the incidence of new crimes committed by parolees. A follow-up study comparing parole outcomes of work-unit and conventional caseloads (of about seventy cases) indicated a lower return-to-prison rate for the work-unit parole population.[31] A cost savings was also demonstrated for programs based on the workload concept.

A study was initiated in Washington, D.C. to obtain information about the offender population under supervision in the Probation Office of the U.S. District Court for the District of Columbia, and to apply this information in devising a more effective case-management approach based on the needs of the offenders and the resources available to the probation officer.[32] Three major objectives of the study were (1) to classify the entire population under supervision, using a multifactor instrument designed to predict the outcome of supervision; (2) to attempt to validate the predictive ability of the instrument by comparing all cases that closed successfully with those closed unsuccessfully during an eighteen-month period; and (3) to use the data to set up differential caseload sizes based on high or low success potential.

A total of 1210 cases were divided into three groups: 43 percent of the entire caseload were rated A, for high potential for favorable adjustment; 44 percent were rated B, for medium potential; and 13 percent were rated C, for low potential. Each of the seventeen field officers had an unequal distribution of As, Bs, and Cs in his caseload. Phase II found a closing rate of 63 percent success, with 93 percent of the A group successfully completing their probation while 56 percent of the B group and 17 percent of the C group were successful. Phase III revealed a low number of individuals with a C rating, a result attributed to the screening process employed by the probation staff at the time of the presentence investigation. More than half (52 percent) of those recommended for probation were rated A, while nearly two-thirds (62 percent) of those not recommended for probation were rated C.

On the basis of the findings of this study the following recommendations were made. The Base Expectancy 61-A scoring instrument should be used when preparing the presentence investigation report because of its high accuracy in predicting adjustment. Individuals rated A should be placed in caseloads receiving minimal supervision, while C offenders should receive intensive supervision. Officers responsible for supervising those rated A should handle caseloads of at least two hundred cases each. A counseling unit of field officers should supervise offenders rated B, and a "crash unit" should be created to work exclusively with low potential offenders in caseloads of a maximum of thirty to thirty-five persons each.

The implications of research on differential or work-unit caseloads for the "deprisonization" effort are clear. If offenders with a high potential for success on probation can be moved out into very large, minimally supervised caseloads (or be given suspended sentences without supervision, fines, restitution orders, or other nonprobation dispositions), the probation system will be freed to concentrate its efforts on medium- and poor-risk probationers as well as to absorb that group of offenders now sent to prison or training school because the authorities believe normal probation supervision to be insufficient for them. Not all offenders currently institutionalized are poor risks (in the District of Columbia study, 38 percent of persons not recommended for probation were rated other than C), so not all offenders diverted from incarceration will require placement in the intensive-supervision programs developed for the poor-risk group. Classification must occur before decisions are made as to appropriate disposition.

Probation for the Serious Offender

Many offenders currently are sent to prison or training school because traditional probation supervision is believed insufficient for their control or rehabilitation. Thus, while greater use of suspended sentences, fines, and regular probation will contribute to the reduction of prison populations, any plans to maximize the use of community alternatives will have to deal with the question of what to do with those offenders who appear to need more supervision, services, or assistance in order to remain out of trouble with the law. Although these individuals are not dangerous (the small minority of offenders who are truly dangerous will be incarcerated) they are likely to repeat offenses and to have difficulty adjusting successfully in the community.

A broad range of services and programs has been provided for the treatment of offenders who require more intensive services than regular supervision. Group or family counseling may be offered as a service of the court; the offender may be referred to community service agencies for additional assistance; probation officers may meet with selected probationers in frequent group sessions; the juvenile probationer may be required to attend daycare centers, or centers providing remedial education or vocational training; and juveniles for whom living with their families is contraindicated because of undesirable home situations may be placed in foster or group homes. Adult offenders also may be required to live in a community residence or halfway house as a condition of probation. Many courts have utilized local volunteers to work with offenders in various capacities, providing tutoring assistance, foster homes, group discussion sessions, counseling, or simply a supportive relationship with a community resident. Most of these programs have not been evaluated. Assessments of effectiveness, where they have been attempted at all, frequently are not very useful: no control group is used, the groups are not comparable, or assignment is not random. Many descriptive studies merely report the subjective judgments of staff or the observed changes over time in arrest patterns of project participants. This means that much of the "community treatment" literature must be interpreted cautiously, although it may still be useful in suggesting the kinds of intervention alternatives that have been tried and that may be duplicated elsewhere.

The variety of services available as an adjunct to probation has permitted some courts greater flexibility in their disposition of offenders for whom neither institutionalization nor regular probation supervision is considered suitable. However, in many jurisdictions the court simply has no available alternative to incarceration, and many offenders are sent to prison or training school who do not need to be there. State subsidy programs have been instituted in an attempt to reduce costs and overcrowding in state institutions by retaining more offenders in the community at the county level. Some of the savings resulting from reduced commitments are diverted to the counties for the purpose of expanding and upgrading probation services for these offenders.

State Subsidy Programs

In 1965 the California State Legislature passed legislation that provided a state subsidy to county probation departments to set up special supervision programs, to increase the degree of supervision of individual cases, and to develop and improve supervisional practices.[33] Reduced commitment of offenders to state correctional institutions was made a mandatory condition for the receipt of subsidy monies. The enabling legislation was the result of the recommendation of a 1964 Board of Corrections probation study undertaken to determine how state costs could be reduced while county probation programs were improved. This study determined that 25 percent of state correctional commitments could be maintained safely and effectively within county systems if probation services were improved. The subsidy plan that was ultimately adopted provided for reimbursement by the state to the counties in proportion to the number of cases retained in the county exceeding the existing rate. A sliding scale was developed to avoid penalizing counties that already had low commitment rates. The following assumptions are among those that influenced the character of the legislation:

1. The most effective correctional services are provided in local communities.
2. Straight probation (without jail) is the least costly service available.
3. Probation is at least as effective as most institutional forms of care.
4. Probation grants can be increased without increasing recidivism.
5. The actual rate of probation grants is determined by the decisions of probation officers, and probation decision-making can be altered by rewarding approved behavior.

6. Costs for improved probation supervision can be offset by savings at the state level.

By 1970-71 forty-five counties (over 97 percent of the state population) were operating approved subsidy programs.[34] Commitments to state institutions had decreased markedly: during that year the state received 4500 to 5000 fewer commitments than would have been expected had the program not been in operation. Although the more than $18 million in subsidy funds paid to the counties was a new high for the five years of the program, it was still considerably less than what it would have cost to keep those offenders in prisons or training schools. The reduction of commitments also has sharply reduced the need to build new institutions—a potential savings of millions of dollars. Construction of juvenile institutions has come to a halt, and several existing training schools have been closed down.

One example of the county programs developed under the California state subsidy is the Special Supervision Unit Program of the Santa Barbara County Probation Department.[35] This program provides intensive, individualized supervision as an alternative to institutionalization. Caseloads are limited to forty-two cases per officer. Each officer receives training in classification and diagnosis. All cases are classified by I-Level methods on a scale that determines the individual's level of social integration. Methods of treatment vary with type of offender, but the basic goal of early confrontation and intensive involvement with the probationer is standard. Typically, the offender is seen two to four times per month; in addition, he participates in group counseling, a public agency therapy program, or a special unit program (such as the work project) one-half day per week. Minor violations may be handled in the unit or by modification of probation, thus serving as a lesson in rehabilitation.

Serious attempts to evaluate the state subsidy program have only just begun. The California Youth Authority, which administers the program for both adults and juveniles, is setting up a basic information system that will provide considerable data on subsidy probationers. Description and some evaluation of the various treatment approaches initiated under the program have also begun. Preliminary reports on some programs have been issued; for example, the Community Oriented Youthful Offender Program (COYOP), one of the Los Angeles County Probation Department's Community Retention Programs.[36] The rate of favorable departures from COYOP is at least as good as that of nonsubsidy probation caseloads, even though COYOP caseloads are comprised of more serious offenders. A California Criminal Statistics Bureau study of the statewide subsidy population reports a 55.5 percent success rate for subsidy-caseload probationers, which compares well with the 65 percent success rate for regular caseloads of less serious offenders.[37]

California's probation subsidy program has demonstrated that serious offenders, normally not eligible for probation, can be retained successfully in the community under special supervision programs without jeopardizing public safety, and that this can be accomplished at considerable savings of taxpayers' dollars. Other states (e.g., Washington, Pennsylvania, Colorado) have introduced state subsidy programs, not necessarily on the California model. The Washington program, in operation since January 1970, allows for state subsidy of county probation supervision for juveniles who are eligible for commitment to state institutions. State commitments by participating counties decreased 42.8 percent during the first year, while nonparticipating counties showed increases. Participating counties also implemented new programs, and have made better use of existing resources.[38] Not all state subsidy monies have been used to upgrade or modify probation supervision. In Oregon, state funds were used to develop small group-home facilities, and in Philadelphia a day center was established.[39] The concept of the state subsidy to county probation departments or, as in Oregon, to the public or private agency operating the program, is a flexible tool that could be used not only to finance improvements in probation service, but also to provide the means for developing a wide range of other community programs for offenders.

Intensive Intervention Programs

When alternatives to incarceration in prison or training school are considered, it is commonly assumed that some special program of intensive supervision, services, or treatment will be required for the successful handling of offenders who are candidates for institutionalization. Research and experimentation have indicated, however, that there are certain types of offenders (some of those currently on probation and some of those imprisoned) who are likely to fail on probation unless considerable effort is invested in their rehabilitation. Programs developed for this group of serious, habitual, or poor-risk offenders, while they may technically be probation programs in that participation is made a condition of probation, generally entail a much greater involvement with the offender than simple supervision and counseling, and may attempt to achieve a considerable modification of attitudes and behaviors that extends beyond the prevention of law violations. More than the probation-plus-services or the small specialized caseload approach, these "intensive intervention" programs are frequently distinguished by their coherent theoretical base, or by their very comprehensive approach to changing the life styles of offenders assigned to them. Because intensive intervention might easily be construed as interference, and because such programs are certainly more costly than regular probation or other dispositions of lower intervention level, assignment to such programs should be preceded by a determination that an offender (1) needs the services or treatment and (2) is able to benefit from them.

Intensive intervention programs appear to use either of two approaches to offender rehabilitation or reintegration: One emphasizes treatment or attitude and behavior modification, and the other focuses on the provision of services (vocational training, job-finding, medical care, financial assistance or guidance). There may be an element of both in any given program. The argument for services as opposed to treatment for offenders derives from the observation that treatment programs—at least under the coercive circumstances of the correction system—do not work. A recent survey of 231 treatment program evaluations published from 1945 to 1967 indicated that the outlook for successful treatment of offenders is bleak.[40] Others have supported this finding,[41] and some suggested that correction should either reduce its operations to a minimum[42] or concentrate on providing those services that the offender himself identifies as useful to him. One author has even suggested that the implementation of a voucher system, in which offenders would be given wide discretion in designing their own rehabilitation programs through the voluntary choice and purchase of services.[43] Another has recommended a correctional policy of minimizing harm or interference and maximizing help to the offender (job training, placement services, parole income, free psychiatric help if requested) in a crime control approach that emphasizes not offender correction but public protection and victim compensation.[44] Intensive intervention programs, whether service or treatment oriented or both, must be viewed in the light of current thinking in correction (less—not more—intervention, the inutility of coercive programs, offender participation in selection of services, etc.) and the evidence that no treatment effort has yet been unambiguously successful.

Despite repeated claims that nothing works, intensive community intervention still generates considerable interest, and treatment programs, both residential and nonresidential, have been established and operated with apparent success. The important point that has been made by the operation of such programs is that community-based alternatives to incarceration can handle the institutional candidate at least as effectively as imprisonment, without serious risk to public safety, at less expense, and with less destructive impact on the offender and his family. These community programs may be residential, requiring the offender to live in a group home, halfway house, or community correction center; or nonresidential, enabling the offender to live at home while participating in the program. Because many believe nonresidential programs to be preferred for their less disruptive effect on the normal lives of offenders, the two types of program are treated separately here. Only a few models are highlighted. Representing the nonresidential community program are the California Youth Authority Department's Community Treatment Project, an example of intensive differential treatment of juveniles; the guided group interaction programs, illustrating peer-group efforts to change juvenile behavior and life styles; and NCCD's "second-offender" project, which utilizes both treatment and service approaches to deal with second-felony recidivists. Group-home projects and Minnesota's PORT program are residential, as is the Community Integration Project in Easton, Pennsylvania.

Many other programs could be mentioned. Massachusetts, in seeking alternatives to the state's now inactivated training schools, has developed a youth advocate system, which provides for an alternate residence at the home of a youth advocate, enrollment in school or special education program, assistance in obtaining employment, contact with courts and community agencies, work with families, and participation of youths in developing their own individualized programs. This program and a range of other residential and nonresidential alternatives to training schools were discussed at a conference held in June 1972.[45] An innovative program being developed in Minnesota for offenders rejected for regular probation will provide for the formulation of an explicit restitution plan involving the offender, an agent of the criminal-justice system, and, whenever possible, the victim. Implementation of the plan will include group or individual monitoring of the extent to which the agreement is fulfilled; discharge from custody (and from residence in a community correction center) will immediately follow an offender's completion of the program. Offenders will be offered the option of participating in the program, which is essentially a contractual reconciliation through negotiated settlement by the parties involved, mediated by a representative of the correctional system.[46] The Minneapolis Rehabilitation Center provides a service-oriented program for parolees that could be adapted for probationers who require more extensive assistance to remain out of prison. A three-year demonstration project was undertaken to test the impact of comprehensive social, psychological, and vocational services on recidivism rates, vocational stability, and personal adjustment of parolees referred to the Center. The project involved the cooperation of private and public agencies and an interdisciplinary team approach to the coordination of correctional and vocational services. Experimentals were given the services of social worker, vocational counselor, and clinical psychologist, besides referral opportunities to consult with a physician, psychiatrist, and other professional personnel as needed. Financial assistance was also provided. It was found that experimentals committed significantly fewer and less serious offenses than controls.[47]

Nonresidential Community Intervention

Community Treatment Project

One of the most widely known experiments in community alternatives to institutionalization, the California Youth Authority Department's Community Treatment Project (CTP), has applied the concepts of offender classification and individualized treatment to a program designed to extend the use of community supervision to offenders who would normally be incarcerated.[48] The original objectives of the project were to test the feasibility of substituting intensive supervision of juveniles in the community for the regular program of institutionalization plus parole, and to develop optimum treatment/control plans for each type of offender identified. Since its inception in 1961, the CTP has been investigating many of the questions about differential management raised by its own and other research. While all phases of the project have been based on caseloads of twelve to fifteen clients, the research has suggested that caseload size is only one of many factors responsible for the demonstrated success of the community program. Factors identified as associated with the superior effectiveness of the community-based program include offender classification and differential treatment-relevant decision-making. Intensive or extensive intervention made possible by reduced caseloads and matching of offender types with agent types are also considered important.

Since 1961 the Community Treatment Project has handled seriously delinquent male and female offenders who have been committed from the juvenile courts in California to the state correctional system. Rather than being institutionalized in state training schools, these youths are placed directly on parole in the community program. After commitment to the reception center, wards are assigned randomly either to a control group, to be given the regular program of institutionalization plus parole, or to the experimental group, to be released immediately to small specialized caseloads in the community. The experimentals, after being classified according to Interpersonal Maturity Level (I-Level) and matched with a parole agent, receive differential or individualized long-term treatment.

The CTP progress reports have been consistently positive in their evaluation of the experimental program. During phase I, the overall success rate of project participants was found to be significantly higher than that of youths in the regular Youth Authority program. Differential success rates were reported: certain types of youth appeared to do especially well under the given treatment conditions, while others did about as well as they would have done in an institution or on parole. In addition, psychological tests scores indicated that experimentals achieved greater positive change than control subjects and a higher level of personal and social adjustment. Throughout phase II, follow-up of study subjects from both phases continued to indicate large differences favoring experimentals over controls. Fifteen-month follow-up data showed that 30 percent of male experimentals had violated parole or been unfavorably discharged, as compared with 51 percent of male controls (and 45 percent of regular statewide Youth Authority releasees). At twenty-four months, these outcomes were 43 percent and 63 percent respectively, again favoring the experimental group.

The CTP findings on recidivism, which indicated that the community program is more effective than imprisonment, have been challenged by James Robison and others who conclude from analysis of the CTP data that recidivism rates have been managed in such a way as to make the experimentals appear favorable. These authors explain that recidivism rates can be influenced, within certain parameters, by the decision-making authorities, and that in the CTP an ideological belief in the effectiveness of community treatment apparently altered the experimental results.[49] In a reexamination of the data, Lerman found that the response to experimentals' offenses was less likely to be revocation unless the offense was of high severity. Experimentals were no less delinquent than controls, but they were significantly less likely to have their paroles revoked for offenses of low or moderate severity.[50]

Regardless of the validity of such criticism, the Community Treatment Project has made some important contributions to both theory and practice in community correction. Providing a composite of diagnostic categories and treatment modalities, the CTP represents an evolving, practical intervention program for delinquency control and a clear alternative to institutionalization for juveniles. The experimental program has been able to handle a large majority of eligible youth (90 percent) at least as effectively as the regular institutional program, while 10 percent have been shown to do better in the traditional program.

Phase III (1969-74) of the Community Treatment Project is concentrating on the development of more effective techniques for working with the 25 percent of youths who seem to do poorly in both the traditional and the community-based programs. A CTP residential facility has been utilized to test the impact of an initial residential placement for these youths. Another objective of this phase has been to determine whether the CTP approach can be applied successfully to a wider range of offenders than has been handled to date—such as those committed from adult courts or for seriously assaultive offenses. In this experiment, eligible youths are studied by a clinic team of treatment and research personnel, who assign each ward to one of two statuses: Status I youths are predicted to perform better if treatment begins within the CTP residential treatment center; Status II youths are those for whom it is believed treatment should begin within the community. Wards are then randomly assigned to either the community setting or the residential setting. The resulting four separate study groups are later compared on growth, parole adjustment, and other outcome measures. Preliminary analyses have suggested that Status I youths who began their treatment within the CTP residential facility performed considerably better following initial release to parole than Status I youths who began treatment in the community. Status II youths (wards seen as not needing initial residential treatment) who began treatment within the residential facility performed somewhat worse than Status II youths who were released directly to the community.[51] Though tentative, these findings indicate that neither institutionalization nor community treatment is equally effective with all types of juveniles. The CTP thus continues to refine its typologies of offenders and treatment strategies, and to expand the application of differential management to include a wider range of both.

Meanwhile, the Community Treatment Project and others such as the

Community Delinquency Control Project[52] and the San Francisco Rehabilitation Project for Adult Offenders[53] have already demonstrated that community programs can effectively handle both juvenile and adult candidates for incarceration. While none of these projects has provided unqualified support for the superior effectiveness of its program, the significant increase in the use of community correction over the last decade in California has been associated with no recorded increase at all in serious crime among those supervised.[54]

Guided Group Interaction Programs

Of the various kinds of nonresidential programs that have been experimented with, one group of programs can be distinguished by a common theoretical orientation. These are the guided group interaction (GGI) programs, which are concerned primarily with peer-group dynamics and the operation of the group in restructuring the offender subculture around socially acceptable norms. These programs also depend to a sometimes considerable extent on the offender's involvement in his own rehabilitation. While other nonresidential programs frequently incorporate the group session into the daily program, less emphasis is placed on the peer group as a major treatment resource.

GGI programs involve the offender in frequent and intensive group discussions of his own and other members' current problems and experiences. Based on the theory that antisocial behavior receives the approval and support of the delinquent peer group, and that substituting acceptable norms for delinquent values also requires peer-group support, these programs foster development of a group culture and encourage members to accept responsibility for helping and controlling one another. As the group culture develops and the group begins to show greater responsibility, the staff group leader allows the group a greater degree of decision-making power. Ultimately, the group's responsibility may extend to decisions involving disciplinary measures imposed on members or determination of a member's readiness for release. Peer-group programs have been developed for use primarily with juvenile offenders, although there have been some recent examples of programs for adults that make use of peer groups and behavior-modification principles.

Projects based on the use of peer-group dynamics derive their program content from the Highfields project, established in New Jersey in 1949.[55] Highfields was a short-term residential program for boys involving work during the day and participation in group sessions in the evening. The program was judged to be as successful as training school in controlling recidivism, and much less costly. The basic principles of Highfields have been applied in nonresidential settings with apparent success, with Essexfields, Collegefields, and the Provo experiment as the best-known examples.

The Provo experiment, initiated in 1959 in Provo, Utah, was divided into two phases. Phase I involved twenty boys at a time in an intensive daily program including work or school and guided group interaction sessions. Each day, following paid employment or school, the boys went to the program center for group sessions, returning at night to their homes. Phase II was designed to aid a boy after release from the intensive phase I program: an effort was made to provide reference group support for the boys and to generate community action to help them find employment. Group development was given high priority since the group, rather than staff alone, was given major responsibility for controlling member behavior and working out solutions to individual or group problems. No length of stay in the program was specified, since release depended not only upon an individual's behavior but on the maturation processes that his group experienced. Release generally occurred between four and seven months. There were no formal rules other than the requirements of appearing each day and working hard on the job. Offenders assigned to the experimental program were compared to two control groups, one under regular probation supervision, the other incarcerated in a training school. Before the experiment, only about 50 to 55 percent of the kinds of persistent offenders who participated in the program were succeeding on probation. Six months after release 73 percent of those initially assigned and 84 percent of those who completed the program had no record of arrest. During the same period the success rate for regular probationers also rose, to 73 percent for offenders initially assigned and 77 percent for those who completed probation. Of the offenders sent to training school, however, 58 percent had been rearrested, and half of those had been arrested two or more times. Youths released from the reformatory appeared to be nearly twice as likely to commit an offense as were program graduates.[56]

Phase II of the Community Treatment Project was concerned with demonstrating the effectiveness of "Provo-type" treatment and comparing it with differential treatment in the community. Experimentals in San Francisco were assigned randomly to either a Differential Treatment Unit (DTU) or a GGI unit. The GGI Unit did not use differential diagnosis as a basis for treatment, although I-Level classification was made for research purposes. Wards in GGI units participated in full-time school or work and attended guided group interaction meetings. Average caseload size was fifteen. Detailed analyses of the rap-sheets (presenting a rundown of all police contact, etc.) of all DTU and GGI males who were part of the San Francisco Community Treatment Project (1965-69) study sample revealed that DTU discharges performed better than their GGI counterparts on twelve-month follow-up, although most of the differences had washed out by the eighteen-month follow-up. Combining the results of the two follow-up cohorts, DTU subjects performed slightly but not significantly better than GGI subjects, but a large difference was found with respect to severe offenses. By twelve months the percentage of discharges who had committed at least one severe offense was more than six times greater within the GGI sample, and by eighteen months 55 percent of the GGI group and only 10 percent of the

DTU group had been involved in at least one severe offense. A twenty-four-month follow-up is being made to test the reliability of this finding.[57]

The Essexfields Rehabilitation Project was established in 1959 in Essex County (Newark), New Jersey, on assumptions similar to those of the Provo experiment. The program was limited to twenty boys at a time, who had been referred to the program as a condition of probation. Five days a week the boys participated in the program from seven in the morning to ten at night, working during the day and attending group sessions in the evening. Length of stay in the program was indeterminate, but was usually from four to five months. The program was evaluated by comparing recidivism rates of Essexfields boys with the rates of groups on probation, in residential group centers, and in the state reformatory. Despite the potential hazards of the high-delinquency area in which it was located, Essexfields demonstrated a rate of in-program failure that was slightly lower than that of the residential group center. Recidivism rates indicated that reformatory boys would do no worse and might do better at Essexfields or in the group centers.[58]

Collegefields, established in Newark, New Jersey, in 1965, developed out of the same theoretical base as Essexfields and Provo, but in addition, a major goal of this project was to alter the educational experience of delinquent boys. Each weekday twenty-five boys attended academic classes in the morning and group sessions in the afternoon. The basic curriculum of the public school system was modified to meet individual student needs, and remedial instruction was provided. During stays of from four to seven months in the program, boys advanced in achievement by as many as three academic years. Comparison of outcome of experimental subjects with two control groups on probation demonstrated greater gains for the Collegefields boys on IQ, attitudes toward school, realistic self-assessment, and achievement motivation, but no difference in recidivism rates was found.[59]

Despite the somewhat uncertain nature of the findings on effectiveness of guided group interaction, none of the research results contradicts the overall conclusions that intensive intervention in the community is at least as effective as incarceration, or that offenders normally sent to an institution can be retained in the community as safely when special services are provided.

The Kentfields program of the Kent County, Michigan, Juvenile Court, initiated in 1970, is demonstrating the cost-effectiveness of behavior-modification techniques with "hard-core" delinquents. The cost of treating a boy at Kentfields for one year is about $400—several thousand dollars less than the cost of training school placement. In addition, the program provides labor for local units of county government at the $1.60 minimum or $3 average wage rates. Follow-up information collected from probation officers and validated by parents showed that, of the fifty-four boys who graduated from the program during the first year, only two had committed offenses serious enough to warrant commitment to training school. A majority were at home and working or attending school.[60] The data suggest that behavior-modification techniques can be used successfully with serious delinquents, and that it is not always necessary to spend large amounts of money to deal effectively with chronic juvenile offenders.

Community Treatment for Recidivists

The National Council on Crime and Delinquency, in conjunction with the Oakland County (Michigan) Circuit Court, established the Community Treatment for Recidivist Offenders Project in 1971 to demonstrate that second-felony adult offenders can be retained and treated in the community at no greater risk to public safety, and with considerable savings in resources. It was believed that concentrating on offenders who have already demonstrated a tendency toward repeated offending, rather than on the first-offender group (many of whom will not commit another offense), would have a greater impact on the system of correctional services. The target group consists of adult offenders who have been convicted of at least one prior felony, or whose prior conviction was for a misdemeanor reduced from a felony charge. For purposes of evaluative research, 50 percent of second-felony offenders are sent to prison and 50 percent are referred to the project. A special service unit was created within the probation department to implement the project. Intensive casework and group services are provided as needed for offenders in caseloads not exceeding thirty-five cases per officer. Peer-group influence toward positive change is accomplished by means of peer task groups which meet to assist members in identifying problems, planning remedial treatment, and monitoring progress toward stated goals. Project staff function as service brokers, obtaining individual and group services to meet identified offender needs. Community resources are inventoried to assist in the matching of offenders with appropriate resources. Citizen volunteers are utilized whenever their special services will contribute to offender reintegration. Services are purchased when they cannot be obtained from volunteers or social service agencies. (See Chapter 7 for a detailed account of this program.)

Referrals to the project as of December 1972 totaled 290, of which 144 had been selected randomly for project supervision and 146 for either regular probation or prison. The 144 cases assigned for project supervision include eighty-one offenders who would have received regular probation and sixty-three who would have been incarcerated. Initial trends indicate that the project is achieving positive results. It had had only nine failures as of December 1972, with failure defined as a prison sentence for a new offense or a probation violation during project supervision. Of particular significance is the fact that only one of the nine failures was from the group of offenders diverted from prison.[61]

The Community Treatment for Recidivist Offenders Project will merit careful attention. Community intervention programs have not been utilized frequently for adult prison candidates, especially for second-felony recidivists. Evaluation of the project will run from termination in June 1973 to December 1973. Comparisons will be made with control groups derived from the selection process, and a retrospective sample of all offenders released from probation from 1968 through 1970 will be taken. The data will be examined to ascertain criminal patterns, characteristics of successes and failures, and the effectiveness of conventional probation.

Residential Community Programs

Group Homes for Delinquents

Jurisdictions in which the courts do not have access to sufficient resources frequently institutionalize juveniles whose homes are not considered conducive to their rehabilitation, simply because the judge sees no alternative. Group-home programs for delinquents have been devised to provide such alternatives. These programs are developed and administered under various arrangements. The contract group home is operated by an organization such as a church or civic group or by private individuals and financed through a contract with the state agency. Agency-operated homes are staffed by employees of the agency responsible for placing the offenders in the program.[62] Most of the latter are halfway houses for parolees from institutions, but there is an increasing use of such facilities as the initial placement in lieu of incarceration. Many states are currently considering opening group homes and halfway houses as alternatives to the increasingly unpopular correctional institution. Many Model Cities utilized funds made available under that program to develop such facilities.[63]

The Silverlake Experiment in Los Angeles was a group-home project providing a program similar to that of Provo, Highfields, and Essexfields, in that an effort was made to create a nondelinquent culture through peer-group interaction and to involve offenders in decision-making. Seriously delinquent boys, aged sixteen to eighteen, were diverted from training school and placed in a large family residence in a middle-class neighborhood. Up to twenty boys at a time lived in the residence during the week and attended school daily; weekends were spent at home. The daily group meeting was the major formal mechanism for implementing program goals. The objective was to structure a social system in which emerging norms, and their observance, were a function of collaborative client-staff decision-making. A study of the extent of actual collaboration between staff and boys found that information about problem behavior was shared freely, and that the effectiveness of the program culture as a social control measure increased over time.[64]

The Attention Home program of Boulder, Colorado, which opened its first group home in 1966, is a distinctly different kind of group-home program in concept, organization, and operation. The major difference is that the program is completely locally supported. The homes are operated by a nonprofit, nongovernmental corporation and managed by a board of directors composed of interested county residents. The basic idea is broad community involvement in and support of programs to curtail delinquency without resorting to institutionalization. Because of extensive volunteer support in services and materials, the Attention Homes cost considerably less than comparably sized government-supported group-home programs.[65]

The Group Home Project of the California Youth Authority was undertaken to develop and test temporary confinement facilities with varying and controllable atmospheres. This project was an integral part of the Community Treatment Project, which has made wide use of out-of-home placements to facilitate the emergence of nondelinquent patterns in CTP wards. The objectives of the project were to classify home environments according to structure, nature of rewards and penalties, and type of houseparents, and to evaluate the effectiveness of each type of home and of group homes generally. The study sample consisted of adolescents committed to the state correctional system after an average of five police arrests and placed in the CTP. Eight boys' homes (six for long-term placement and two for temporary care) and one girls' home were established. The homes were operated by nonprofessionally trained husband/wife teams who worked in conjunction with one or more CTP parole agents. During the three years (1966-69) of the project, ninety-three separate placements were made (fifty-one for long-term and forty-two for temporary care).

The temporary-care home appeared to have definite advantages over most other placement alternatives (e.g., independent placement, relatives, foster homes). From an operational standpoint there appeared to be two quite successful boys' group homes, while others were moderately successful and at least two were unsuccessful. The final report of the Group Home Project outlines the differential effectiveness of the various group-home models, provides descriptions of home atmospheres and personnel types, and identifies problems encountered in establishing and operating these homes.[66]

Probationed Offenders Rehabilitation Training

Probationed Offenders Rehabilitation Training (PORT), established in 1969 in Rochester, Minnesota, is a live-in, community-based, community supported and directed program for both juvenile and adult offenders.[67] The program provides an alternative for those offenders who require greater control and attention than probation can offer and who, without PORT, would have been sent to training school or prison. Through December 1971 PORT has accepted sixty male residents, ranging in age from thirteen to forty-seven and in offenses from truancy to armed robbery. All but three would have been incarcerated. Entrance into the program is voluntary: the candidate spends a three-week evaluation period in residence at PORT while he and the screening committee determine whether the program is the choice of both. The committee performs more of a catalytic than a screening function, and so far it has not rejected any applicant.

The core of the program is a combination of group treatment and behavior modification. Behavior modification was added after a year of operation, when it was found that the group alone was insufficient. A point system is used to mete out levels of freedom systematically, based on measured performance in tangible areas. The newcomer starts out at the lowest level of a group-evolved classification system, with categories ranging from I (minimum freedom) to V (freedom equal to that of an individual of the same age in the community). Through a process of demonstrating performance to the group and earnings on the point system, the resident gradually gains the freedoms and responsibilities accorded a normal person of his age. The "peer group" of PORT residents assists its members in identifying problems and setting goals and evaluates each individual's readiness for increased freedom and eventual release. Twelve to fifteen resident counselors, mostly college students, live in the building and room with the offenders, in effect replacing the guard/counselor staff of the institution.

A key to the success of the program is the involvement of the community and the heavy use of existing local resources. Educational, vocational, employment, and mental-health services and other resources are not duplicated in PORT as they are in an institution. The community actually runs PORT through a corporate board of directors which hires staff and sets policy. Public support and voluntary service contributions to PORT programs are obtained through the PORT Advisory Committee, a group of about sixty-five Rochester citizens.

While it is too early to state with complete assurance that the concepts employed at PORT are effective, the program appears promising. Of the sixty residents served by the program as of December 1971, thirty-four have been discharged, six as failures (sent to institutions) and twenty-eight who are now living in the community. The following conclusions have been drawn from experience to date: (1) The mixing of juveniles and adults is not only practical but preferred. (2) Community involvement and support from the start is essential. (3) Most existing community resources can be utilized and need not be duplicated. (4) The program can be operated at a cost of less than $3000 per year per bed. (5) The dual treatment method of group therapy and behavior modification seems to be the most successful both in affording control and in achieving individual goals.

It is the intention of PORT not only to provide an effective correctional service in Rochester but to develop a model program that can be transferred to other communities throughout the state and nation.[68] Three other Minnesota communities have already set up programs modeled after PORT.

Community Integration Project

The Community Integration Project in Easton, Pennsylvania, is an experimental research project with the goal of proving that convicted young adult offenders who meet stringent selection criteria can be controlled and treated more effectively and less expensively in a community residence than in prison. Offenders classed as eligible for the project are randomly assigned to the residence group or the control group (sent to prison). Each participant lives in the residence for about six months, after which he becomes an outresident and lives at home. All participants are employed in the metropolitan area in jobs that pay the federal minimum wage. Program staff members help residents to find and maintain career-oriented positions. From wages earned, residents pay room and board, make at least partial restitution to victims, contribute to the support of their dependents, and pay taxes. Therapeutic, vocational, and academic counseling are provided as needed. The research/evaluation component of the three-year project, which was designed and is being operated by the National Council on Crime and Delinquency, will examine cost-effectiveness and the impact on family stability and community safety.

The Community Integration Project is intended to serve as one among several alternatives to incarceration. There are probably many offenders who do not need and cannot benefit from the degree of control and supervision provided by the program. On the other hand, functioning as a kind of work-release center or halfway house, it can play a useful role in demonstrating that viable alternatives to the traditional prison do exist.

The Community Correction Center

As federal and state governments begin to turn away from the traditional prison and training school and toward community alternatives to institutionalization, one of the alternatives most frequently put forward as a model for future development is the community correction center. One of the strongest pushes in this direction has come from the Federal Bureau of Prisons, whose ten-year building program is aimed at replacing existing prisons with smaller ones. In addition, the Bureau operates more than a dozen Community Treatment Centers, which function primarily as halfway houses for offenders on prerelease status but also accept selected short-sentence prisoners and female offenders.[69] The states have also begun to incorporate "community-based" treatment facilities (small, minimum-security institutions) into their overall correctional systems. Illinois has selected locations for four new community correction centers for adult male felons. It is expected that the creation of these new centers will reduce overcrowding in the state's three maximum security prisons and provide opportunities for offenders to move from maximum to medium to minimum security facilities as they are prepared to do so. Location of these new facilities in the more densely populated areas of the state is designed to facilitate community involvement and citizen participation as volunteers.[70]

Washington State, which has expressed its intention of not financing large institutions any longer than necessary, views the small institution, located in the community it serves, as the model for future correction facilities. The Washington Corrections Center at Shelton is an ultramodern facility surrounded by a fence instead of a wall. Inmates live in individual rooms instead of cells, and there are many activities to combat idleness. Younger first offenders are sent there and the center serves a reception and diagnostic function for all sentenced inmates. At the Treatment Center for Women, residents occupy private rooms in residence cottages with all the modern conveniences. Each woman has a key to her room and many of them leave the institution during the day to work or attend classes in nearby communities.[71] These facilities are products of a new trend toward attractive, homelike, nonsecure correctional institutions that are placed in the community in order to overcome the disadvantages of isolation from community resources and opportunities. An institution situated in the locale which supplies the offender population is better able to draw upon the social, educational, employment, and health services and resources of that community and to involve community residents and the offender's family in the reintegration process.

Despite the vast improvement over the maximum-security prison represented by these new facilities, the rapid development of these "nonprisons" could present a real threat to the movement to deinstitutionalize correction. With modern, well-equipped facilities readily available, will the development of noninstitutional community programs be viewed as essential? How many potential prison inmates will be diverted to probation when the pressures of unbearable prison conditions are lifted? Will some of those persons now placed on probation be referred instead to "community residences" for that extra degree of supervision and control? Will these new institutions be plagued by many of the same problems now facing prisons? Are they any more effective than (less expensive) nonresidential programs? Are they necessary?

The community correction center or community-located institution may have a place in a fully diversified correction system. As a minimum security institution it may provide the degree of supervision and control that some offenders require. But care should be taken that, in reallocating correctional resources, investment in these small institutions is not made at the expense of the development of community resources at a lower level of intervention.

Conclusion

In the California study of the effects of criminal penalties it was concluded that since severe penalties do not deter more effectively, since prisons do not rehabilitate, and since the criminal-justice system is inconsistent and has little quantitative impact on crime, the best rehabilitative possibilities would appear to be in the community.[72]

This reasoning typifies much current thinking in correction and illustrates the kind of cognitive leap on which enthusiasm for "community treatment" is based. If prisons do not rehabilitate, and if the goal of correction is to reduce recidivism through integration of offender and community, it seems axiomatic that treating the offender without removing him from society will be more effective. Unfortunately, while one may express the opinion that, since prisons are not effective (a validated observation) then one might as well retain offenders in the community, one cannot assume without the support of adequate research that the best rehabilitative possibilities are to be found in the community. The most rigorous research designs generally have found that offenders eligible for supervision in the community in lieu of incarceration do as well in the community as they do in prison or training school. When intervening variables are controlled, recidivism rates usually appear to be about the same.

This is not to derogate community alternatives to institutionalization, since it is a most important finding: A large number of offenders who are candidates for incarceration may be retained in the community as safely, as effectively, and at much less expense. Moreover, the observed effects of the overcrowded and isolated institution on the personal and social adjustment of the individual are avoided. It is unnecessary to demonstrate, as most experimental projects appear to feel pressured to do, that recidivism rates are lower when offenders are retained in the community. Given the fact that expensive and overcrowded institutions are not doing the job they are supposed to be doing, it is appropriate to expect that less costly, less personally damaging alternatives will be utilized whenever they are at least as effective as imprisonment.

The historical trend in correction is toward the expansion of community-based alternatives to imprisonment. This has come to mean limiting the use of incarceration to dangerous offenders, and diverting all others to the least drastic alternative at the earliest feasible opportunity in criminal-justice processing. The goal of reducing institutional populations is furthered by legislation decriminalizing victimless crimes, by the informal handling of minor deviance without resort to the courts (e.g., the youth service bureau), by the expanded use of alternatives to jail and detention (release on recognizance, bail), and by increased reliance on deferred prosecution, suspended sentences, fines, restitution orders, and probation. For many offenders who make it as far as an institutional sentence, alternatives such as those described above have been shown to be at least workable alternatives.

A fully diversified correctional system, in which resources are optimally allocated, would provide a range of alternatives sufficient to insure that no individual is subjected to greater control or treatment than he requires or can benefit from, not merely because such a system would concur with modern conceptions of justice but because it would be maximally cost-effective. Because the vast majority of offenders apparently do not require and cannot benefit from imprisonment, this would entail a reallocation of correctional resources to reverse the present 90 percent investment in institutional programs. It will not be sufficient simply to build smaller prisons or community-located institutions, although such institutions might be one component of an overall plan. Because the proportion of offenders who must be incarcerated is as yet unknown, it would appear reasonable to begin by diverting as many offenders as possible to community programs and resources of greater cost-effectiveness, leaving the construction of correctional institutions until it is known how many and what kinds of offenders must be served by institutional programs.

Isolation and banishment have not worked. It is coming to be recognized that unless society is willing to keep a large and growing number of offenders in permanent custody, it must begin to accept greater responsibility in the areas of social control and correction. The evidence obtained from experimental work in community correction—and supported by the results of experience with partial imprisonment and graduated release, the treatment of mental illness, and alternatives to criminal-justice processing—makes it clear that a vast proportion of offenders can be managed in the community or diverted from the justice system entirely, thus returning to the community its responsibility for dealing with behavior it defines as antisocial or deviant.

Until alternatives to institutionalization are demonstrated to be more effective than imprisonment in preventing further crime, an important rationale for the use of community programs will be that correctional costs can be reduced considerably by handling in the community setting a large number of those offenders normally institutionalized. Experimental projects have shown that, for a large proportion of institutional candidates, incarceration is apparently unnecessary. If, in light of this evidence, society is still determined to keep these offenders in prisons and training schools, it must be willing to pay the price. The central question thus becomes: Are the goals of punishment and temporary incapacitation worth the high costs of constructing and maintaining correctional institutions, as well as the personal and social costs incurred through exposing individuals to the institutional experience?

References

1. President's Commission on Law Enforcement and Administration of Justice, *The Challenge of Crime in a Free Society* (Washington, D.C.: U.S. Government Printing Office, 1967), p. 165.

2. Wisconsin Council on Criminal Justice, *Final Report to the Governor of the Citizens' Study Committee on Offender Rehabilitation* (Madison, Wis., 1972).

3. President's Task Force on Prisoner Rehabilitation, *The Criminal Offender—What Should Be Done?* (Washington, D.C.: U.S. Government Printing Office, 1970).

4. California Board of Corrections, *Correctional System Study—Coordinated California Corrections: The System* (Sacramento, Calif., 1971).

5. Board of Trustees, NCCD, "Institutional Construction: A Policy Statement" (Paramus, N.J., 1972).

6. New Jersey Coalition for Penal Reform, "Position Paper," 1972.

7. John Howard Association. *Comprehensive Long Range Master Plan: Department of Juvenile Services*, State of Maryland (Chicago, Ill., 1972).

8. Massachusetts Department of Youth Services, *A Strategy for Youth in Trouble* (Boston, Mass., 1972).

9. California Legislature, Assembly Committee on Criminal Procedure, *Deterrent Effects of Criminal Sanctions* (Sacramento, Calif., 1968).

10. National Advisory Commission on Criminal Justice Standards and Goals, Task Force on Corrections, *Report* (working draft), (Austin, Tex., 1972), ch. 17, "Research and Development, Information and Statistics," p. 8.

11. Robert Martinson, "The Paradox of Prison Reform" (parts I-IV), *New Republic*, 166(14):23-25, 1972; 166(15): 13-15, 1972; 166(16): 17-19, 1972; 166(17): 21-23, 1972.

12. California Legislature, op. cit.

13. Dorothy R. Jaman and Robert M. Dickover, *A Study of Parole Outcome as a Function of Time Served* (Sacramento, Calif.: Department of Corrections, 1969); *A Study of the Characteristics and Recidivism Experiences of California Prisoners* (San Jose, Calif.: Public Systems, Inc., 1970).

14. Robert Martinson, "The Paradox of Prison Reform" (part I), *New Republic*, 166(14):23-25, 1972, p. 25.

15. National Advisory Commission on Criminal Justice Standards and Goals, *Working Papers of the National Conference on Criminal Justice, January 23-26, 1973* (Washington, D.C.: Law Enforcement Assistance Administration, 1973).

16. Ibid., p. C-140.

17. Eleanor Harlow, *Diversion from the Criminal Justice System* (Washington, D.C.: National Institute of Mental Health, 1971); William L. Hickey, "Strategies for Decreasing Jail Populations," *Crime and Delinquency Literature*, 3(1):76-94, 1971; William L. Hickey and Sol Rubin, "Suspended Sentences and Fines," *Crime and Delinquency Literature*, 3(3):413-29, 1971.

18. Eugene Doleschal, "Graduated Release," *Information Review on Crime and Delinquency*, 1(10):1-26, 1969.

19. The Model Sentencing Act establishes criteria for identifying two groups characterized as dangerous: the assaultive criminal and the racketeer. NCCD Council of Judges, Model Sentencing Act (2nd ed.) (Hackensack, N.J., 1972), p. 10.

20. The California Assembly Office of Research estimates that at least 50

percent of the men entering prison each year may be no more serious offenders than many of those placed on probation. California Assembly Office of Research, *Preliminary Report on the Costs and Effects of the California Criminal Justice System and Recommendations for Legislation to Increase Support of Local Police and Corrections Programs* (Sacramento, Calif., 1969).

21. James Robison, *The California Prison, Parole and Probation System* (Sacramento: California Assembly Office of Research, 1969), pp. 27-32.

22. Frank R. Scarpitti and Richard M. Stephenson, "A Study of Probation Effectiveness," *Journal of Criminal Law, Criminology and Police Science*, 59(3):361-69, 1968.

23. Ralph England, "What Is Responsible for Satisfactory Probation and Post-Probation Outcome?" *Journal of Criminal Law, Criminology and Police Science*, 47(6):667-677, 1967; Max Grunhut, Penal Reform (New York: Clarendon, 1958).

24. LaMar T. Empey, *Alternatives to Incarceration* (Washington, D.C.: Office of Juvenile Delinquency and Youth Development, 1967).

25. Michigan Council, NCCD, *Saving People and Money: A Pioneer Michigan Experiment in Probation* (East Lansing, Mich., 1963).

26. Bertram M. Johnson, "The 'Failure' of a Parole Research Project," *California Youth Authority Quarterly*, 18(3):35-39, 1965.

27. California Department of Corrections, Special Intensive Parole Unit, *Research Reports, Phases I-IV* (Sacramento, Calif., 1953-64).

28. University of California School of Criminology, San Francisco Project, *Research Reports* (Berkeley, Calif., 1965-67).

29. James Robison and Gerald Smith, "The Effectiveness of Correctional Programs," *Crime and Delinquency*, 17(1):67-80, 1971.

30. The program is briefly described in the 1971 *Annual Research Review of the California Department of Corrections*, pp. 49-50.

31. Robison and Takagi take issue with this finding, pointing out that Work Unit caseloads were comprised of better-risk parolees and that when controls for parolee risk level were introduced the difference in parole outcome for work-unit and conventional caseloads was erased. J. Robison and P. Takagi, "Case Decisions in a State Parole System," California Department of Corrections, Research Division, 1968, Administrative Abstract Research Report No. 31.

32. Ronald I. Weiner, "Probation Caseload Classification Study in the United States District Court for the District of Columbia" (Washington, D.C.: American University, n.d.).

33. For a description of the origin of state subsidy programs in California and six other states, see Leslie T. Wilkins and Don M. Gottfredson, *Research, Demonstration and Social Action* (Davis, Calif.: NCCD Research Center, 1969), pp. 43-70.

34. Robert L. Smith, *A Quiet Revolution: Probation Subsidy* (Washington, D.C.: Youth Development and Delinquency Prevention Administration, 1971).

35. Santa Barbara County Probation Department, "Special Supervision Unit Program" (Santa Barbara, Calif., 1968).

36. Lawrence Yonemura and others, *Subsidy Evaluation Project: Community Oriented Youthful Offender Program* (Los Angeles: Los Angeles County Probation Department, 1971).

37. "Characteristics, Case Movement, Disposition, Experience of Superior Court Probationers in Regular and Subsidy Caseloads" (Sacramento, Calif.: Criminal Statistics Bureau, 1971).

38. Washington State Institutions Division, "Probation Subsidy in Washington State: Calendar Year 1970," *Research Report*, 3(14):1-24, 1971.

39. Wilkins and Gottfredson, op. cit.

40. Douglas S. Lipton, Robert Martinson, and Judith Wilks, *Effectiveness of Correctional Treatment: A Survey of Treatment Evaluations* (New York: State Office of Crime Control Planning, 1970).

41. Robison and Smith, op. cit.

42. James Robison, *The California Prison, Parole and Probation System*, (Sacramento, 1970, California Assembly Office of Research Technical Supplement No. 2).

43. David F. Greenberg, "A Voucher System for Correction," *Crime and Delinquency*, 19(2):212-17, 1973.

44. Martinson, op. cit.

45. Massachusetts Youth Services Department and Fordham University Institute for Social Research, *Conference Proceedings for "The Closing Down of Institutions and New Strategies in Youth Services,"* June 26-28, 1972, Boston, Mass., 1972.

46. David Fogel, Burt Galaway, and Joe Hudson, "Restitution in Criminal Justice: A Minnesota Experiment," *Criminal Law Bulletin*, 8(8):681-91, 1972.

47. Richard C. Ericson and Daniel O. Moberg, *The Rehabilitation of Parolees* (Minneapolis, Minn.: Minneapolis Rehabilitation Center, 1969).

48. California Youth Authority, Community Treatment Project, *Research Reports* (Sacramento, Calif., 1961-72).

49. Robison and Takagi, op. cit. *See also* Robison and Smith, op. cit.

50. P. Lerman, "Evaluating the Outcome of Institutions for Delinquents," *Social Work*, 13(3):55-64, 1968.

51. Ted Palmer and Eric Werner, *California's Community Treatment Project— The Phase III Experiment: Progress to Date* (Sacramento: California Youth Authority, 1972).

52. *The Los Angeles Community Delinquency Control Project: An Experiment in the Rehabilitation of Delinquents in an Urban Community* (Sacramento: California Youth Authority, 1970).

53. Northern California Service League, *Final Report of the San Francisco Project for Adult Offenders* (San Francisco, Calif., 1968).

54. California Assembly, op. cit.

55. Lloyd W. McCorkle, Albert Elias, and F. Lovell Bixby, *The Highfields*

Story: An Experimental Treatment Project for Youthful Offenders (New York: Henry Holt, 1958).

56. LaMar T. Empey, Maynard Erickson, and Max Scott, "The Provo Experiment: Evaluation of a Community Program," *Correction in the Community: Alternatives to Incarceration* (Sacramento: California Department of Corrections, 1964), pp. 29-38.

57. Ted Palmer and Alice Herrera, *CTP's San Francisco Experiment (1965-69): Post-Discharge Behavior of Differential Treatment and Guided Group Interaction Subjects* (Sacramento: California Youth Authority, 1972).

58. Richard M. Stephenson and Frank R. Scarpitti, "Essexfields: A Non-Residential Experiment in Group Centered Rehabilitation of Delinquents," *American Journal of Correction*, 31(1):12-18, 1969.

59. Saul Pilnick and others, *Collegefields: From Delinquency to Freedom* (Newark, N.J.: Newark State College, 1967).

60. William S. Davidson, *Kentfields Rehabilitation Program: An Alternative to Institutionalization* (Grand Rapids, Mich.: Kent County Juvenile Court, 1971).

61. Community Treatment for Recidivist Offenders Project, *Annual Report: 1972* (Pontiac, Mich.: NCCD and Oakland County Circuit Court, 1973).

62. Experience in Illinois with both state-operated and contract group homes suggests the superiority of the latter with respect to both operational and financial considerations. Illinois Department of Corrections, Juvenile Division, *Project Group Homes: A Report* (Springfield, Ill., 1972).

63. Eugene Doleschal, "Criminal Justice Programs in Model Cities," *Crime and Delinquency Literature*, 4(2):292-328, 1972.

64. LaMar T. Empey and George E. Newland, "Staff-Inmate Collaboration: A Study of Critical Incidents and Consequences in the Silverlake Experiment," *Journal of Research in Crime and Delinquency*, 5(1):1-17, 1968.

65. John E. Hagardine, *The Attention Homes of Boulder, Colorado* (Washington, D.C.: Juvenile Delinquency and Youth Development Office, 1968).

66. Ted Palmer, *The Group Home Project: Differential Placement of Delinquents in Group Homes* (Sacramento: California Youth Authority, 1972).

67. Kenneth F. Schoen, "PORT: A New Concept of Community Based Correction," *Federal Probation*, 36(3):35-40, 1973.

68. See *PORT Handbook: A Manual for Effective Community Action with the Criminal Offender* (St. Paul: Minnesota Corrections Department, 1972).

69. *The Residential Center: Corrections in the Community* (Washington, D.C.: U.S. Bureau of Prisons, 1968).

70. Illinois Department of Corrections, Planning Task Force on Community-Based Treatment Facilities, *Planning for Community-Based Corrections* (Chicago, Ill., 1972).

71. Robert Schuman, "Washington's Institutions: Rehabilitation Stressed in Programs, New Units," *American Journal of Correction*, 34(6):29,37, 1972.

72. California Legislature, op. cit.

6

Volunteers in Probation: Not Just a Band-Aid Story

Judge Keith J. Leenhouts[a]

Once there was a mythical city of 100,000 people in the United States. It had no city hospital for seriously injured people, so emergency cases were taken to a nearby state hospital. However, the state hospital was so badly operated, poorly conceived, and overcrowded that most injured people who were taken there did not get better. Rather, nearly all of them got worse. Many of them died in the hospital, either physically or emotionally. Those who died there emotionally were sometimes even worse off than those who physically died there. Those who stayed there for a short period of time and were treated and released were nearly always hurt more than they were helped. The vast majority of those who were released returned to the hospital over and over again, each time in worse condition than before because the hospital was such a poor institution. When someone had an injured or dying friend or relative, he almost hoped that the ambulance would not take him to the hospital. It was so overcrowded, understaffed, dirty, inefficient, and terrible. The alternative, to let him die without being taken to the hospital, often seemed even better. Yet they kept taking the injured to the hospital. Because there were always an increasing number of people living in the city, more and more people were injured and it got worse and worse. Finally one man got an idea. "Why don't we train a lot of our citizens in first aid? Then, when there is an accident, the injured could be treated without going to the hospital, where about eighty percent of the injured only get worse. Maybe, he reasoned, "if we truly knew how to help the injured person with first aid right here in the community—in the city—then he would not have to go to the hospital, where the chances are that he will not get better but only get worse."

Most of the people of the city laughed at him when he asked five of his friends to join him and learn how to give first aid to the injured. However, the few people who started to learn how to give first aid to the injured decided that if they could only help two people out of ten, it would be better than the hospital which, at best, only helped one person out of ten. How they laughed at the six citizens. They even gave them a name that made them sound ridiculous. They called them the "Band-Aiders." They scornfully gave them this name to

[a]Judge Keith J. Leenhouts was Municipal District Court Judge in Royal Oak, Michigan from 1959 to 1969 and Director of Volunteers in Probation, a division of the National Council on Crime and Delinquency, since 1969.

make it sound silly to try to help a severely injured person with Band-Aids. However, the six people sort of liked the name that had been given to them, so they called themselves the Band-Aiders.

Folks in the city did not laugh quite so much when, after a few years, hundreds of citizens were trained and became very good at first aid. Slowly, they began to realize that, although some 90 percent of the injured taken to the hospital got infected even more severely and went on to worse problems, most of those who got first aid from the Band-Aiders got better and did not have to go to the hospital at all.

After many years, the city began to realize that putting on Band-Aids was not all that silly. Sure, there probably were times when the Band-Aiders did more harm than good. But not nearly as many times as the hospital hurt more than it helped. Finally it got to the point where only the most seriously injured were taken to the hospital. They are still being hurt more than they are being helped. The rest, who are not quite so seriously injured, are getting Band-Aids now. Most of them get better.

The story—and the analogy—is not really mythical at all. The hospital is, of course, the prison. The injured are the apprehended criminals. The Band-Aiders are the volunteers, who, working under the direction, supervision, surveillance, support, and guidance of professionals, are becoming extremely effective.

Volunteers in the criminal-justice system can, and are, doing exactly what our mythical Band-Aiders did. They are keeping many young offenders from going to prison, knowing that once there, there is little hope for the future. To be more specific, in a six-month period in 1959, before one court started using volunteers, thirty-one felony cases were brought to the Municipal Court for preliminary examination to determine if a crime had been committed and if the defendant probably committed the crime. If the lower court, the Municipal Court, found that those two factors did occur, then the case was sent to the higher, adult felony court, for trial and final determination of guilt and innocence. If guilt was determined, then the higher court would sentence the defendant, often to prison. Thirty out of the thirty-one cases were sent to the higher court for trial and possible prison sentences. Only one case, for lack of evidence, was not sent on to the higher court. Six years later, in 1965, also during a six-month period, thirty-five cases were brought before the same court. Of those thirty-five cases, ten were reduced to misdemeanors. Two factors are highly significant. First, while the total population and number of felonies increased greatly from 1959 to 1965, nationwide, the number of cases processed as felonies stayed about the same in that city. The Band-Aiders were keeping the number down. Hundreds of lay and professional volunteers, doing everything from serving as friends to working in group psychotherapy, became involved. Second, almost 30 percent of the cases brought to the court were reduced from felonies to misdemeanors and were not sent on for trial and possible prison terms in the adult felony court. Like the Band-Aiders who kept many injured people from going to the hospital, where the injured nearly always only got worse, so the volunteers were keeping many apprehended criminals from going to prison, where they almost always got more hurt, scarred, and dangerous than before.

As a further indication of the effectiveness of the volunteers, so many cases were reduced from felonies to misdemeanors that the parole officer in charge of the state parole office of the county in which that particular city was located noted a great decrease in the number of cases that were sent on to the higher court and received a prison and parole sentence. The operation of the parole office was materially changed because of the reduced number on parole, following a prison term. How is it that the volunteers, working under the direction of professionals, were so effective? A few simple but extremely important facts stand out. First, the great majority of felonies are not characterized by extreme violence. A few of them are, but the great majority are not.

Murder, rape, and armed robbery are the three violent felonies that come before the court most often. They involve extreme violence. However, less than 10 percent of all felonies involve acts that give rise to the crime of murder, rape, and armed robbery. This means that the vast majority of felonies do not involve extreme violence. What they do involve are acts of less violence or of fraud and deceit. In this category are such crimes as larceny from an automobile, larceny from a building, breaking and entering, unlawfully driving away from a motor vehicle accident, etc. In the vast majority of states in the United States, all felonies, including but not limited to the most violent felonies, first go to a lower court for a preliminary examination. Unless that lower court, often called a city court or a municipal court, finds that a crime was committed and that there is probable cause for believing the defendant did commit the crime, then the defendant is not sent for trial to the higher court. The function of the lower court is an adult misdemeanant court, excepting only for the preliminary examination in felonies. The function of the higher court is to handle felonies in adult cases, but only after the lower court rules that there is sufficient evidence for the higher court to do so. Thus, there is a preliminary step where the lower court can, upon the request and petition of the police and prosecutor, reduce the crime from a felony to a misdemeanor. It is also possible for the court, alone, to do this in extreme cases without the petition and consent of the law enforcement agencies, but those cases are not very common. Thus, when a lower court really mobilizes the resources of the community, the police and the prosecutor will often see fit to write a misdemeanor charge instead of a felony charge in the first place or will be likely to reduce felony charges to a misdemeanor in other cases. (Many acts give rise to either a felony or misdemeanor charge. Often, either can be processed.) This is exactly what happened on numerous occasions in the city referred to above. Thus, it came to be that many cases were never presented by the prosecutor's office as felonies, and many other cases originally presented as felonies were reduced to misdemeanors. In view of the fact that about 80 to 90 percent of those committing felonies first commit misdemeanors and appear before our lower court, and also considering the fact that felonies originally go to the lower court for preliminary examinations, it is obvious that if the lower court really does the job then we can substantially reduce the number of felony cases that are processed to the higher courts and on to prison and parole sentences. This is true for a very simple reason. The lower, adult misdemeanant court in that city developed services which the higher, adult felony court simply did not have. The reason this lower court, with virtually no funds whatsoever, did develop these services is that it did not equate rehabilitative services with money and budget. In the higher court in the county referred to in this chapter, money meant services. If you had one dollar's worth of money, you gave one dollar's worth of services. Never did you give any more. In the lower, adult misdemeanant court, money was not equated to services. Because of the volunteers, about one quarter of a million dollars in services was furnished its citizens on an extremely low budget of less than $18,000 a year.

The lower court having established these services, what would you do if you were a prosecutor in a few of the following examples? A young seventeen-year-old youth has just driven away an automobile without permission. As you check into the case you find out that he has no prior record but he is extremely lonely. His father is alcoholic and his mother works outside of the home. He dropped out of high school and has never really had a good positive influence in his life. It is obvious to you that he needs a one-to-one friend who will listen to him, give him counseling and guidance, do for him what one friend does for another, help him find a job, spend leisure time with him and help him gain dignity, pride, and self-respect by enhancing his dignity through the art of listening, sharing, and caring. Obviously, the professional probation officer in the higher court does not have time to do this, since he has a caseload of over seventy-five probationers. Also, because he is so busy with presentence investigations and administration, he only spends about 10 percent of his time counseling and supervising probationers. The vast majority of his time is spent in administration, management, and investigations.

In the lower court, the volunteer can spend several hours each week, if necessary, since he has a caseload of just one probationer. Also, he is blessed with a number of professionals who can guide him, counsel him, and share frustrations, failures, and successes along the way.

What would you do if you were that prosecutor? Would you send the young man to the higher court for minimal probation or possibly on to prison, followed by parole that would not really give him any help. Or would you seek to have the case handled as a misdemeanor, so that one of the hundreds of one-to-one volunteers in that lower court could work with him on an individual basis? The answer is obvious, particularly when it has been your experience as prosecutor to know that the recidivism rate and general success rate of the one-to-one volunteer under such circumstances is far better than the professional probation officer, overburdened and understaffed, in the higher court. Or perhaps you have a young woman who has been guilty of larceny from an automobile. She stole a transistor radio from the front seat of a car. As you investigate the matter, you find that she has attempted suicide on two previous occasions. The attorney for the defendant urges you to do what you can to solve the psychiatric problem that has caused her to become a menace to herself and to society. You know that if the case is processed as a felony, absolutely no court or prison psychiatric services will be available to her because of her lack of money. However, the adult misdemeanant court in the city has a group of volunteer psychiatrists and psychologists who are willing to work with her on a one-to-one basis without any fee. They also have a group psychotherapy program, in which a small number of approximately eight to twelve defendants who have emotional problems can meet on a group basis for two hours a week with a volunteer psychiatrist. You know full well that if she is referred to the higher courts and convicted, probation will simply mean a two- or three-minute meeting once a month with the probation officer of the higher court or she will receive a prison-parole term. You know that there is no chance she will get psychiatric help in that court or prison. Do you think that you would have incentive, as a prosecutor, to process the case as a misdemeanor rather than a felony?

The next defendant who appears before you is an alcoholic. He broke into a store while drunk simply to steal a submarine sandwich and a bottle of beer. After he drank half of the beer and ate half of the sandwich, he passed out on the floor. The next morning the owner found the store had been broken into and discovered the defendant on the floor. The charge would normally be breaking and entering, a felony. You know that in the lower court, the adult misdemeanant court, the rehabilitative services include the assistance of a presentence investigator who is a recovered alcoholic. He can make referrals to an alcohol information school and to the program of Alcoholic Anonymous, which is directed by a recovered alcoholic who was previously referred to the court A.A. program by the judge. You know that the program is extremely effective, for rarely can anyone but a recovered alcoholic succeed with an alcoholic. You also know that in certain extreme cases, volunteer medical doctors will prescribe Antibuse, which is extremely effective in the limited number of cases where it is utilized. You also know that in the higher court the probation officer, in the two or three minutes a month that he would have time to spend with the alcoholic, is unable to give him any real services. Prison, of course, will only make the situation worse. Are you going to send him on to the higher court with a felony charge, or will you seek to process the case in the lower court as a misdemeanor, even if it has to be reduced from a felony, so that the defendant can receive the assistance which he so desperately needs?

Or what if you are faced with a defendant who has need for professional services. Perhaps his teeth are crooked and dirty and cause him to have extreme halitosis. Perhaps he is badly in need of marriage counseling, his marriage being in a complete shambles, which causes him great emotional turmoil. Perhaps it is a case in which you suspect mild brain damage. Or maybe it is a case in which the legal problems of the defendant have become so desperate that he is beyond the point of control. Perhaps it is a case in which the I.Q. is relatively high but achievement is extremely low and there has never been an eye examination. Are you going to send them to the higher court on a felony charge and then on to prison or to that one helpless probation officer? Or are you going to reduce the cases from felonies, or present them as misdemeanors in the first case, so that the lower court of the city, which has volunteer dentists, medical doctors, marriage counselors, lawyers, and optometrists who freely give of their services even to defendants who cannot afford professional assistance, will really solve the problem? Or perhaps it is a case in which the defendant obviously needs intensive professional counseling. Because of volunteers, the adult misdemeanant court has intensive professional services where well-trained professionals can meet with the probationer for several hours a month, at no cost to the defendant. You know that their services are extremely effective, for you have seen what has been and is being done in your city. Are you going to present the case to the court as a felony, and insist that it be processed as a felony and sent to the higher court for minimal probation services or a prison term? Or are you going to have the matter handled as a misdemeanor where adequate professional services are possible? Or perhaps you have an early offender who has never committed an offense before. You feel that it is a case in which the offender has really lived a reasonably good life but committed a sudden stupid act for no reason. Would you be interested in a diversionary program where the early offender could earn dignity, pride, self-respect, and a dismissal, or would you like to have him sent to the higher court for a possible prison term?

You know that the vast majority of cases that are handled in a diversionary manner are done so very successfully because the program is tough, realistic, intelligent, and thoroughly administered by volunteer retirees. You know that only about 2 percent of the apprehended offenders who are referred to this program have failed to comply with the terms of the diverted procedure. The rest of them have earned dismissals and have gone on to the higher court or even come back to the lower court again. Are you going to insist that these persons be handled as felons and sent to the higher court for a very minimal probation experience with virtually no rehabilitative services, or possibly on to a prison sentence? Or are you going to do what you know is effective and process the case as a misdemeanor? The answer, of course, is obvious. It was obvious to the prosecutor and to the police of the City of Royal Oak, Michigan, which we have been using as our example, This city of 100,000 people in the Detroit Metropolitan area did experience the things that are set forth above. There are many different areas in which we have to be extremely effective as we work in the criminal-justice system. Some of us find ourselves working with juveniles before they commit offenses, some with juveniles who have committed offenses, some with forgotten prisoners who are languishing in our prisons, some with parolees and others in bringing about systems change. All of these are extremely vital and important. One of the very vital areas of concern in criminal justice is the young-adult misdemeanant. Nearly all felons, nearly all prisoners and parolees, are first misdemeanants. Many times an act that can be processed either as a misdemeanor or as a felony should be handled as a misdemeanor, for many reasons.

All of us can participate to involve the volunteer and the professional in intensive, intelligent, and individualized probationary services at the adult misdemeanant court level, so that many offenders will not even be sent to a court where a prison term is possible. We can also volunteer. Like the Band-Aiders in our example, volunteers and professionals, working together, can successfully accomplish this goal. When we do this on a massive, nationwide scale we will greatly reduce the number of offenders who are sent to prison. Since prison almost inevitably does more harm than good, it is important that this be one goal that we achieve in the near future. As indicated above, the key words seem to begin with the letter I—*intensive, individualized,* and *intelligent* rehabilitative services. By intensive, we mean that several hours a month should be given to the needs of each probationer; depending, of course, upon what those needs are. In some cases it might involve as many as ten hours a month in services. Sometimes the need for that amount of time continues or diminishes as the probation period goes to its conclusion. Those who say that probation is not successful should know that the term "probation" usually refers to a very minimal type of supervision where the defendant reports by telephone, letter, or, at best, in person for only a very few minutes once every one to six months, or perhaps even only once a year. It would be good if we had a different name for that minimal type of probation. To call that method of probation and the kind of probation which we have been talking about, where the volunteer and professional combine to give intensive services for many hours per month, by the same name is like calling a sand-lot game involving six-year olds and a major league game the one name of baseball. We are talking about two entirely different things.

The second tremendous need for effective probation is to give *individualized* services. This means that we should spend five to twenty hours after guilt is determined but before sentencing to investigate the case and accomplish the following goals:

1. Gather information to help the judge sentence the defendant.

2. Evaluate this information and prepare a probation plan of rehabilitative services.

3. Divert cases in which the problem is medical or emotional or involves some

other difficulty that makes it inappropriate for court action. For example, some cases are psychiatric cases and should be treated medically by competent professionals, and not be in court at all. These cases should be diverted out of the court system.

4. Prepare the defendant for a probation department that will really share, care, and, with firmness, discipline and, intelligence, give love to the offender.

5. Recommend in each case what is needed and constantly demand that the Probation Department increase and expand its services until they are total and complete.

The last requirement is *intelligence.* This means that volunteers must be carefully recruited, screened, oriented, trained, supervised, supported, etc. All kinds of problems are presented to the court. It is necessary that we have all kinds of resources in solving those problems. There is no way the court can buy all the resources it needs, which involve psychiatrists, psychologists, lawyers, medical doctors, dentists, professional counselors, one-to-one volunteers serving as friends, experts in alcoholism, marriage counselors, etc. The only way the court can receive these services is by and through the intelligent, intensive, and individualized use of volunteers. We need both professional and lay volunteers. When we bring all this together, we are extremely effective in reducing the necessity to process many apprehended felony offenders to prisons. Whenever anyone is diverted from a prison term, we greatly increase the possibility that he will make a successful adjustment to society and to a better and happier life. (And at tremendous savings to taxpayers.)

One of the things that became evident in Royal Oak was that many hours had to be spent in the proper administration and management of a volunteer-professional rehabilitative program. In 1959, one man, the judge, spent one-fourth of his time, or five hundred hours a year, on the total criminal court process in our city. By 1965, about five hundred citizens, nearly all of them volunteers, were giving fifty thousand hours a year to the same process. Of those fifty thousand hours, 14 thousand were spent in the administration of the program by seven retirees, who worked full time for the court. The cost to the taxpayer for their administrative services was zero; some of them volunteered their time and others were paid by contributions from businessmen who believed in the necessity of the proper administration and management of the program. This chapter began with a fantasy—and if it had been written only ten years ago, it would have ended in one. No one would have believed that it was possible to harness the citizen power of a community to give *intensive, intelligent,* and *individualized—* and inspired—rehabilitative misdemeanant court services. What we are suggesting is not pretend or make-believe. In the past ten years the number of citizens involved as volunteers in courts and corrections has grown from virtually zero to about one-third of a million volunteers involved in some two thousand programs in courts, jails, prisons, and juvenile institutions. In another three to five years one million of our citizens will be involved. Most of these volunteers give their time to juvenile and adult misdemeanant courts. We can work hard, involve the citizens of our community, and develop rehabilitative court services that will save many offenders from felony convictions and prison terms. "Band-Aids" are effective. This is what hundreds of communities are doing now, and what thousands of our communities must do in the future if we are going to solve the problem and the challenge of crime in a free society.

Research of the Program

In April 1965, the Royal Oak Municipal Court received a grant from the National Institutes of Mental Health to study the effectiveness of a complete rehabilitative service based upon citizen participation and volunteer action in Royal Oak, Michigan. The basic idea of the grant was to study the Royal Oak program and the program of a reasonably comparable court, to ascertain the effectiveness of extensive probationary services. This was done by testing the defendants who appeared before the Royal Oak court and the other court, which we will call Court A. The defendants in each court received a series of tests to study their hostility, aggressiveness, belligerence, and antisocial attitudes. One of the tests used was the Minnesota Multi-Phasic Personality Inventory.

At the end of eighteen months the same defendants were tested again. If their attitude and behavioral concepts had changed about the same in both courts, then intensive probation would make no difference. We are now through with the testing and retesting program and can evaluate the results of the research study, which have been most gratifying from the standpoint of the Royal Oak Municipal Court and the use of intensive probation.

In Royal Oak, of the 94 youthful offenders tested, all between the ages of seventeen and twenty-five and all white males, 9 tested normally both before and after the testing program and were eliminated. Of the 85 left, 62 showed definite improvement, 13 showed no change, and 10 regressed. This means that 73.8 percent improved, 15.3 percent showed no change, and 11.7 percent regressed.

In Court A 82 were tested. Nine were eliminated because they tested normal before and after. Of the 73 remaining, 13 improved, 25 showed no change, and 35 regressed—17.8 percent improved, 34.2 percent showed no change and 48.0 percent regressed. Almost 3 out of 4 showed improvement in Royal Oak—1 out of 5 showed improvement in Court A. Less than 1 out of 8 in Royal Oak regressed—nearly 1 out of 2 regressed in Court A.

Both Royal Oak and Court A have a budget from the city of about $17,000. Court A runs the typical type of probation where the probationers report once a month, usually in writing. Royal Oak has intensive follow-up, which usually includes weekly meetings for all or at least a substantial part of the probationary period.

While Court A has only one paid professional probation officer and one secretary on the $17,000-a-year budget, Royal Oak has six retired citizens who serve as full-time administrators, and some five hundred volunteers who give services valued at some $300,000 a year. Royal Oak features individual and group psychotherapy, a court-related Alcoholics Anonymous program, individual counseling, volunteer inspirational personalities to act somewhat akin to Big Brothers, employment counseling, marriage counseling, and other services, such as educational counseling. Some retired citizens are paid, what Social Security allows for their full-time services, others are unpaid.

The courts are located in cities with similar populations. Court A is slightly larger and is located in another state. Royal Oak is in a larger (Detroit) metropolitan area. Both have about the same potential caseload of about six hundred probationers a year.

The grant is particularly interesting, for it shows what Royal Oak would be doing if it operated a traditional probation program, as distinguished from the unique citizen participation and volunteer program involving some five hundred people in the community. There is no doubt of its effectiveness. The credit properly goes not to one person or a small group of persons but to the spirit of the citizens of the City of Royal Oak. See "Concerned Citizens and a City Criminal Court," a fifty-page booklet; the book *First Offender*, published by Funk and Wagnalls, and other literature available on the Royal Oak program.

One major aspect of the project is the psychological testing program which is being used for data-gathering and measuring the degree of emotional disturbance, hostility, and other social attributes in roughly one hundred court research cases described above. By comparing test-retest data of these research subjects with those of the Royal Oak Court research subjects, significant differences in improvement can be measured and evaluated properly. Such comparisons do demonstrate the value and success of the extensive Royal Oak probation system. The test battery is composed of intellectual, biographical, and psychological data-gathering devices, and is administered to each probationer in all study courts.

Examination of these groups reveals a definite trend showing improvement of retest scores over the initial test scores in the case of the research subjects in the Royal Oak group (see graphs attached) where intensive individual and/or group counseling by volunteers or professionals played major roles in the probation program. This is not the case with the Court A group who were unexposed to the treatment during the eighteen-month study period. At best, Court A offered only a short monthly meeting to its probationers, often lasting five minutes or less. Many probationers reported monthly by mail only.

Thus, concrete evidence has developed which supports the principle that rehabilitation of the young misdemeanant can be effected through the intensive, intelligent, individualized and inspired use of professional and lay volunteers. Further information will be furnished by request, from Volunteers in Probation, Inc., 200 Washington Square Plaza, Royal Oak, Michigan 48067.

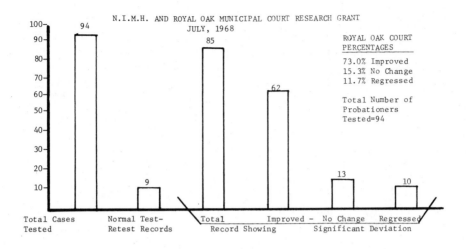

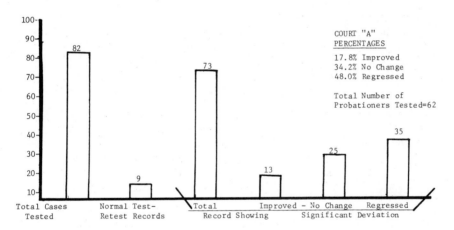

Figure 6-1. NIMH and Royal Oak Municipal Court Research Grant
July 1968

Although a simple test of recidivism—how many committed a second offense after being put on probation—has many limitations, the various studies completed over the years on the Royal Oak citizen participation probation program indicates a success ratio of about 93 percent. This means that 7 percent commit a second violation in our jurisdiction while under court supervision. This compares to a 75 percent success ratio, which is considered good for the routine type of probation program. The most significant fact is that the 73.8 to 17.8 percent success ratio in the attitudinal research study bears a reasonable relationship to the 93 to 25 percent recidivism results, and adds validity to both tests.

References

Leenhouts, Judge Keith J. "Getting Started in Volunteer Programs" (Audio Tape) Volunteers in Probation, Royal Oak, Mich., 1972.

Morris, Joe Alex, *First Offender.* Funk and Wagnalls, New York, N.Y., 1970.

_____ , "Royal Oak Aids Its Problem Youth," *Reader's Digest*, October 1965, reprint, pp. 2-6.

_____ , "Big Help For Small Offenders," *Reader's Digest*, April 1968, reprint, pp. 2-6.

National Council on Crime and Delinquency, "Help Me Please" (Film), Volunteers in Probation, Royal Oak, Mich., 1970.

National Council on Crime and Delinquency, "Big Help For Small Offenders" (Film), Volunteers in Probation, Royal Oak, Mich., 1971.

National Council on Crime and Delinquency, "Royal Oak, City With a Heart" (Film), Volunteers in Probation, Royal Oak, Mich., 1970.

National Council on Crime and Delinquency, "Don't Curse The Darkness" (Film), Volunteers in Probation, Royal Oak, Mich., 1971.

National Information Center on Volunteerism, "Volunteer Courts Newsletter," "Information Brochure," "National Directory Volunteer Courts in America," "Consultant Programs" (Pamphlets).

Royal Oak Department of Municipal Court Probation, *Concerned Citizens and A City Criminal Court*, Royal Oak, Mich.

U.S. Department of Health, Education and Welfare, *National Institutes of Mental Health and The Royal Oak Municipal Research Study Report*, Washington, D.C.: July 1968.

Other Resource People:

Judge William Burnett, County Court, Denver, Colo.

Mr. Charles Cameron, Chief Juvenile Officer, Boulder County Juvenile Court, Boulder, Colo.

Mr. Harold Dyer, Director, Kalamazoo County Juvenile Court, Kalamazoo, Mich.

Mr. Leonard Flynn, Director of Community Services, Tallahassee, Fla.

Mr. Robert Hamm, Volunteer Coordinator, Boulder County Juvenile Court, Boulder, Colo.

Judge Horace B. Holmes, Boulder County Juvenile Court, Boulder, Colo.

Professor G. LaMarr Howard, Assistant Professor of Criminal Justice, Georgia State University, Atlanta, Ga.

Judge Montague Hunt, Ferndale, Mich.

Mrs. Lois Johnson, Assistant Director, Kalamazoo County Juvenile Court, Kalamazoo, Mich.

Professor James Jorgensen, Graduate School of Social Work, University of Denver, Denver, Colo.

Mrs. Phyllis Lake, Director of Volunteers, Washington, D.C.

Judge Keith J. Leenhouts, Volunteers in Probation of the National Council On Crime and Delinquency, Royal Oak, Mich.

Mr. Bob Moffitt, Director, Partners Project, Denver, Colo.

Dr. Leonard J. Pinto, Professor, Department of Sociology, University of Colorado, Boulder, Colo.

Mr. Loren Ranton, Director, Training Center, National Council on Crime and Delinquency, Hackensack, N.J.

Dr. Ernest Shelley, Ingham County Probate Court, Children's Service, Lansing, Mich.

Dr. Ivan H. Scheier, Director, National Information Center on Volunteers.

Mrs. Marie Thomson, Clerk of the County Court, County Court of Jefferson County, Golden, Colo.

Mr. Robert D. Trujillo, Director of Corrections, Denver, Colo.

Mrs. Ruth Wedden, Director Broward County Division of Youth Services, Fort Lauderdale, Fla.

7 Instead of Prison

Michael J. Mahoney[a]

The Problem

The repeat offender is the forgotten person in the criminal justice process. Most probation programs concentrate on the first-time offender whom judges usually give a "break" and place on probation. But in direct proportion to the frequency in which a repeat offender is brought before the court, the judge will reject the alternative of probation and sentence him to a prison term.

This was the situation in Oakland County, Michigan, in 1971. Offenders with prior records accounted for almost two-thirds of those arrested, convicted, and sentenced by the Circuit Court. Of the 530 offenders sentenced in that year, 25 percent of the first offenders were sent to institutions, 44 percent of offenders with one prior conviction went to prison, and 75 percent of offenders with two or more prior convictions were imprisoned.

Oakland County is typical of many areas in the United States. A booming suburban region with a population of nearly 1 million, the county was experiencing the rapid growth of crime typical of the 1960s. Drug use was widespread, crime was spilling over into the county from the ghettos of nearby Detroit, and Pontiac, the county seat, with a population of 80,000, had typical urban crime problems.

Response

The judges of the Oakland County Circuit Court were casting about for ways to help cut crime. They were seeking to strengthen alternatives to prison sentences. At the same time the National Council on Crime and Delinquency was looking for a site to test a project for repeat offenders. NCCD felt that if a Community Treatment Project for Repeat Offenders could demonstrate that repeat felony offenders can be retained and treated in the community at no significant risk to public safety, and if the cycle of offense arrest, conviction, and incarceration could be broken, substantial savings in money, manpower, and human resources

[a]Michael J. Mahoney was Midwest Regional Director for the National Council on Crime and Delinquency in Chicago, Illinois. He is a master's program graduate of the University of Louisville and formerly a member of the staff of the Louisville Metropolitan Social Services Department. He was Project Director for the Oakland County Project. He is presently Assistant Director, John Howard Association, Chicago, Ill.

would result. Because Oakland County has the depth and variety of social service resources needed to augment successful intensive probationary programs, NCCD felt that it was a suitable site to undertake the project.

The judges, probation department, prosecuting attorney, and county commissioners; the State Corrections Department and Office of Criminal Justice Programs; the NCCD and the Sachem Foundation forged a working relationship to design the program.

The project received funding amounting to $199,986 in April 1971. Sachem contributed $86,000; the county commissioners, $41,000, and the Michigan Office of Criminal Justice Programs, $62,900.

A Citizens' Advisory Committee, with the concurrence of local officials, selected Michael J. Mahoney, a well-qualified corrections professional, to direct the program. Mahoney joined the NCCD staff and under his supervision a special unit within the county probation department was organized. Mahoney recruited a staff of four probation officers, a research assistant, and two clerks. (Currently, the professional staff consists of five probation officers and two university students, the latter working two days a week). The project began taking offenders in July 1971 and has been operating continuously since that time.

How the Program Works

The project seeks to aid offenders and maintain them in the community in a number of ways:

It provides casework and group services for offenders in small caseloads, not exceeding thirty-five per probation officer. Besides intensive one-to-one supervision, offenders are assigned to small task groups of six to ten offenders. These groups meet periodically to help participants identify problems contributing to their criminal behavior and to plan a course of remedial treatment. This part of the project is described in greater detail below.

The project refers clients to a large variety of governmental and private services. These include drug-abuse treatment, vocational rehabilitation, mental health, educational equivalency, technical and job training, college courses, family counseling, and employment. Through a grant from the Michigan Office of Criminal Justice Programs, the project also purchases a number of services for clients. These include fees for tuition in educational programs, medical examinations, psychological testing, and certain kinds of counseling.

The project utilizes volunteer services. The project brings in lawyers to provide personal and group legal counseling. A teacher donates his time giving individual and group general equivalency education tutoring. A banker furnishes personal financial and small-business counseling. Doctors give free physical examinations. An architect provides vocational information. An optometrist examines clients. A real estate broker from time to time gives counseling on his field. Seminarians from a local college give individual counseling and include project clients in ther organized recreational activities program.

Who the Project Helps

The clients participating in the project have typically been convicted of such crimes as burglaries, stealing cars, creating disturbances, shoplifting, and assaultive behavior. A large number of crimes relates to drug or drinking problems. The offenders are generally in their twenties. They are repeat offenders, but are not generally violent or dangerous. Rather, they are often confused and immature persons with histories of disrupted family life or poverty. They don't really belong in prison, but because they repeatedly commit crimes they are destined to receive prison terms—unless a special program such as this one can intercede.

In administering the project, NCCD found that not all probationers in the project need intensive supervision. The amount and kind of supervision really depends a great deal on the individual's needs and his problems. In some cases, it's not necessary for a probation officer to see a client more than once a month. In others, the officer has to be in touch with probationers three or four times a week.

Here are some true case histories (only the names are fictitious) taken from the files on the project.

William

William, twenty, was convicted of larceny in a building and placed on probation. He had a long record of juvenile offenses, truancy, possession of alcoholic beverages, violence, and reckless driving. Two weeks after his latest conviction he was in violation of probation, having been found drunk and apparently attempting a second break and entry. The judge gave him a good tongue-lashing, but because a project probation officer interceded in his behalf the judge continued probation. Otherwise he would have received three to five years in prison, the officer said.

According to the probation officer, the youth was so grateful that he gave "100 percent attention to the group meetings which he attended." Due to the group's encouragement, he got a steady job and went back to school. The group encouraged him to continue school despite being constantly cut down by his mother.

"We are advocates for our clients as opposed to being surveillance and enforcement people, as is the case in many probation departments," the officer remarked. "Our work is treatment and prevention oriented."

Joseph D.

Black and fifty-six years old, Joseph D. has been in prison half his life. His record began back in 1928, when he was institutionalized for truancy. Most of his prison sentences stemmed from a long history of charges involving larcenies and purse-snatching. Finally, an Oakland County judge placed him on five years' probation and fined him $1000 for an attempted breaking and entering. "He had family trouble and an unhappy childhood," a probation officer reported. "He has a drinking problem."

In a two-month span he had seven contacts with his project probation officer, four office interviews, and three group meetings. "The causes of his problem have not gone away and the circumstances are the same," his probation officer reported recently. "But he is keeping out of trouble and we are still working with him. He is a help to us. He has found jobs for five people in the project."

Dan

Dan, a twenty-nine-year-old black of "dull normal" intelligence, lives with a family composed of fourteen brothers, sisters, nieces, and nephews. He has never been married, and has an out-of-wedlock child. He has been unemployed for three or four years. He has a record that includes larceny, aggravated assault, possession of an unregistered gun, and two traffic violations.

Dan was referred to the project in November 1971 for attempted larceny. Through the project's individual and group counseling sessions at the Pontiac Neighborhood Service Center he began to focus on his drug-related problems, employment possibilities, physical and health impairments, and job-training programs. Through use of many community resources, he has successfully completed the methadone maintenance program, and has had his hearing deficiency treated. Upon early discharge from probation, he will be employed by GMC Truck and Coach Division.

He also wishes to become actively involved in a future responsible role as an assistant in group counseling with project black offenders in the service center. He plans on marrying his girl friend and assuming a father role with his out-of-wedlock son.

Terry D.

Terry D., Caucasian male, nineteen and married, has a juvenile criminal record and was in the State Boys' Training School from age sixteen until his nineteenth birthday. Prior to that he had been placed on probation with the juvenile court, and violated that probation. He ran away from the training school on several occasions. Through the efforts of the project, he has seen a psychiatrist, and has been identified as having a possible personality disorder. The project saw to it that he was enrolled in a drug therapy program, because he is a self-proclaimed heroin addict.

He passed the general education equivalency program and is now enrolled in the Diesel Training Institute.

Group Counseling Sessions

It's a sociological fact that individuals are greatly influenced by their peers. For this reason, task discussion groups are an integral part of the project. These groups meet periodically to help participants identify problems contributing to their criminal behavior, and to plan a course of remedial action. The group then monitors individuals' progress toward solving their problems.

Attendance is flexible, depending on the individuals' needs and schedules. Usually a client will start out attending once a week. Then the attendance can taper off somewhat, depending on the client's progress. Group sessions are held in community locations in Pontiac and Detroit, besides project headquarters in Royal Oak.

The discussion groups can perhaps best be explained by an account of an actual meeting.

It was a Wednesday night counseling session. Eight clients, all in their early twenties, at least three with drug problems, were "rapping." Attention turned to one participant, who seemed to be talking loudest. He was wearing a comical-looking felt hat. They commented on the hat.

Pete enjoyed the attention. He continued to talk loudly, basking in his role as the center of attraction.

Probation Officer Tom Jacks, a group coordinator, now began to deftly turn the rapping into a real discussion.

First, he asked Jim to explain the differences between group counseling and rap sessions. Jim repeated that participants in counseling sessions explain, are responsible for self and others, concerned about doing things and making changes, and listen; and each is himself. Members of rap sessions explain away, avoid responsibility, and do what is safest in the group.

Everyone nodded in agreement.

Turning toward Pete, Jacks declared, "You're acting very strangely tonight. Why?"

"I racked up my car the other night," Pete replied. "I guess it's bothering me. Besides, what's wrong with me? Can't I have some fun?"

The participants took their cue from Jacks. They questioned Pete sharply.

Pete gradually admitted that he took an illicit drug and while he was high smashed his car. Luckily, no one was hurt, and the police made no arrest. But his auto sustained several hundred dollars' worth of damage.

When the pressure gets to be too much, Pete turns to drugs. Born of middle-class parents, Pete had a normal childhood, on the surface at least, but he began to turn to drugs at the age of thirteen, winding up hooked on heroin. He was in a methadone maintenance program for three years. Just when he seemed to be coming around he'd get impatient and blow it. He'd get a fix—and steal a car or attempt a burglary.

Pete is married and has one small child. His wife is hooked on heroin. She is expecting another child. She recently attempted to take her life. The authorities took away her child. Through the program, Pete has obtained the services of a lawyer to help him get his child back.

Things are tough for Pete. But he did get one break, following his latest arrest and conviction. Instead of being sent to prison, where he would get no individual attention, he was referred to the project.

He began attending group sessions. Through the efforts of the project, the Department of Vocational Rehabilitation advanced him funds to enable him to attend a technical school to learn dental technology.

"Let's face it. I hate to say it, but I have middle-class values. I want the same things. . . . There's good money in making false teeth."

Pete is doing well enough in school, but he's disappointed in himself. "That instructor takes a real interest in me; he really feels bad when I miss a class. He says I'm doing okay, but I don't feel really with it. I know that I can do better."

Pete tries to make excuses. "I haven't really done anything wrong," he says with a lilt in his voice. He is still high from a drug. "If only my parents didn't nag me."

The participants are not sympathetic.

"You can't blame your parents for being upset."

"Do you want to blow this chance you're getting?"

"You're just trying to kid yourself and look for an easy way out."

Pete looks for understanding. He explains that he gets depressed and continues to lack confidence in himself. "I know that I'm doing the wrong things," he finally admits in a crestfallen voice. "I really want to succeed, but then I go out and do a stupid thing like this."

The conversation turns to another participant, who confesses to what might be developing into a drinking problem. "I go out drinking every night. I drink too much. I think I'm becoming an alcoholic," he explains.

Another talks about the methadone maintenance program he is in. He seems to be setting himself straight. He holds a regular job as an auto mechanic.

The conversation turns back to Pete. "We understand your problems," Jacks says sympathetically. "But there is a solution. You've got to keep trying. You can't give up."

The participants agree. All seem to take heart. The meeting adjourns, and hopefully the participants have derived enough sustenance to help them get through another week.

"Man, this is a beautiful program," a probationer remarks as the group leaves. Others agree. "Before this, I never met a probation officer who really cared."

Project Achieves Recognition

Oakland County officials are convinced the project is working for them. Following completion of the two-year demonstration, the county agreed to take over supervision and financing of the project.

After having studied preliminary results, the State Department of Corrections and the Michigan Office of Criminal Justice Programs have endorsed the project and are planning to install it on a statewide basis. As a first step, funds are being sought to open similar projects in Michigan's urban areas. News about the project results is being discussed in professional circles. And now other states are showing interest in replication.

8 Wilderness Training as an Alternative to Incarceration

Joseph Nold and Mary Wilpers[a]

"I didn't think I could do it. But once I did it, I realized I could do more than I thought I could." Danny Nelson, sixteen years old, an adjudicated delinquent from the Juvenile Court of Denver on probation to Outward Bound, was recounting his experience of the rappel. This was a mountaineering exercise where he had descended a sheer 110-foot cliff by sliding down a long nylon rope, a bare 7/16" thick, while dangling out in space.

/ The essence of "wilderness therapy" is in this experience: challenge, the overcoming of a seemingly impossible task, the confrontation of fear, a success experience. It is an opportunity to gain self-reliance, to prove one's worth, to define one's manhood. The results are immediate. The task is clear, definable, unavoidable. It is an act of interpersonal interaction as well, for while Danny stepped nervously off the cliff, he was secured by a safety rope, held firmly in the hands of another member of his climbing team. That night sitting around the campfire, with his group and their leader, they recounted the incident. Danny was able to admit his fear and yet not be considered "chicken." Bringing the intense emotions of the day to a conscious level, he could integrate his success into his image of himself, reinforce the positive action, clarify his values.

Outward Bound, the model for many adventure-centered programs, uses the challenge of wilderness training and service activities to give people a greater sense of their own potentiality, and opportunities for group interaction and leadership, to strengthen their commitment to society and a sense of themselves in a religious or universal perspective.[1]

Since 1962, over five hundred delinquent youngsters, boys and girls, have taken part in the program, interspersed with the normal student population coming from a wide cross-section of American society, from all backgrounds and walks of life. The program, lasting approximately three weeks, has four phases: basic skills training; a long expedition; the solo, a three-day period of solitude; and the final testing events. In basic training the skills necessary to survive and travel in a wilderness environment are taught, depending on the school

[a]Joseph Nold, president of the Colorado Outward Bound School, studied in Scotland and England and received his M.A. from Columbia University, consultant to educators, corrections leaders, and other human service representatives. Mary Wilpers is a graduate of the University of Massachusetts, with an M.A. for Education. She is a research assistant with Outward Bound School and an instructor at the Hurricane Island Outward Bound School in Maine.

location—forests of a national park, high mountains, the sea, canoe country, the desert. This is followed by a long expedition that has clear objectives—to climb so many peaks, to canoe so many lakes, to explore so many islands. There is a sense of purpose, a fixed destination, clear-cut goals. Solo, usually three days alone in a remote setting, with a minimum of food and shelter, provides a period of contemplation. And finally there are experiences that test fitness, skills, and teamwork, such as small groups expeditioning through unfamiliar terrain without an instructor. A long-distance marathon event is the final personal challenge.

Certain program principles are common to all programs. Activities are planned that provide stretching experiences. The difficulties become progressively greater; success is built upon previous success. The small group is the prime social unit, nine to twelve members living together, acting as a team, needing to develop cooperative efforts and group decision-making abilities in order to succeed. Team activities are programed, such as the wall—a thirteen-foot obstacle that must be scaled by *all* members, an impossible task without teamwork. Morning readings, evening discussions, group sessions, underline the purpose of the activities, emphasize the values, and bring conflicts to the surface. The activities are not an end in themselves, but merely the vehicle through which personal growth can take place. They provide opportunities for value-forming experiences.

What does such an experience offer problem youth? The character traits of the delinquent have been summarized as follows: low self-esteem, lack of confidence in his ability to effectively cope with and manipulate his environment; inability to communicate, alienation from and resentment toward others; inability to delay gratification or pursue long-range goals; low threshold of frustration—impulsiveness; inability to cooperate, to form mutual-trust relationships; and lack of information and skills related to successful adult functioning, lack of knowledge of community resources.[2]

Most delinquent youth are teachable and have the energy and desire to learn, and adventure-centered wilderness training speaks to their needs. A wilderness environment, with which an inner-city youth is totally unfamiliar, and the new skills required to cope with it, offer a fresh chance to develop self-confidence and the ability to manipulate the environment by living successfully with it. The obvious need for skills—tent-pitching, camp cooking, direction-finding, climbing techniques, and first aid—permit learning to take place in a nonauthoritarian setting. Feedback is immediate—porridge is burned if it's improperly cooked; a sleeping bag gets wet if a tent is inadequately pitched. Problem-solving techniques are learned through day-to-day living tasks as well as the specially contrived initiative tests, problems presented to a group that require planning and teamwork through resolve. An individual shares in the success that is only possible through cooperation, persistence, and teamwork. The experiences provide opportunities to be successful, to help and to be helped. Sharing is essential, and communications are improved. Stress situations compel a student to face his own reactions, his abilities and inabilities, and to make decisions for himself. Rock climbing and rappelling are high-risk controlled situations of immediate confrontation. Frustration will not help one get up a rock face, and it quite often impossible to back down. Persistence is rewarded by the arrival at one's destination, finally achieving the summit. Peak ascents demand delayed gratification, are the culmination of several days' expenditure of energy and group effort. The accomplishments are personal successes; the reward is from within.

Mutual trust is developed on an adventurous expedition. This is particularly important for the delinquent, as many have had few opportunities to experience "being trusted," or trusting one another. Students are taught to "belay" the climber. That means that the student personally must assume responsibility for another person's life. Simultaneously, the climbing student must trust the fellow student. whom he has just met, with his life. It is a serious and meaningful experience.

Self-reliance and independence are boosted by the experience of solo. The three days of solitude are a time to take a good, long, undistracted look at one's self. Being alone in the wilderness not only stimulates an awareness of the natural setting but also triggers deep thoughts about one's past, present, and future. For many this is the most difficult and demanding part of the course. It can also be the most rewarding.

Does it work? The one major source of documentation is a study by Kelly and Baer[3] carried out for the Massachusetts Department of Youth Services, funded by an Office of Juvenile Delinquency grant. Their report presents the results of a two-year demonstration project which involved 120 delinquent boys, sixty who attended Outward Bound schools and sixty who were treated in a routine manner by the juvenile corrections authorities. Effectiveness was measured primarily by comparing the recidivism rates between two matched groups one year after parole. The subjects of the study were boys fifteen to seventeen years of age, in good health without any severe physical disability or severe psychological problems. Each participant was administered a series of tests before and after the course.

Psychologists served as participant observers at each of the schools where they recorded their impressions of the program, the instruction, and the impact on delinquents. Not only is it rich in statistical data, but the narrative account also provides a valuable qualitative critique.

Recidivism among the experimental group who attended Outward Bound was only 20 percent after one year on parole, while 42 percent of the comparison group had returned. Results supported the expectation that Outward Bound was more effective in reducing recidivism than the routine rehabilitative methods of institutions at that time.

Kelly and Baer tested for certain background variables found to be related to recidivism. They included the number of previous commitments, the type of offense, the presence of parents in the home, age at the first court appearance and first commitment. Variables such as I.Q., race, religion, and residence were not found to be significant. It was found that the Outward Bound experience had a greater influence on those delinquents who were committed for the first time than for those who had had previous periods of institutionalization. There was a greater effect on the delinquent whose first court appearance occurred following the onset of adolescence. This suggests that Outward Bound provides an opportunity for youth to resolve their identity crises. There was a positive influence on boys whose delinquency was a response to home conflict, but it was found more successful with those who act out in the community than with those who act out at home. So, for a period of one year at least, Outward Bound training was demonstrated to have a positive effect.

However, this is not the full story. Kelly is currently doing a five-year follow-up study, which is not yet published. Preliminary results indicate that using the rate of recidivism as the sole criteria, the differences between the Outward Bound group and the control group narrow each year, so that after five years there is no significant difference between the two groups. Kelly does find though a significant "qualitative" difference. The Outward Bound group commits significantly less number of crimes; they are less serious; they spend less time in detention; there is a significant saving in the cost of remedial and custodial care required by the state. Kelly concludes that this form of treatment is indeed helpful, though far from a panacea; and he points to the need for follow-up activity to reinforce the positive growth that has taken place to nurture and sustain the experience.

Most Outward Bound courses have been open to delinquent youth, and many are sent, many on scholarships raised by Outward Bound and their communities. Organizations that have found the experience valuable for their wards include the Michigan Office of Youth Services, the Colorado Division of Youth Services, the Juvenile Court of Denver, the Department of Human Resources of Chicago. Private agencies that have a commitment to working with problem youth have also participated: the New York Urban League, the IMPACT program in Newark, Darrow Hall in St. Louis, Job Corps, Young Life, the Boys' Clubs, Creative Living Foundation of Phoenix, Ute Tribal Court, the Federal Youth Center in Englewood, Colorado.

How important is it to mix delinquents with other students? The opportunities for positive peer pressure within a mixed group are obvious, and have often proven to be highly beneficial. This has been particularly true of those delinquents with leadership skills, who are assertive, adaptive, and truly confident and can make the adjustment to middle-class social norms and achievement goals.[4]

There is evidence, however, that many delinquents benefit as much from a modified program, designed specifically for a special group, geared to their needs, expectations, and physical capabilities. Kelly and Baer's research in Massachusetts would indicate there is little difference in the long-range impact of both programs.[5] The Florida Ocean Sciences Institute (FOSI) near Fort Lauderdale uses ocean experiences as a delinquent-rehabilitation environment. In four years of research with 344 boys, recidivists rates were 11.5 percent for the 121 graduates and 14 percent for 158 more who survived a rough 30 day orientation program.

Whether in mixed or homogenous groups, delinquent youth do require special attention if they are to be successful. One is expecting a tremendous adjustment on the part of the student. There is much that is threatening, and realistically so, for there is a very real chance of injury. Not every person can respond to such challenge. Without proper preparation the failure rate can be high.,[6] as much as 50 percent, when 3 percent would be the expected drop-out rate for a regular group, or one that was well prepared.

A study was done into the reasons for such a high percentage of students dropping out, and these factors have been identified as being important for the success of students who are referred to Outward Bound as a means of rehabilitation.

1. The selection and orientation of students is critical. All too often they are corralled into the program with promises of summer-camp experiences, complete with golf courses, swimming pools, and horseback riding. The primitive conditions under which Outward Bound courses are run add to the "culture shock." Those referring students and selecting them need to have a full understanding of what the experience is about; indeed, it helps if the referring person can have experienced it himself. Students need to be psychologically prepared for what they are getting into, not shanghaied into it.

2. A well thought-out orientation is necessary. Students should be given the Outward Bound literature to read and digest and discuss, and good films can be shown of the various programs. There is a complicated medical form to be filled out. For some this may represent their first trip to a doctor and their first exposure to shots, in itself a cause for anxiety. Precourse dental attention is recommended. There is warm clothing to be bought, boots to be fitted. A precourse training program of fitness involving running a mile a day, ten push-ups, etc., is also a necessary preparation for the strenuous program to follow.

All of these come fairly naturally and easily to a typical middle-class student, for whom the program has been designed, but they can become confusing obstacles for a boy whose personal and family life is in a state of chaos. For such students, the orientation phase should be successfully designed as a program in itself, which has great value and merit quite aside from the preparation it provides for the wilderness experience.

3. Continuity between the selection and orientation process and the Outward Bound program has also proven to be helpful. It is recommended that groups of

delinquents be accompanied by their own street workers or probation officers where possible, for then there is a strengthening of the purposes of the agency or institution and the experience of Outward Bound itself. It also helps cut down on the scapegoating that can often take place by those who waver, who claim that they were misinformed, that this isn't what they were told, that they have been hoodwinked into a program, that they didn't know what they were getting into.

4. Outward Bound group leaders have sometimes had difficulty coping with delinquent youth in the program. There is a commitment to those students who have come because they have identified with the challenge, they want to be there, they identify with the virtues and values of strenuous outdoor activity. Not every delinquent can rise to the same challenge. When they isolate themselves, either through acting out or withdrawal, it can provide great difficulties for an instructor whose job it is to create a team with a sense of identity and unity out of each group. Where delinquents have been put into groups made up totally of students with similar backgrounds, some Outward Bound instructors who come primarily from middle-class backgrounds have lacked the insight, the experience, and the group skills to work effectively with them. Some need special training to be effective with delinquents, as do other professionals, teachers, counselors, and social workers. The Hurricane Island, Maine, Outward Bound School has been particularly effective in training minority leaders, recruited from the streets, in Outward Bound skills.

Short-Term Program Models

The twelve years of experience that Outward Bound has had working with delinquents would indicate two things: that adventure training does work for certain sorts of problem youth who have been properly selected and oriented; and that a program can be designed to be run exclusively for a delinquent population. If the program, however, is to benefit those in most need of it, it needs to be implemented by those who have a prime institutional commitment to work in this area. There is already an impressive number of programs of this nature.

The "Homeward Bound" program was established in 1970 by the Massachusetts Division of Youth Services located at the Stephen L. French Youth Forestry Camp near Nickerson State Park on Cape Cod.[7] Formerly a work therapy camp, they developed a six-week program very similar to Outward Bound in design. Initially staffed by Outward Bound professionals, it is now operated by state employees. During its first full year of operation it was offered to three hundred boys. Referrals are made directly from the courts. Much time and effort have gone into explaining the program to judges, juvenile police officers, probation officers, and school counselors. The program is carefully explained to each boy and his family—that it is rugged, it is voluntary, once begun it must be completed, that there are only a limited number of openings, that once it is completed the boy will be parolled directly home. They are shown slides of the program and required to visit the camp.

The first phase of the program is based on the lodge at the camp. Thirty-two boys go through the program at a time, divided into groups of eight, led by a group leader, and an assistant, usually a boy who has gone through the program itself. For two weeks they engage in outdoor-skills training, backpacking, camping, first aid, map and compass. They build up their fitness level through daily calisthenics, obstacle courses, hikes along the seashore. Evenings are spent in classes; much has to be learned in a short period of time. There is an all-night hike. Each boy is counseled in developing a plan for his postrelease period.

The second phase is a deeper immersion in adventure experience. The training is more intensive and specialized leading to a land or sea expedition. Instruction is given in knot-tying, rock climbing, rappelling. An overnight shakedown expedition tests the equipment and their ability to use it. This is followed by a three-day hike, which leads to a major expedition—ten days along the Appalachian Trail, on snowshoes in winter, to ten days at sea in a pulling boat, landing to explore and camp at night. Toward the end of the expedition is the three-day solo, the long marathon run, and the final "graduating ceremonies."

After the program a detached worker continues to work with a boy back in the community, with his family, the schools, and court officials to help him on the problems of reentering, to see that the experience is reinforced by meaningful adults, to help him build on his success.

The follow-up study demonstrated results almost identical to the Kelly and Baer study of Outward Bound's impact. After seven to fourteen months, 20.8 percent of the Homeward Bound group recidivated, as opposed to 42.7 percent of a control group. It is significant, too, that when Jerome Miller closed the youth institutions in Massachusetts, the Homeward Bound program was continued. The staff have continued to experiment with both the activities and the length of program. The original six weeks has been shortened to four, and found to be as effective. Psychological testing has indicated that most of the change takes place in the first two weeks, and a study is under way to measure the impact of the shorter program.

The Stockton Community Parole Center, operated by the California Youth Authority, has run a similar program since July 1971, funded by a federal grant.[8] They have five trips a year in the Sierra Nevada, using the same basic program: backpacking, camping, outdoor survival skills, rock climbing, expeditioning, and the solo. There is also a heavy emphasis on group process. The staff has been trained in transactional analysis, and they use the frustrations of the adventure experience, the tensions of group living, to create counseling moments. The joyousness and the camaraderie of simple living enhance and reinforce the good feelings generated. After the experience boys spend sixty days in a group home where they receive further counseling in personal growth, furthering their education, and finding jobs.

The Arkansas Rehabilitation Services, in cooperation with Adlersgate Methodist Camp and Arkansas Research and Training Center, has developed a similar program on an experimental basis.[9] They stated that the majority of rehabilitation programs for problem youths have been usually oriented toward just the intellectual (educational and vocational training) or just the emotional (counseling and guidance), with little emphasis placed upon the physical, or on an integrated "total" program to effect all three life spheres. They sought to develop a program that integrated these dimensions with systematic, functional, challenging experiences, consolidating therapy with direct experience. Their program lasted three weeks and consisted of four stages: basic training, a backpacking expedition, counseling, and follow-through experiences. They worked in groups of six. "Survival camping" was used to provide a vehicle for learning and creating success experiences as a result of physical challenge that they believed to have therapeutic value. They sought increased awareness of themselves and their bodies, increased skills and abilities that were seen as the springboard for further development upon their return to the community. Twenty-one boys started the program, and nineteen successfully completed it. Follow-up results have not been reported.

Project Wingspread,[10] operated in 1974 by the Phillips Research Foundation under contract for the Illinois Department of Children and Family Services, has a program for boys fourteen to seventeen years of age, based on the traditional Outward Bound concept of psychological education, which uses a cattle ranch in northwest Illinois for its base. A twenty-three-day training phase for two groups of eight boys each, with an instructor and an assistant, introduces students to outdoor living skills, group life, and adventure experience, with a focus on self-concept, peer interaction, and authority relationships. This is followed by a twenty-eight-day intensive adventure program in the Southern Illinois University Outdoor Laboratory "Underway" program, where they engage in rock-climbing, spellunking, canoeing, solo experiences, and expeditioning. A five-day phase-out period, back on the ranch, prepares students to return to their communities.

Programs of a similar nature are being developed by state agencies in Connecticut, Maine, Oregon, and Wisconsin. The National Outdoor Leadership Training School in Wyoming has conducted successful experiences with prison authorities.

Salesmanship Club of Dallas:
A Long-Term Program Model

The Salesmanship Boys' Camp of Dallas, Texas, has developed a unique program, using the natural problems arising around outdoor living as a therapeutic process.

Campbell Loughmiller's book *Wilderness Road* is an imaginative, sensitive, and articulate description of the program.[11] They work with boys from the ages of six through sixteen for a period ranging from one to two years. The program is a combination of primitive outdoor living in a very natural setting, intensive use of group process, and adventure activities.

The campsite of 840 acres, ninety miles east of Dallas, is a wooded, largely undeveloped piece of property with streams, springs, and open spaces. Boys are organized into small primary groups of ten with two counselors in a total living program. They live in tents that they themselves design and build. They cook at least half of their own meals on outdoor cooking facilities. Modern facilities, electricity, cabins have been deliberately left out so that the problems of primitive living provide opportunities for activity and interaction.

Each group has a high degree of autonomy to organize its own life, plan its own activities, and develop a natural flow of living experiences that are not broken up or segmented, where its problems have precedence. Individuals have a stake in the planning and evaluating of their own activities. Outdoor activities such as hiking, woodcutting, exploring, fishing, make up the "basic curriculum." Buses provide mobility for the group to take field trips, which can last from three days to three weeks. Planning ranges from the problems of logistics to the schedule for visiting ranches, factories, government agencies, natural wonders. The trip is always something that arises out of the interest of the group and reflects its own goals and capabilities in carrying it out. Formal academic instruction has been deliberately excluded, as almost all boys have been failures in their schools, of they wouldn't be in the program. However, a great deal of academic learning does take place through the planning and preparation for such trips, measuring food, quantities, and calories, planning itineraries, budgeting, reading Chamber of Commerce brochures, research in the camp library into background information. Adventure training is introduced into the program as a group achieves a degree of cohesiveness. Trips are planned canoeing to the Gulf of Mexico, distances of three hundred to eight hundred miles, some groups ending up at the mouth of the Mississippi River. On rafting trips students not only plan their routes, including points of interest they wish to visit and study along the way, but construct their rafts as well. They take backpacking expeditions into the mountains of Colorado. Here they encounter hardship, excitement, and situations that often call for an all-out group effort. The expeditions have been particularly effective in helping a boy grow in self-confidence, in learning how to meet successfully and to overcome a wide variety of adversities and emergencies. Expeditions can pull a group together and weld them into a cohesive unit and develop within them a sense of responsibility for others.

Boys are referred by schools, social agencies, psychiatric clinics, private psychiatrists, and others, drawn largely from the Dallas area so that the families can be involved in the program. A boy and his family must visit the camp before he is accepted. The boy must want to come. Monthly visits are made home. The goal of having the boy return home is stressed from the very beginning.

Follow-up counseling back in the community is provided for both the boy and his family. Counselors, the central persons in the program, have a minimum of professional training. They are selected for their own maturity, their warmth, their interest in boys, their own well-roundedness and ability to live comfortably in primitive settings and provide leadership. They are supported by professional staff who give them training in group process and support in dealing with particularly difficult situations. A director of counselor training and a group work supervisor overlap in these functions.

Groups are open-ended; as a boy reaches a point of being able to handle his problems he is returned to his family and community, and a new boy is enrolled, attempting to match his growth needs with the strength of the existing group. There is always peer leadership within the group as the more experienced and mature provide the balance of maturity necessary for the group to function effectively.

Since 1946, in their first eighteen years six hundred boys with serious emotional handicaps have gone through the program, and 70 percent were evaluated as having made satisfactory adjustments in the post camp. An additional 24 percent made appreciable gains.

Community-Based Programs

The efficacy of taking a person out of his community to rehabilitate him is being increasingly challenged. If he is to become a functioning member of society, this can take place best in the real-life context of his own neighborhood. Community-based program models use the wilderness primarily as an ignition phase to the rehabilitative process, a catalyst for further growth and change. The emphasis is on integrating wilderness experience into a total spectrum of support experiences.

The Urban League of New York City has developed a comprehensive model.[12] Funded under the Law Enforcement Assistance Act, the program was set up in 1972 for 550 youth offenders on parole. The staff was predominantly black, recruited from the Upper West Side of Harlem, the community the program was to serve. Many had a past history of conflict with the law themselves. There were four phases to the program. The first was staff training, where the entire staff went through a program at the Hurricane Island Outward Bound School. Their purposes were first to create a strong team among themselves and gain a central commitment to the underlying concepts of the project, which saw the demands of wilderness training providing a prime catalyst for the rest of their program. Second, they sought to gain a better understanding of Outward Bound concepts and training methods and for those who would lead the wilderness program, to improve their skills. Third, it gave them the opportunity to study the suitability of this form of training to their own needs and to design the adaptions that would be necessary for inner-city black youth. Phase 2 was a very thorough and complete program for recruiting, selecting, screening, orienting, and preparing those who would enter the program. Youths who were heavily on drugs were excluded as not being suitable for this program, as were youngsters guilty of major crimes against persons. Referral by the court was a problem until courts fully understood the program. There was also a strike by the probation department, who saw this program as infringing on their professional jurisdiction. Once recruited, students were picked up by an "advocator," whose job it was to walk them through the intricacies of medical examinations, get proper clothing and family permission, and prepare them psychologically and begin a physical fitness training program.

The wilderness program was the third phase, run in a rural setting at Camp Paradox, in the Catskills, only fifty miles from downtown New York. The program included a number of outdoor activities such as camping, rock climbing, sailing, motor boating, and in the winter cross-country skiing and snowshoeing. The pace varied, but where appropriate traditional Outward Bound activities such as the wall and beam, the ropes course,[13] drown-proofing (a method of survival swimming), expeditioning, and solo were used. The high-risk activities were necessarily staffed by program specialists, but continuity was maintained between the street experience and the wilderness experience by having each "advocator" go through it with his group. He knew the background of his students, had been involved in their selection, knew their families, their specific problems, and had a wealth of personal data to work with as background to the intense personal and interpersonal interaction that takes place through the stress, adventure, and exhilaration. In this program, the group leaders were seen not only as instructors and guides capable of leading them through "death-defying feats," but also as figures of trust and security, representing continuity with the student's social background. They, too, were from the Harlem streets.

Back in the community again, phase 4 built on these experiences. The advocator returned to the city with his students and spent a month as a street worker, following up regularly with his group, providing them with personal counseling, building bridges to other support services created by the Urban League in such areas as academic tutoring, school and college placement, job-training opportunities, and job placement. He also acted as an advocate for him with the court, as would a probation officer. Though students were picked up by a broader range of human services, he was still available on a personal basis to provide encouragement and friendly advice. Initial reports on the success of the program have been very promising, though a detailed evaluation has not been made available.

Community-based wilderness programs have been attempted in a number of different settings. The "Outer Limits" Project was initiated by the High IMPACT

Anti-Crime Commission in Newark, New Jersey, in March 1974. Funded under LEAA, it sought to develop an adventure-centered rehabilitation program for court-acquainted youth in the Newark watershed within two hours of the city. Staff would be recruited locally and trained by Outward Bound, who would also provide consultants for program design and specialist support. The "Urban Bound"[14] program developed with the Juvenile Court of Denver in 1967-68 for thirty-two boys involved the schools and the YMCA in follow-up services after an adventure experience. One year later, twenty-one had not been before the court again, and eleven committed subsequent offenses; but of these eleven, three were back in school, two had jobs, and one other was reported relating more effectively. Only five showed little observable benefits. In all, 85 percent of the group benefited positively from the program.

The East Side Multi-Service Center in East Los Angeles has designed a program, "Barrio Outward Bound",[15] run by street workers with eighteen youth who were gang leaders from six different gangs with a history of rivalry including armed warfare. They were brought together and mixed in small groups as a part of a wilderness program in the Mt. Whitney area, involving rock climbing, solo, and a marathon. It was the first time that many of these members from rival gangs had spoken to each other, and the experience of living together and sharing danger and hardship helped develop not only peace but cooperation among them. Young Life has run a similar program with an Outward Bound philosophy at their summer camp at Saranac Village during the summer of 1970. Phoenix House had a group of drug offenders row and sail an open pulling boat from Boston to New York as a part of a rehabilitative program.

Manpower Challenge focuses on prejob training for "the hard-core unemployed."[16] It was developed by the Adolph Coors Company of Golden, Colorado, with the Colorado Outward Bound School. Coors reasoned that few of their employees fail because they lack education or skill, but rather because they lack punctuality, have a high rate of absenteeism, and find difficulty in relating to supervisors. Men were recruited off the welfare rolls, among probationers from the state penitentiary, through the state employment office, and they went through a specially designed Outward Bound course. Foremen from the plant took the same course, sharing tents, food, fun, and frustration with their future employees. The course is followed by a probationary period in the reclamation yard of their recycling plant. Assistance with transportation and counseling in budget planning, consumer economics, and legal problems are provided. They will also be a friendly advocate with the court where necessary. After ninety days they become fulltime employees in production and other jobs in the plant. Since 1968, 107 trainees and 23 supervisors completed the program in the first three years. Of these, 97 had been hired by Coors and 57 are still on the job. Eight of those who have left were known to have found other employment and three were in military service, giving a success-ratio to the program of 71 percent employed.[17]

Not a Panacea

While this chapter has dwelt largely on the successes, one must caution that the program is no panacea. Human nature is too diverse, and in this area of human endeavor one is involved with the most diverse of human natures. Experience belies the effectiveness of any single approach, and cautions one to be humble in one's claims.

Some of the failures have not been without irony and humor. One young joy rider who had a weakness for vintage-age Fords and Chevrolets successfully completed an Outward Bound course and one month later was picked up at a fashionable ski area in a Mercedes Benz. An example of enhanced self-image? In another study the most successful candidate was in the control group. He had been rejected from the Outward Bound group for medical reasons the day before the course began. He went over the fence instead of going to the mountains. For three months he successfully evaded law authorities, got a job as a service-station attendant, found a place to live, and was a productive employee until picked up running a red light in the station's pick-up. Returned to the institution, he was given a battery of psychological tests and came out on top with flying colors for heightened self-concept, improved social adjustment, and motivation. Should one design a program for escapees? This indeed seemed to be the case with the Golden Gate Youth Camp program in Colorado. It is a low-security residential program in an isolated area, where staff depended upon the surrounding mountain wilderness to reduce runaways. After successful training in wilderness survival, three out of ten in one group headed over the hill. Success or failure?

However, the evidence is conclusive that wilderness training can provide a valuable alternative to incarceration, and it can be an effective method of rehabilitation, provided that it is not overinflated in claims and overloaded with unrealistic expectations. Outward Bound and the other organizations with similar programs can make the following claims:

1. A neutral setting, a change of environment, hostility provided not by bars, bricks, and walls, but by the natural forces of nature, demand a change in outlook and an adjustment on the part of the individual that can often catalyze further growth and change.

2. Activities that are challenging, exciting, exhilarating, where the results are immediate and irrevocable, are readily grasped and understood. They speak deeply to their need to feel competent, to exert their large muscles, to assert their "machismo" in socially acceptable ways. The experience is often seen as a *"rite de passage,"* helping to clarify the confusion of emerging manhood.[18]

3. The small-group structure fosters cooperation, and teamwork, and helps build trust in human relations. Where staff has been trained in group process the opportunities for reality counseling are many and powerful.

4. There is the right psychological moment. The high impact, drama, deeply stretching experience, has the greatest effect if planned at critical transition

points. Seen as a catalyst, it opens one to insights into oneself, it opens doors to new experience, it helps one move on. It comes best at the beginning of a longer program of treatment and rehabilitation, or as the transition phase between institutional life and return to society. Or for first offenders, it can be a more viable alternative to the corrosive influences of institutionalization.

5. The program needs to be seen not as an end unto itself, but rather as a part of a continuum. It needs to be seen in the total context of a young person's life, and the treatment prescribed for him in his current difficulties; and the most successful programs are those that, picking him up right from the courts and the streets, can see the program beginning at the point of initial contact and carrying him through the wilderness experience, back to his community, and into the resources of referral and counseling that can further sustain him.

6. Finally and most important, it provides a learning climate that is enhancing both to the helper and the "helpee." It is a program where the professional cannot hide behind façades and jargon. The activities which cause the adrenalin to flow and are exhilarating, breathtaking, uplifting, help build relationships that are warm, intimate, and equal—where two people or ten can interact with each other with respect, dignity, and humanity. Herein lie its secret and its promise.

References

1. Outward Bound was founded in Britain during World War II as a survival school for merchant seamen, stressing both the physical and psychological aspects of survival. Since then it has become an international organization with thirty-one schools. The Colorado Outward Bound School was founded in 1962, followed by schools in Minnesota, Maine, Oregon, North Carolina, and Texas, and an Outward Bound Center at Dartmouth. Student enrollment is nearly five thousand a year in the American schools, including special courses for educators, businessmen, and the socially disadvantaged. Schools are incorporated under Outward Bound, Inc., the headquarters organization, 165 West Putnam Avenue, Greenwich, Connecticut 06830.

2. Richard La Paglia, Los Angeles County Welfare Department, unpublished report, 1973.

3. F.J. Kelly and D.J. Baer, *Outward Bound as an Alternative to Institutionalization for Adolescent Delinquent Boys*, Fandel Press, Boston, 1968. Reprinted by Outward Bound, Inc.

4. "The Outer Limits," a Wolpers Production film, presented by the National Geographic Society, depicts the success of a Chicano street gang leader from Chicago who is parolled to Outward Bound by the court. Available on a rental basis from Outward Bound, Inc., 165 W. Putnam Avenue, Greenwich, Connecticut 06830.

5. F.J. Kelly and D.J. Baer, "Physical Challenge as a Treatment for Delinquency," *Crime and Delinquency*, October 1971, pp. 437-45.

6. The Michigan Office of Youth Services sent a total of twenty-eight students to the Colorado and Minnesota Outward Bound Schools in 1972. Fourteen completed their courses successfully, another three made it beyond the halfway point, and twelve dropped out the first week. In 1973, after a study of the problem and better preparation of students, seven out of a group of nine successfully completed the course.

7. Herb C. Willman, Jr., and Ron Y.F. Chun, "Homeward Bound, An Alternative to the Institutionalization of Adjudicated Juvenile Offenders," *Federal Probation*, September 1973, pp. 52-58.

8. "I'm Okay," film. Extension Media Center, University of California, Berkeley, California 94720.

9. Thomas Collingwood, "Survival Camping: A Therapeutic Mode for Rehabilitation of Problem Youth," unpublished report, 1973.

10. *Project Wingspread*, Phillips Research Foundation, Naperville, Illinois. Unpublished report, 1974.

11. Campbell Loughmiller, *Wilderness Road*, Hogg Foundation for Mental Health, Austin, Texas.

12. New York Urban League, Youth Enrichment Services Center, unpublished report, 1973.

13. Adventure Curriculum: Physical Education, Project Adventure, Hamilton-Wenham, Massachusetts, 1974. A detailed account, complete with diagrams and photographs of ropes courses and initiative games that were developed as an alternative to traditional physical education.

14. *Urban Bound.* Colorado Outward Bound School, Denver, 1969.

15. Richard La Paglia, op. cit.

16. "A Third Chance," film, distributed by the Adolph Coors Company, Golden, Colorado 80401.

17. *Manpower Challenge.*, unpublished report, Colorado Outward Bound School, Denver, 1971.

18. A comparable argument can be made for such programs for girls who also lack opportunities to prove their competence.

9

M-2 (Man-to-Man)
Job Therapy[a]

Edited by Richard J. Simmons[b]

One of the grimmest aspects of the crime problem is the percentage of lawbreakers who are repeaters: men who emerge from prison only to be jailed again within a few months. Prison officials call them "high-crime-risk" offenders. They know that when such prisoners are released with no job, no friends, little money and less acceptance by society, their chances of failure in the outside world may run as high as 90 percent.

These high-crime-risk repeaters are one of the chief reasons why crime costs the U.S.A. at least $30 billion a year—and why law-abiding citizens are afraid to walk the streets at night. *In prison, many of these men have one thing in common: almost complete isolation from the outside world.* They receive no letters. They have no visitors. Their families have disowned them. Sullen and bitter, they live with a festering hate and distrust of society.

Such men have long been considered virtually unredeemable. But in the past ten years an eager young idealist named Richard Simmons has proved that a high proportion of such offenders *can* be salvaged—if ordinary, everyday citizens will somehow find the time, concern, and courage (it does take courage) to go into the prison or penitentiary, single out one of these lonely misfits, and offer him friendship and moral support simply because he is a fellow human being.

In 1963, having served four years as a Presbyterian minister in conventional parishes, and then having turned to missionary work with teen-age gangs and drug addicts in the slums of New York, Simmons was struck by a strong intuition that there was important work waiting for him in the Seattle area. Then thirty-two, he moved with his family to Snohomish, Washington; "a minister turned layman," he says of himself.

At the request of a friend, he began visiting two young men confined in the nearby Washington State Reformatory at Monroe. Increasingly, he was haunted

---

[a]This part of the Job Therapy story first appeared in the August 1970 issue of *Rotarian* (copyright 1970 by the Readers Digest Association, Inc.) and was condensed in the August 1970 issue of *Reader's Digest*, under the title "They Go to Prison on Purpose." It is used here by permission of both publishers and the author, Arthur Gordon, who is editor of *Guideposts* and former editor of *Good Housekeeping* and of *Cosmopolitan*. Reprints are available from *Reader's Digest*.

[b]Richard J. Simmons attended the University of Washington and San Francisco Theological Seminary (B.D. 1956). He pastored in the Bedford-Stuyvesant area of Brooklyn, New York, where he helped establish one of the first drug clinics in the nation. He is Founder-President of Man-to-Man/Job Therapy, International.

by the loneliness of many of the prisoners: Out of eight hundred men, two hundred never received letters or visitors. Nor could he forget one of his first conversations with an inmate. "When you get out," Simmons had asked, "won't they help you find a job?" "*They?*" said the prisoner bitterly. "There is no *they.*"

Deeply troubled, Simmons began to seek some answers to the problems faced by such forgotten men. He visited prisons in Washington, Oregon, and British Columbia.

In a study of thirty-five after-care programs throughout the world, the single fact that impressed him most was the claim of penal authorities in The Netherlands that released prisoners had a 90 percent chance of succeeding on parole.

Noting that in the U.S.A. the figure was barely 50 percent, Simmons dug deeper, and found that the Dutch were using more than nine thousand volunteers in its army of rehabilitation workers who concerned themselves with the welfare and morale of prisoners, not only after they were released, but while they were still in jail.

Simmons could not get this concept of volunteer sponsors out of his mind. "You know," he said to his wife, "Holland has only twelve million people, but there are almost nine thousand volunteers. The country has only fifteen hundred inmates in maximum security, while our own State of Washington, with three million people, has more than three thousand. If our ratio were equal to Holland's we'd have only three hundred-seventy-five prisoners in maximum security instead of three thousand. That would mean an annual saving in manpower of two thousand six-hundred-twenty-five lives, and a saving in wasted taxes of at least eight million dollars!"

Simmons called a meeting of a few friends: a bank president, a physician, a parole officer, a contractor, and the editor of the local newspaper. "This is a tremendous problem," he told them, "not just here in Washington, but all over the country. I know there are only six of us. But somebody has to make a start somewhere. I've been trying to work out a program."

Simmons explained that since the greatest need of released felons was jobs, the program should emphasize job therapy. "But," he said, "we've got to get to the prisoner *before* he's released, and help him build some worthwhile, hopeful, positive attitudes. I'm convinced that this can only be done on a man-to-man basis, with the free man going to visit the imprisoned man for one reason only: because he *cares.* This volunteer effort behind those bars will be the heart of our program. I'd like to call it M-2—Man-to-Man."

The discussions that followed were long and searching. Would ordinary citizens take on such a responsibility? Might they not be afraid to associate with hardened criminals? Would prison officials welcome such an offer—or even tolerate it? In the end, a plan for a multiphase citizen-action program was submitted to Dr. Garrett Heyns, then Director of Institutions for the State of

Washington. Dr. Heyns gave his approval, and in March 1965, a nonprofit corporation was chartered under the official title Simmons had chosen: Job Therapy, Inc.

One of the first volunteers to sponsor an inmate was Bill Bates, editor and publisher of the Snohomish County *Tribune*.

"In the beginning," he says, "none of us really knew what we were getting into. Dick Simmons believed in trying to match the sponsor with the inmate in terms of some common interest. So I was matched with Louie, a twenty-two-year-old printer trainee under sentence for second-degree assault. The first ten minutes were the worst. I don't know which of us was more nervous. I tried to talk about printing, but Louie was tongue-tied. Finally he blurted out, 'Say, what are you doing this for, anyway?' I just stared at him. Finally I said, 'I don't know. When I find out, I'll tell you!' "

For over a year, Bill Bates came to visit Louie at least once a month. When he was finally released, Bill invited Louie to stay in his home—and offered him a job with the *Tribune*. "We almost lost Louie the very first night," Bill says. "A police car cruised past the house a couple of times and spooked him so badly that he simply ran away. But we got him back, and today he's a valued member of the *Tribune* staff. He's got a lot to be proud of—and so have we."

In the last ten years, Job Therapy projects in five different states have recruited, screened, and matched over 5000 reputable business, laboring, and professional men as volunteer citizen-sponsors of almost 6000 confined men. At first some inmates viewed such volunteers with suspicion. But sponsors have found that there are almost no prisoners who do not respond, sooner or later, to friendly interest and kindness.

An inmate named Gary graphically described his own case: "As I look back, I find it almost impossible to believe that a person could be as I was then and not even realize that he was all twisted inside. I believed that problems were to be laughed at, and work was for suckers. My philosophy was that everybody was out for what he could get; the bottom dog gets chewed up, so burn the other fellow before he burns you.

"When I was asked if I'd like a sponsor, I figured, well, this guy will be just another jukebox. You know, when the money stops, he stops. I think deep inside, I was really scared. I might just be leaving myself open to getting hurt—again. But I've come a long way. This man, once I gave him a chance, has literally knocked the foundations out from under my old life, leaving me with no choice but to build a new one. To be sure, some of my old problems have merely given way to new ones. But the faith I am able to put in another person—for the first time in my memory—is the basis for a whole new way of life for me."

Like Gary, many inmates have found in their sponsors substitutes for the fathers they never had. Psychologists say that the need of such men for father-figures to identify with is acute. Prisoners seldom make such identification with prison advisors or counselors because they are paid employees of the correctional system. But they have no such resistance to unpaid volunteers. Now that word of Job Therapy/Man-to-Man has spread to other West Coast prisons, the demand for sponsors is running far ahead of the supply.

Some volunteers, trying to convey a touch of family warmth, bring their wives and children on visits to the prison. "I want to thank you," wrote one inmate to his sponsor, "for coming up on my birthday and bringing the kids. It was the first time in five years that anyone I knew has been with me on my birthday."

Less visible than the impact on the offender, but perhaps no less important, is the effect on the sponsor himself and his family. Said one young businessman, "Seeing what growing up without a father has done to these boys has made me try to be a better father to my own children. A year ago, when I'd come home from work, the first thing I'd pick up was the newspaper. Now the first thing I pick up is one of our kids!"

Job Therapy recruits its candidates for the M-2 program in a variety of ways. On Sundays, Dick Simmons and his staff speak at various churches, challenging the members to put their faith into visible practice by becoming M-2 sponsors. On weekdays they may address a civic club, asking anyone who is interested to leave his card. News coverage in the press also attracts volunteers.

Would-be sponsors are carefully screened. Each applicant must fill out a searching questionnaire and attend two orientation seminars. Job Therapy also checks with the applicant's neighbors and pastor. "We really ask three basic questions," says an official of the organization. "Is this person responsible? Is he attractive in his responsibility?—a person can be responsible, but also cold and forbidding, you know. And finally, Will he stick with it? There's really no cut-off point in the relationship. Once you take the plunge, you may find yourself walking step by step with your adopted felon for years."

Although the number of visits usually depends on the action of the parole board, applicants for the role of sponsor are warned that they may have to wait two or three years before the prisoner becomes a parolee. In a typical case a sponsor makes prison visits for about a year, usually once or twice a month.

For many sponsors, the acid test comes when the offender is finally released from prison. Each sponsor signs a pledge that on release day he will escort his friend from the institution and remain with him throughout his first day in free society. He is also pledged to assist him with all of the problems of reentry into the community—and often there are many.

Recently a Seattle sponsor dropped by his parolee's home, to find him facing eviction, with his furniture being carted off by an auction company. "Jim's landlord and creditors were ready to tar and feather him. I suggested that maybe we all had a mutual problem here. We, meaning all of us law-abiding citizens, could continue to try to bust Jim, and then support him and his family to the tune of about $12,000 per year. Or we could work together to help him get on his feet and let him support himself and pay his debts. They finally agreed that the second alternative was the best. For $40 I got his furniture back. Then we found some rent-free lodging for him temporarily. The next day I negotiated a return to his welding job. Little by little, step by step—but I believe that Jim will make it as a mature, responsible citizen in our society one day."

Generally laboring, business, or professional men from the middle-income salary range accept the man-to-man challenge. Occasionally, a top executive like Charles Loomis, president of the Loomis Armored Car Corporation, will accept the time-consuming responsibility of an M-2 relationship. He is a leading member of the Downtown Rotary Club of Seattle. As a sponsor, Chuck was paired with Roy, a twenty-five-year-old, imprisoned for armed robbery at Washington State Reformatory in Monroe. During that time Chuck visited Roy about once a month, and saw him complete four years of high school, participate in football and baseball, and also preside over the Sportmen's Club in prison. When Roy came out, Chuck was there to help, but could not, according to the policy of his company, offer him a job in the firm. He did, however, give Roy the courage to seek his own employment, to enroll in a heavy equipment school, where he trained to be a logger. He is hard at work in a shingle mill, has saved money, and appears stable and determined to succeed. Chuck helped Roy open a savings account and a checking account, find a small house in which to live close to his job, and get a car and renewal of his driver's license. Roy is often a guest in the Loomis household, where Chuck and his wife and three children, aged fifteen, twenty, and twenty-two, make the young man feel perfectly at home, even taking him on family vacations.

Still another executive deeply involved in M-2 sponsorship is Paul Waterman, owner of Ravenna Motors in Seattle. Mrs. Waterman shares this involvement, the two of them going together to visit their "boys" at Washington State Reformatory. One of these is Dan B, who was confined on a manslaughter count resulting from an automobile accident. Trained in body work, Dan went to Paul's Revenna Motors on being parolled. He has subsequently married, attends church regularly, and seems to have his feet on the ground. Dan, in fact, lived at the Waterman home upon his release. "This is a very rewarding business to be in," says Paul. "In some ways the sponsor gets more reward out of it than the parolee." He believes, however, that *both* a husband and wife should be involved in the program. "After all, we *are* substitute parents, and cannot do a job if only one is present and accounted for anymore than real parents can be effective if there is only one of them."

Less dramatic than the M-2 program, but just as important, is the job-placement service that Job Therapy offers at its Seattle headquarters. Statistics show that if an ex-offender is employed full time, his chances of completing his parole successfully are 87 percent. If he works part time, that percentage drops to 55. If he works only occasionally, his chances fall to 27 percent.

"Part of our whole purpose," says Simmons, "is to persuade the public—and that includes employers—not to judge the ex-offender by his unfavorable past, but by his present attitudes and accomplishments and his future potential." Job Therapy has been highly successful at this. The persuasive and energetic staff of Simmons, with a well-trained volunteer team of retired men, canvasses Seattle firms, emphasizing that it is not only humane but often economically advantageous to hire men who have had specialized training while in prison. At the moment, seven hundred companies are actively cooperating. Periodically, Job Therapy sends out to these firms—and five hundred others—a printed brochure called "Futures Wanted," listing thumbnail biographies of prisoners soon to be released, with a resumé of their skills. In 1973, 771 of 1540 applicants were placed in suitable jobs.

Simmons figures that the cost per man for the Job Therapy program is a fraction over $700. "When you remember," he says, "that it costs the State of Washington fifty-five hundred dollars a year to keep a man in custody, plus another fifty-five hundred dollars for welfare for his wife and children if he's married, you can see what enormous savings our volunteers can produce. If we're successful in keeping, say, one hundred married men and two hundred single men out of jail, that's a savings of over a million dollars each year." In this sort of work, the cost of failure vastly exceeds the price of success.

From the start, adequate financing has been a problem for Simmons and the small Job Therapy staff. Their budget for 1968, mostly made up of contributions from foundations, churches, and industrial firms, was less than $35,000. Over the last three years Job Therapy's operational costs have increased to over $250,000 per year. This fiscal growth came primarily from grants awarded by the State Planning Office of the Federal LEAA program. The Corrections Division of the state's super-social-agency DSHS (Department of Social and Health Services) contracted with Job Therapy to provide sponsors and job-finding services for inmates and parolees of state correctional institutions. These services are awarded in a fee-for-service basis at a cost of $400 per client, or $200 per service.

High officials throughout the State of Washington endorse and support Simmons's work. "It really pays off three ways," says Governor Daniel J. Evans. "The ex-offender is encouraged and helped to become a useful citizen, the taxpayer is saved a great deal of money, and the volunteer sponsor himself becomes a bigger and better person."

The former pastor of Seattle's largest congregation, Dr. Robert Munger of the University Presbyterian Church, sees in M-2 a valuable channel for church-generated energies. "A lot of us ministers," he says with a smile, "keep telling our parishoners to be good Christians, but we don't always tell them how to go about it. The M-2 program offers a readymade blueprint for anyone who really wants to do what he can to make this a better world."

Bruce Johnson, Chairman of the State Board of Prison Terms and Paroles, admits that at first he was skeptical about Job Therapy. "In the past," he says,

"we've had our share of well-meaning volunteers who were either too senti-
mental or too emotional or who simply didn't follow through. But the sponsors
recruited by Job Therapy are different. They're concerned about what happens
to people, not just as inmates or parolees, but as individuals who need to be
helped to reach their maximum potential."

The late Dr. Garrett Heyns, former Director of Institutions, said flatly: "The
services of Job Therapy are critically needed. It could well serve as a model
program for our entire nation."

Such enlightened efforts, with volunteers leading the way, are strictly in
accord with a philosophy that seems to be gaining momentum all over the U.S.:
the conviction that big government has gone as far as it can go with social
reform; that from here on it must be the concerned citizen, not the bureaucrat,
who carries the burden. It's the man-to-man job-oriented approach that seems to
succeed where all else fails.

"If it hadn't been for my white sponsor," said a former black inmate of
Monroe, now working as a reporter in Seattle, "I'd probably be an enraged black
militant today. I don't think this approach has to be limited to prisons, either. I
think it would work in the ghettos, or anywhere people will go out of their way
to show other people that they care about them as individuals. I mean, really
care."

Things are not always perfect at Job Therapy, of course. Sometimes a parolee
will drift away from his sponsor and not be heard from again. Sometimes, in
prison, an inmate will find the pain of relating to someone after years of
self-absorption more than he can bear and will break off the relationship. Once
in a while sponsor and inmate will turn out to have been mismatched in terms of
interests or personality.

But no one is discouraged by such lapses. "I really don't feel that we have any
failures," Simmons says cheerfully, "because in every case one human being is
showing concern for another. There's always love in action, and that's what
counts."

W-2 (Women-to-Women) Friendship Therapy[c]

The M-2 Program is now matched by the W-2 (Women-to-Women) project. The
first W-2 matches were made at Walla Walla Penitentiary, with sponsor-candi-
dates flying to the Southeast Washington city. The program was transferred to
Purdy two months later when the Center opened there.

Much preparation goes into the first matching.

[c]This part of the Job Therapy story was written by Anne Wyne, who is a W-2 sponsor and a
free-lance writer for the *Northwest Progress Newspaper*. This edited version of her
contribution is reprinted by permission.

Most sponsors first hear of the program through speakers appearing before potentially interested groups. Although the largest response comes from church-related groups, the program attempts to avoid making that the main orientation.

Interested persons are given inquiry cards and those who fill out the cards are invited to detailed orientation sessions. At the session, persons are asked to fill out a form requesting personal information (like a credit-card application) and to explain motives. (Experience has shown that those who are merely curious about prison life and the prisoners make poor sponsors—the residents call them "phonies." You don't walk up to a woman and ask her what she's serving time for.)

References are carefully checked. One very important sponsor characteristic is stability. It is a terrible disappointment to a resident when she finds a "terrific" sponsor and the woman never shows up again.

Finally, after learning details and experiences of other sponsors as well as undergoing the background reviews, the prospective sponsor is ready to be matched with a resident. This is accomplished person to person at a party or meeting on a week night at Purdy.

The prospective sponsor gets dressed up and drives the hour from Seattle to Purdy with as much trepidation as a girl going to her first grown-up party ("Will anyone want me for a partner?"). She joins a group of women in which it is hard to tell which are the residents (as prisoners there are referred to). They are often better dressed and groomed than those visiting, thanks to sewing, hair, and charm classes offered since they've been there.

Meeting as new friends would at any party, prospective sponsors and residents talk, and those who find themselves compatible mutually decide to form a sponsor-resident relationship.

The first surface relationship of the sponsor and resident at the Purdy Women's Treatment Center starts with an exchange of letters, visits, perhaps once a week or once a month, small gifts or personal needs, supplies, perhaps a box of home-baked cookies. The sponsor learns it is important not to "come laden" with gifts; friendship can't be bought, and too many gifts can put a strain on a relationship.

At an all-day seminar held at Purdy, moderated by Jerry Kelly, associate professor of social work at the University of Washington, the sponsor of the meeting, an attempt was made to define this friendship. The residents spelled out how they regard a sponsor—"someone from the outside, who is not a police symbol." And what they want from a sponsor—a friend, "someone I can trust." They stressed that someone should maintain the confidentiality of the relationship, and that it should be non-conditional. (They are saying, "No matter what I have done, she should still like me.")

The friendship should have long-term potential and durability and the sponsor should be dependable. This is asking more than most friendships offer on the outside, but these girls tend to idealize goals, making them harder to achieve. Yet, idealistic as this relationship is to the residents and difficult as it is for the realistic sponsor, honest and sincere friendships do develop.

Marion, a prisoner at the Women's Treatment Center at Purdy, at thirty-five, is still an attractive woman. She is a mother eight times over, with youngsters ranging from seven to eighteen years of age. Her husband is incarcerated at the Washington State Reformatory, and their children have been placed in five different foster homes.

Another year must pass before Marion becomes eligible for parole. In spite of the many problems created by her incarceration, Marion considers herself one of the more fortunate women at Purdy. She has a W-2 sponsor; someone who cares for her, visits her, and discusses her problems with her. As a result of this relationship, Marion remains, to a noticeable degree, in control of her family.

Marion is a child of a broken family; her parents were divorced when she was merely a child. She was married at sixteen, to a serviceman at Fort Lewis. Their first child came during their first year of marriage, and others followed regularly in spite of periods of unemployment of her husband. He was not a good provider for their steadily increasing family. During their twenty years of marriage the family has been on the welfare rolls for almost fifteen years.

Marion's husband frequently ran afoul of the law. His most recent brush with the law led him to the reformatory. Marion was beside him in court as he was sentenced. A half-hour later she was notified of the death of her grandmother; the only person in the world to whom she could turn. After twenty years of marriage her husband left her with eight youngsters to care for, an accumulation of past-due bills, no income, and a total of forty-five cents.

From county jail to funeral, to a home filled with eight hungry children, went Marion. She had no job, no friends, and no money with which to feed her children. The double shock was too much for any woman to bear. Marion went out and wrote bad checks to buy food for her children. The end result was her incarceration at Purdy.

The children became wards of the court and were sent to various foster homes. Marion's anxiety, frustration, and loneliness were very real, but were not intensified by her imprisonment, because of her sponsor relationship.

Marion's need to verbalize her fears and anxieties grew within her until they reached a near bursting point. Joan, her sponsor, held out her hand, and Marion reached for it. To her, Marion bared her innermost feelings. Joan has been there when needed ever since.

Joan gathers Marion's children together at least once a month. With Marion's eight and her own five she drives to Purdy for regular visits. Between visits she relays messages from Marion to each of her youngsters, in an effort to maintain as close a family unit as is possible under the circumstances.

The bond between these women grows stronger each day. Joan is truly a sister to Marion, and has set an example that Marion plans to follow to eliminate any possibility of a future separation of the family.

At the seminar the discussion of the sponsor role included many more practical things than a simple friendship. The sponsor is an advocate—with the counselor within the center, with the parole board (a letter from the sponsor, a responsible citizen on the outside who has gotten to know the girl carries a lot of weight), and with prospective employers. She may sponsor her friend for a furlough, receiving her into her own home for a day or a weekend. Not everyone is eligible for a furlough. The system at Purdy is carefully monitored. The resident cannot go on furlough until she has seen the parole board and obtained permission. Then weeks go by until she actually is furloughed. The person and place to which she is furloughed are also carefully checked out, just as the sponsor originally was checked. The sponsor will perhaps pick her up on her first day on the outside and stay with her, helping her get adjusted. That first day is the difficult one. (Old acquaintances, experiences, and environments are often yearned for.)

Most cannot expect to change a girl. But they can try to be an example of another kind of life. The women may have been committed for any type of crime. The most common seem to be drugs and forgery, but they range to armed robbery and murder.

Most of the women come from poor and even depraved backgrounds. The prospective sponsor must make up her mind beforehand that her attitude toward a girl will not be affected by her crime, her background, or even the language she uses.

Sponsors, too, come in all shapes and sizes. One carpool leaving Seattle every month on visiting evening includes a housewife, a nun, a young secretary, and a recently retired grandmother. All are responding in their own way to the loneliness of prison life. For, in spite of the euphemism now in use, Purdy Treatment Center still is a prison.

The beautiful grounds, referred to as the "campus," still are the "yard" to the women there. The "resident" still is confined to that center. The counselor still is a guard. And the entire area may not be surrounded by a wall with machine-gun mounts, as in the past, but it is still ringed by radar.

If a girl has no contact with the outside world and no one cares, there is little reason to try to change a life at cross-purposes with the laws of society. With encouragement, goals can be formulated, such as education, getting a high-school diploma, starting college work, learning a trade, improving sanitation, grooming, and hair care, and simply learning to get along with others. Thus, with encouragement, the start of a whole new life might be achieved.

Personal Benefits of Job Therapy[d]

There are over three thousand men in my state who have worked hard at caring to insure the success of the men in our institutions. Typically they drive

---

[d]This section was written by Gordon Cameron and excerpted from a speech he made before the National Conference on Volunteers in Probation at Detroit, Michigan. Mr. Cameron is assistant vice-president of the Prudential Savings Bank, Seattle, Washington, and President of the Board of Directors of Job Therapy, Inc.

hundreds of miles a year to visit, share birthdays and Christmas, encourage men to take and complete vocational training, help find jobs, and invite them into their homes. They will take on anyone who wants and needs help.

An insurance man volunteered to sponsor a man who since the age of nineteen had been in prison—fifteen years. His record was three bank robberies and two violations on narcotics. His attitude was, "Go ahead, Judge, sentence me to as many years as you like. I couldn't care less." This prisoner has received over one hundred shock treatments as a psychopathic case at a prison in Springfield. This insurance man not only visited him but researched his entire case, worked with a prison counselor, the parole board and the Department of Vocational Rehabilitation. This inmate started college last week, instead of completing his sentence to the year 2015.

A bailiff from Seattle's Municipal Court drove 276 miles to visit a man who at the age of thirty-nine had spent thirty of those years in institutions, to visit a man who had refused parole, a man who had accepted the absolute fact that he would spend the rest of his life in prison. The result of the visit was that the inmate told the sponsor, "Forget it and don't come back." This volunteer drove home and wrote the man a letter and told him he was going to drive that 276 miles and come back anyway! He did, and today that parolee has been out over a year, and has been active in speaking in churches and before civic groups to help find his buddies volunteer sponsors.

Sponsors are tenacious. A printer stuck with a young man who violated parole three times. Recently he paid a sixty-five dollar traffic ticket out of his one hundred-sixty dollar weekly take-home pay so his man wouldn't be returned a fourth time. His comment was, "This young man has been in institutions since he was ten years old and never learned about responsibility. I figure it will take him about one more year to grow up." This volunteer is not going to give up—he is going to help that twenty-three-year-old man with fifteen-year-old emotions to grow up.

A lineman for the telephone company volunteered his friendship to an Indian with an alcoholic problem. When this inmate was on parole, he got into trouble by drinking too much. He went to see the judge, who said "I have just ten minutes," but was so impressed with this man's sincerity and the man-to-man program that he canceled an appointment and spent one and a half hours discussing the problem. The outcome was that the sponsor accepted personal responsibility for this man. Today this parolee is married and has a baby girl.

Does it seem unreasonable that a banker would give the key to his front door to a man who had spent time for burglary in New Mexico, Louisiana, and Washington? My relationship with Frank was such that it never occurred to me to say No when he came to live in my home.

Regardless of background or occupation, prison volunteers have one thing in common. They really care about men like Pete, an inmate at McNiel Island Federal Penitentiary, who said, "I see two roads ahead of me. Die of peace of mind, or die by crime. I know the road I want. I need just a little help to stay on it by some passerby."

A View from the Inside

The following is the story of one inmate who relates his experiences with Job Therapy.

It's been ten months now since my sponsors and I were first introduced to one another, and they have been ten of the most pleasant and gratifying months of my life.

In August, I heard some of the other inmates talking of the sponsorship program, and out of a deep sense of personal need asked my counselor some questions about it and if it would be possible for me to take part. He said that he would make an application and put my name on the waiting list.

As the days and weeks passed with no word, I began to think nothing more would be heard on the subject. My mental state then was one of confusion and apprehension. I was feeling terribly sorry for myself, and just contemplating the next three years of my life behind bars made things appear fairly hopeless.

In this frame of mind I began asking my counselor for some concrete evidence that all was not hopeless in regards to obtaining a sponsor. All the while, efforts were being made in that direction. Persistence and a great effort on the part of my counselor paid off, for in February of the next year, I was told that a family had agreed to correspond and come to the institution periodically for visits.

Ten months later, the relationship this family and I had developed had blossomed into something more fulfilling than could have been imagined. It's still a bit difficult to accept the idea that there can be such selfless people as these are! The interest and devotion they showed in me and their efforts to help salvage my life had a profound effect. This genuine interest by them has generated a new interest in myself; one that's helped me to establish some realistic goals. They have also shown, by example, that things really aren't as hopeless as I'd thought previously.

Before meeting and coming to know them the world was quite a narrow and confining place. The concern they've shown has opened new vistas of interest that otherwise may have forever remained closed.

Before good fortune brought us together I wouldn't have given anyone a plugged nickle as to my chances for making it when released. Their giving so freely of their time and the way they made me feel that they really care sparked a new feeling of hope within and lent that something extra that will be the deciding factor in shaping my future in the months and years to come. God bless them.

Reflections of an Ideal M-2 Sponsor
A letter from John W. Maas, Sponsor

Dear Dick,

As I reflect on the past eight years I have much to be thankful for. I had the privilege of meeting you and being with the M-2 program from its beginning. Since then I have officially served as sponsor for five of the residents in Monroe and worked with others in an unofficial capacity. As far as I know, all of those who have been released and are now on parole have not returned to confinement.

The first one I visited was Chuck. His mental capacity was much below average. Both Mr. Maxwell (Superintendent of Washington State Reformatory) and Mr. Wood indicated he was likely the *most unmanageable they ever had in Monroe.* Mr. Wood said to me, "If we can't handle him here where else can he go?" Later, Mr. Wood thanked me at least three times for visiting him because the change had been so great. When Chuck sensed we were sincere in our visits he became so excited about it he wrote us as many as five letters in one day. Chuck jumped his parole and went to California. However, he kept in contact with me and has done so ever since. He is now in a place for rehabilitation and speaks highly of those who work with him. Knowing how Chuck had been at first when I visited him, such an attitude toward others like such folks is almost a miracle. Last Christmas, I sent him a colored picture of our family.

Another one I visited has gone back to school. His mother wanted him to do this but she could not seem to persuade him. I was thankful that after a few visits he had quite a different attitude.

Still another has started his own business. It was quite a struggle but his mother told me she was very proud of him. He bought an old truck and was cutting and delivering wood for fireplaces and such. I bought some wood from him, also, to help him along.

The last one I visited is now working in Falls City, Washington. His parents had shown little interest in him. However, when they realized someone else was concerned they became more interested also. At the end, they welcomed him home and got a job for him. They also provided a vehicle for him to go to work.

I thought perhaps you would appreciate my reflections on these past years. I wish to thank the Lord for whatever good I may have done for others. I wish to thank you also. You are the one who had the vision and saw the need. You began the program so I could work in it. Thank you, Dick. Thank you much. May the Lord continue to give you strength and wisdom to continue in His Name. May the Lord bless your staff and the Board. I will be praying for you.

Sincerely,
s/ JOHN W. MAAS

The following letter from Reverend Maas' first inmate, Chuck, indicates how psychologically severely damaged this young man had become through years of parental neglect and incarceration. His case counselor, Mr. Annis, hesitantly asked the M-2 staff to find Roy a sponsor. The counselor warned that the relationship would be difficult and was likely to fail. Chuck had not been able to relate to any of the staff, spent a good deal of his time in his cell writing letters threatening those whom he disliked.

Chuck was notified by a personal visit from Mr. Stevens on Christmas Day of 1965, that they would like to get him a special gift for Christmas—someone to visit and write to him. Chuck's second note to his counselor indicates his response. Mr. Annis, his counselor, said this was the first time Chuck had ever said "thank you" to anyone on the staff. Once Mr. Maas and his wife and three children started visiting, Chuck would write every day to every member of the family. Later he told Mr. Stevens—"before Rev. Maas started visiting me, I wanted to get a gun and shoot people, but now I want to forgive them, since Mr. Maas has forgiven me."

"I DON'T LIKE YOUR PUNKY GAME"
(A disturbed inmates letter to his parents, showing his need)

your the reason   BORN TO LOSE

Dear Dad

how are things. This is my last letter. you better tell mother too only one weak Before Christmas and this is her last chance to get up or hell with her, you must think Im a clam Duck, your the one who will quack mark those words. Its been a long time Mr Amm's my case worker came down said he shoat a letter out too mother But she did not answer this letter is tell you and mother that if I dont get a Package for Christmas your is tight and You can hang it up. Its been two months two day since we had a note two months 15 days since we had a letter let me tell you I dont like your Punky game. So make your mind up you might think you dont stink I can smell it from here If I dont get a visit Christmas I eve such I dont have too long in this Joint Mr I will haunt you. I will drive you nuts — call you evvry hour on the hour. I will send a list what I want I will chase

Talk to me

Trouble in Mind

KRD

ON BEING ASSIGNED TO AN M-2 MAN-TO-MAN SPONSOR
(Note to Institution Counselor in anticipation of being assigned)

Mr. Anris

I want to say thanks a lot for having mr Stevens come up and tell me about what he is going to do for me they are one out of a Billion there are a lot better than my family I find it real hard to understand why my family would not help me to have someone I never saw before come up and will try and find somone to write me and come up Mr Aunas I will close and hope to see you and tell mr Stevens thanks a million, for what he can do, But I know he will try his Best and I thank him and would like to hear From him.,

September 26, 1965

Correction Officer Incident Report
Self Mutilation

At 8:00 p.m., this date, while on routine check of cellhouse 111-A, the undersigned found inmate   MLR   lying apparently unconscious on the floor of his cell. Both of his forearms had been cut and scratched with a razor blade.

Yes, I cut myself, I have been trying to contact my Dad and girl, but they won't write me. My brother wrote me and told me not to bother my Dad and girl friend and not even come home when I get out.

I understand my brother, but not my Dad. I don't care anymore. I sat down on my bunk and took the razor in my hand and I don't remember anything else. Some of the inmates have been pressuring me for my medication (Dilantin with Phenobarbital).

Isolation 5 to 20 years, suspended 30 days.

Richard J. Simmons
Director of M-2
2210 North 45th Street
Seattle, Washington 98103

February 21, 1970

Dear Mr. Simmons:

Please allow me to introduce myself. My name is Thomas T. K   , and I
would like to say that I am in great need to be given some kind understanding
from one of your members of M-2. I have just left from seeing your members,
and I do need someone to visit me so I can get to understand myself, and I guess
other people.

I'm here on bank robbery, and also my last case was bank robbery. So you
see there must be something for me to do or feel. Something. *What has been in
my mind for so long is to better myself for a bigger and better robbery.* Yeah,
me. But I know that this hate is no good, and it may kill me. Please answer soon
Mr. Simmons.

Thank you very much.

Thomas T.K. (name fictitious)

**The Correctional Impact
of M-2 (Job Therapy)**[e]

As the crime statistics of the past few years indicate, there has never been a
greater need in this country for developing a correctional system that is both
humane and effective. Alarming as those crime figures may be, there are
indications of substantial progress in corrections, and much of the thanks goes to
men and women like Man-to-Man Sponsors, who realize that all elements of
society have an important role to play in bringing about the necessary changes.

Fortunately, increasing numbers of citizens are devoting their time and
energies to organizations such as Job Therapy. Spurred by motives that range
from the humanitarian to the pragmatic, many Americans are beginning to take
note of the fact that a criminal-justice system cannot be stronger than its
weakest link. Without a doubt, corrections has been the weakest component in
this nation's criminal-justice system for an intolerably long time.

Valuable work is being done by Job Therapy and similar volunteer programs
throughout the country. The efforts of Job Therapy to find employment for
ex-offenders and the Man-to-Man Program are two outstanding examples of the
kind of contribution to corrections that most properly comes from concerned
citizens of this country.

[e]This section is excerpted from a speech by Norman Carlson, Director, Federal Bureau of
Prisons, Department of Justice, given before the annual Recognition Banquet of Job
Therapy, Inc., March 15, 1974.

As we work to bring strength to a correctional system that has been weakened by decades of apathy and neglect, each of us can play a varying, yet equally important role. While professional correctional administrators and citizens share a common goal—that of making corrections catch up with the realities of the twentieth century—we often find that day-to-day pressures dictate a different ordering of priorities. The innovative and worthwhile efforts of the Job Therapy organization are a type that can only successfully come from the private sector. Offenders and ex-offenders alike are often suspicious of those who work for government agencies, and frequently are more receptive to efforts from concerned representatives of the community at large; men and women who speak not in an official capacity but man-to-man, person-to-person. There is a pressing need for those who put into daily practice the golden rule that so many others simply talk about.

Warden Rauch of the U.S. Penitentiary, McNeil Island, Washington, and his staff join me in expressing appreciation to Job Therapy for the fine work that has been done at our federal facility, both in the M-2 Program and in job placement.

Since its inception in 1970 over two hundred sponsors have been matched with inmates in the M-2 program at McNeil Island. The sponsors have gone out of their way not only to provide help and understanding to the men at McNeil Island, but on frequent occasions have provided transportation, food, temporary lodging, and other assistance to offenders' families.

The response in job placement for men leaving McNeil Island has been equally gratifying. Many sponsors have acted as go-betweens, finding jobs and setting up interviews with prospective employers, and some have even provided work for ex-offenders in their own businesses. Job Therapy is one of the more effective volunteer programs now being conducted in any correctional system.

Future Goals of Job Therapy
Toward a State Without Prisons

The governor and the legislators of the State of Washington are planning toward and have hired correctional leadership for the expressed purpose of phasing out our large fortress prisons. If we are to kick the prison habit, then we must provide and develop an entire system of sound community-based alternatives which can effectively service the estimated 50 to 75 percent of the offenders who do not need rigid confinement for their own or society's protection.

As part of a total system of community-based correctional services by a whole array of private and government agencies, Man-to-Man/Job Therapy is seeking to develop a package of pretrial diversional services designed to be a *volunteer* and *industrial* alternative to traditional incarceration. The client offender would be sentenced to on-the-job training within the community under the supervision of an M-2 job advisor.

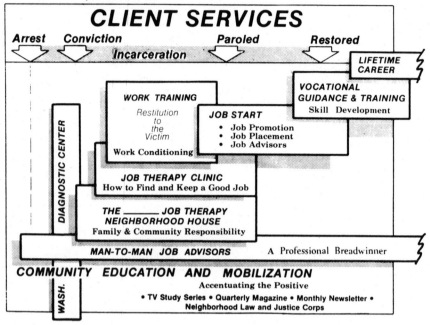

Figure 9-1. Job Therapy of Washington. Localized Community-Based Corrections—Client Services

This package is summarized in Figures 9-1 and 9-2, and Tables 9-1 and 9-2. The entire package offers employment-related services. The offender would be referred to other agencies for treatment of personal problems that are not directly related to employment, such as drugs, alcohol, mental illness, remedial reading, medical-dental, etc. M-2 Job Therapy would provide personalized employment services, once it was determined the client was employable. To foist them into the labor market prematurely would destroy both the client and the cooperative relationship Job Therapy enjoys with its affiliate employers and labor.

M-2 Job Therapy seeks to prepare the client for responsible employment through its *job prep* services. These preparatory services can all be conducted while the offender awaits his trial and sentence. If he is retained in the community and sentenced to M-2 Job Therapy, then he may be placed in an on-the-job training slot, provided by an affiliate employer. After he has completed the first phase of the Job Success Clinic and proven himself in a work-training situation, then the goal of the next phase, Jobstart, is to help him find a job on the regular market that is commensurate with his abilities and interests.

Once the trial is over and his sentence is definite, then he may be matched

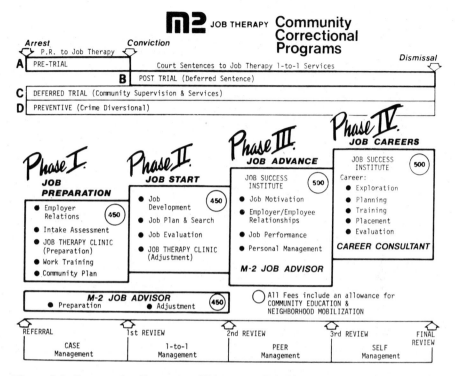

Figure 9-2. Community Correctional Programs—Job Therapy

with an M-2 Man-to-Man (or W-2) *job advisor*, who agrees to coach him on a weekly basis in how to find and keep a suitable job. The M-2 Job Advisor meets for a minimum of three hours each week with his job client on a one-to-one or group basis.

Step by step, following a workbook guide, the volunteer job advisor guides his client in his quest for a productive job future. This one-to-one weekly workshop with his own private job-tutor provides the offender-client with the *intensive guidance* that is now lacking in the present penal system, and that only volunteer citizens can give effectively.

After three months of successful and satisfying employment, the client-advisor relationship and training program moves into the *job advance* phase, designed to upgrade his motivation and work habits on the job. He continues to meet regularly with his M-2 Job Advisor, on a biweekly basis. After six months of a successful job experience, during which the client has definitely advanced in employment attitudes and work habits, then and only then, he will be encouraged to request of the presiding judge that he be promoted into the *job careers* phase. Here he will receive vocational guidance and training designed to lead him into a lifetime career with a trade of his choice.

Table 9-1
Phase I, Job Preparation–Phase II, Job Start

Phase I, Job Preparation Client Services	Phase II, Job Start Client Services
#1 Employer Relations $100/Client —Mobilize Employer Affiliates (Sales/ Briefings) —Employer & Job Analysis (Operations & Needs) —Employer Training & Communication	#6 Job Development & Control $100/Client —Central Job Bank (Coded & Updates) —Order Control System (File Search) —Employer/Employee Arbitration
#2 Intake Assessment $ 50/Client —Review Applications —Diagnostic Interview (employability) —Field Investigation (verification)	#7 Job Search & Placement $100/Client —Implementation of Plan —Resume Review and Distribution —Job Referral and Placement 　Pre-screening for Employers
#3 Job Preparation Clinic $100/Client —How to Get the Right Job —How to Succeed On the Job —Community Survival Tactics	Interview Scheduling 　Job Finding Escort —Support Services 　Tools, clothing, housing, transportation, etc.
#4 Work Training (On-the-Job) $100/Client —Develop Work Habits —Conditioned to Work —Self Support and Restitution	#8 Evaluation (30, 60, 90 days) $100/Client —Employee Monthly Follow-up —Employer Monthly Follow-up —Job Performance Analysis
#5 Community Employment Plan $ 50/Client —Develop Realistic Job Plan —Institutional Coordination —Court Representation & Negotiation —Appropriate Treatment Referrals	#9 Job Adjustment Clinic $100/Client —Diagnosis of Problem Areas —Proposed Remedies —Community Survival
#10 M-2 (Man-to-Man) Job Advisor	$600/Client
—Preparation 　Recruiting 　Training 　Community Liaison	—Adjustment 　In-Service Training 　Weekly 3 Hours Workshops 　Weekly Programs Review

The immediate goal of the M-2 Job Package is a six-month experience of *job success*. The ultimate goal is to start the client on the road to a definite *job career*.

To maintain visibility and evaluate the client's continuing progress, each volunteer Job Advisor must report in writing progress achieved in each weekly

Table 9-2
Personalized Service Contracts

● Optimum Service Package:		(Total Cost — $1,400 for 6 Months)	
Add:	Service #10	M-2 (Man-to-Man) Job Advisor**	Cost to Agency $900. per client
● Medium Service Package:		(Total Cost — $800. for 6 Months)	
Add:	Service #3	Job Success Clinic — Preparation	Cost to Agency $600. per client
	Service #4	Work Training (On-the-Job)	
	Service #9	Job Success Clinic — Adjustment	
● Minimum Service Package:		(Total Cost — $500. for 6 Months)	
	Service #1	Employer Relations*	
	Service #2	Intake Assessment	
	Service #5	Community & Job Plan	Cost to Agency $300. per client
	Service #6	Job Development*	
	Service #7	Job Search & Placement	
	Service #8	Evaluation (30, 60, 90 days)	

*Cost incurred by Job Therapy
**50% of the cost incurred by Job Therapy

visit with his client. He is interviewed by phone once every month by the Volunteer Coordinator on the M-2 Job Therapy staff to clarify his weekly client progress reports and offer professional assistance and guidance where needed. At the end of each quarter, the job client and his job advisor prepare their progress report for the presiding judge. The client chronology and progress summary are verified by his job advisor and submitted to the judge with the job advisor's recommendations. This quarterly review is cleared for release by the M-2 Volunteer Coordinator before submittal to the judge.

Such a system of job-related services we believe to be the best total alternative to traditional incarceration. It will cost substantially to train and supervise the volunteers adequately (see Figures 9-1, 9-2, and Tables 9-1 and 9-2), but we believe such a project can accomplish in one year what traditional methods fail to do in two to six years of imprisonment.

Our present system is problem and crisis oriented. It focuses on the man's failure and weaknesses. In the M-2 Job Therapy package we employ the industrial method of management by objectives, focusing on the client's strengths and potentials. The traditional probation officer with excessive caseloads can only give him fifteen minutes each month—more time only if he is in trouble or has violated his provation. In the M-2 package the client receives three hours of positive goal-oriented personalized counseling every week. The goal of this intensive program of M-2 services and supervision will be to maximize his potential by helping him set and attain practical job and vocational goals.

The M-2 Job Therapy approach provides the sound community alternative which, when fully instituted within each county of a state, would starve the existing fortress prisons out of existence in a safe and orderly fashion. This is the type alternative judges have been pleading for—a well-supervised, goal-oriented, highly structured package of employment services, designed to build the offender's sense of responsibility and make him a self-sufficient individual.

M-2 (Man-to-Man) Concept Developed in Other Areas

Since the publication of the M-2 article in the August 1970 issue of *Reader's Digest*, there have been calls from several states for assistance in starting M-2 Man-to-Man/Job Therapy projects. Following is a list of the states and private projects that have established a formal organization of volunteers currently delivering M-2 services.

State	Title of Agency	Headquarters
Washington	M-2 Man-to-Man/Job Therapy	Seattle
Oregon	Job Therapy of Oregon	Portland
California	Job Therapy, California	Hayward
Oklahoma	Volunteers in Corrections	Oklahoma City
Kansas	Heart of America Job Therapy	Kansas City
Iowa	Man-to-Man	Des Moines
Nevada	Job Therapy of Nevada	Reno
New Mexico	(Being developed)	Albuquerque
New York	The Bridge	Buffalo
Washington, D.C.	Man-to-Man	Washington, D.C.
British Columbia	Job Therapy of Canada	Vancouver, B.C.
South Korea	Man-to-Man	Seoul

Research Concerned with the Effects of Job Therapy on Recidivism[f]

The introduction of the volunteer sponsor into the prisoner's experiences is an added factor that is not a part of the nonsponsored inmate's experiences, and is

[f]A summary of the procedures used and conclusions drawn by a thesis submitted by Alfred Gordon Lawyer in satisfaction of requirements for a Master of Arts, University of Washington, 1970. Copies of this thesis are available through (M-2) Man-to-Man/Job Therapy office at 150 John Street, Seattle, Washington 98109 ($2.00 per copy).

therefore subject to evaluation. It was the purpose of this thesis study to compare the parole failure rates of a group of inmates who have received the added social attention of a sponsor with the failure rates of another group who did not have this additional outside contact. The sponsored subjects studied were released between January 1, 1966 and March 31, 1968. The parole duration cut-off date was set at April 1, 1970, giving a mean release time of thirty-three months.

The ninety members of the *sponsored group* were obtained from the files of Job Therapy, and were restricted to those sponsored inmates who were released on parole from the Washington State Reformatory. The *comparison group* of 90 was selected from 925 inmates released on parole during this period. The two variables, lack of social contact (visits and correspondence), and time on parole, were considered of such significance with respect to the probability of parole failure that these were used as the basis for matching comparison group cases to the sponsored subjects.

Of the total population of 925 parolees, 364 were returned to an institution and classed as failures. This was a failure rate of 39.3 percent, and may be used as a base rate upon which to make comparisons.

Gordon Lawyer first surveyed the percentage of parole failures in the total population by contact through visits and correspondence, demonstrating that the greater the level of outside contacts, the greater the probability of parole success. The data collected strongly suggested that neglect of inmates by families or friends outside the institution is a factor in the high rate of parole failures (25.5 percent of the total population received no visits during their entire incarceration).

Lawyer then compared percentages of sponsored and nonsponsored subjects in total population according to level of visits and letters received, demonstrating that *inmates chosen for sponsorship* were the most alienated, maintaining a low level of contact with relatives and others outside the institution.

In comparing the failures and successes in both the sponsored group and the balance of the population, it revealed little significant difference. This suggests, then, that *the sponsors' visits and letters made up for the lack of primary contact.* Hence, it may be that sponsors' visits and letters served to "bring up" a previously "disadvantaged" group to the level of the entire inmate population.

Therefore, to see more directly the impact of the program, it became necessary to compare the sponsored group with an equally disadvantaged group that did not receive the sponsor contact. The *disadvantaged comparison group* had a failure rate considerably higher than the total population, and consequently a much higher failure rate than the sponsored group.

Summary of Findings

1. There is a relationship between rates of parole failure and the degree of outside contact in the overall population of parolees.

2. The sponsored group was taken from the lower levels of outside contact, yet it did not fail at a greater rate than the overall population of parolees, as it might have had it not been for the sponsorship.

3. When compared with a group whose level of outside contact was the same as the sponsored group before the visits and letters were received from the sponsor, the rate of parole failure was *significantly lower* (52.5 to 33.3 percent), despite the fact that

4. The two groups do not significantly differ on ten other variables related to rates of recidivism.

Admitting the limitations of any ex post facto study, from the data collected and compared we can infer man-to-man was highly successful. The difference between the sponsored and comparison groups could well be attributed to the increased level of social contact from the sponsor.

For this particular sample, it was shown that the rate of parole failure has been reduced from 39.3 percent (for the total population of parolees), to 33.3 percent for the sponsored group. But, when comparing this sample with an equivalent group, matched on the two critical variables of time on parole and social contact (visits and letters) with persons on the outside, the comparison group had a rate of 52.2 percent compared with the sponsored group rate of 33.2 percent.

It appears that, with the controls available, there is a reduction of 18.9 percent in the parole failure rate in the sponsored group. Considering the failure rate of the comparison group as unity, this reduction in failure is an impressive *36 percent.*

From Figure 9-3, it can be seen that the sponsored group had a net gain in raw percentage of 18.9 in success rate. However, the forty-three successes in the comparison group constitute 100 percent of the successes in that category, which can be presumed to be the predicted success rate of the sponsored group had it not been for the factor of sponsorship. Since, in fact, the sponsored group had not 18.9 percent, but 17/43, or 39.5 percent. The percentages of 18.9 and 47.8 may be substituted for the numerical values in this computation, with the same result of 39.5 percent.[g]

Sponsored group: 60 Successes   139.5%

Comparison group: ___   =   _____   = 39.5% Increase
  with no sponsors: 43 Successes   100%   attributed to
                                                      M-2 Sponsorship

---

[g]In the test of the thesis, the emphasis was on reduction of parole failure rather than on increase in parole success, so the percentage of parole failures was computed from a different base; i.e., 100 percent of the parole failures in the comparison group numbered 47, and decreased to 30 in the sponsored group, still a difference of 17/47 equals 36.1 percent.

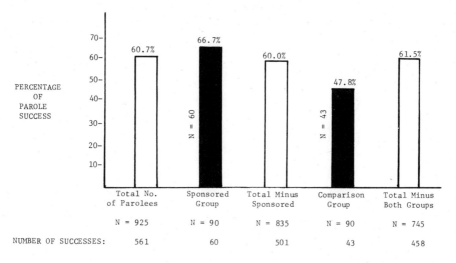

COMPARISON OF SUCCESS RATES BETWEEN VARIOUS GROUPS

Figure 9-3. Comparison of Success Rates Between Various Groups

References

1. "M-2 New Formula for Wasted Lives" reprinted by permission of author. Material appeared in *Reader's Digest*, August 1970, under title "They Go To Prison on Purpose." Reprinted by permission of publisher.

2. "W-2 (Woman-to-Woman) Friendship Therapy" reprinted by permission of author. Material appeared in *Northwest Progress*, March 31, 1972. Reprinted by permission of publisher.

3. "Personal Benefits of (M-2) Man-to-Man" reprinted by permission of author.

4. "The Correctional Impact of M-2 (Job Therapy)" reprinted by permission of author.

5. "The Critical and Essential Need for Man-to-Man" reprinted by permission of author.

6. "Research Concerned with the Effects of Job Therapy of Recidivism" ("The Effects of Social Attention of Recidivism") reprinted by permission of author.

10

The Halfway House as an Alternative

Calvert R. Dodge[a]

Small-group homes, or as they are more commonly called, halfway houses, were first introduced into the United States during the early part of the 1800s. Religious and private volunteer groups usually provided the sponsorship impetus rather than government. Their purpose was to provide such services as a temporary place of shelter, food, clothing, friendly advice, and sometimes efforts to assist the ex-law-offender in securing employment. The early halfway houses were self-contained, and isolated from correctional staffs and other services. They were not really a part of corrections, and while this factor was attractive to the ex-offender it may have been the reason they did not grow rapidly during the eighties.

Early halfway houses included one opened in Boston in 1864 for women that had a twenty-year history of operation; a Quaker-sponsored halfway house in New York City which still survives as the Isaac T. Hopper House; The House of Industry, established in Philadelphia in 1889, also still in existence; and Hope Hall, established in 1896 by Maud Booth and her husband in New York City. Hope halls were established in Chicago in 1903 and the group sponsoring this movement started halfway houses in other states as well. At a time in the nation's history when "punishment" was a very significant word in terms of criminal rehabilitation, the halfway-house movement in the nineteenth century was indeed a pioneer movement. Their founders were often met with hostility and indifference by both officials and publics. But they had started an alternative to imprisonment that would take root in the nation. The movement was dormant, however, until the fifties, when revival came in the founding of such facilities as St. Leonard's House, Dismas House, and 308 West Residence. Awareness of the high recidivism rates of ex-offenders and the many problems they face when released from prison provided the spark that set the movement in motion again.

Whether or not the group home can be considered either as a replacement for or an alternative to prison depends upon who is observing the phenomena. Mueller suggested that placement in a group home is simply a "diversion" from the mainstream of the sanctioning process, as are work-release, probation, parole, etc.[1] Mueller states that the lack of imaginative experimentation with

[a]With special acknowledgment to E.B. Henderson, III, Executive Assistant, Talbert House, Cincinnati, Ohio, for editorial assistance.

197

alternatives to imprisonment, however, is surprising. Perhaps it may be that, in the past, "the better minds of the bar—as the Supreme Court itself—shunned any preoccupation with sanctions, that reputable scientists found better employment in more productive enterprises than prison systems and that the community saw no use in the expenditure of funds for an inevitable apparatus meant to restrain hopeless cases."[2]

Even to the extent that extramural alternatives to imprisonment were invented, like alcoholics' treatment projects, [drug] addiction treatment facilities, court employment projects, etc. We have the uneasy feeling that the underlying motivation frequently was not the desire to rehabilitate and to help but, rather, administrative frustration over the system's inability to handle growing caseloads within the mainstream of the system. This is [of course] in no way intended to disparage the humanitarianism of those who have designed the newer correctional diversion systems.[3]

From Mueller's tone, we can assume that those persons interested in developing alternatives such as group homes are somewhat limited in the utilization of creativeness. The judicial structure, court process, sentencing requirements make it mandatory for some people to go to prison. If an alternative is created, therefore, it either must aim at the potential crime committer or it must become a partial victim of the system and create programs for the person already convicted. Group homes (except foster homes) for those in trouble with the law usually fall within this "after-the-fact-of-conviction" category. Still, if they reduce time spent behind bars in the present penal system, they should have merit. To their founders and supporters they offer "purpose" in work, some intangible "rewards" to egos. A good example of dedication to these intangibles is John Mahers, Delancey Street Foundation in San Francisco where ex-drug addicts contribute one-hundred percent of their income and valuables as a "condition" of being a member of The Delancey Street "Family." To their residents they may be all that is left to the "hope" of tomorrow. To systems, they often are headaches, often scapegoats, sometimes rescuers.

 Talbert House and the Talbert House system in Cincinnati, Ohio is one example of the group home as an alternative.

In the sixties, Dr. Jack S. Brown was a professor of psychiatry at the University of Cincinnati. Like others he was disturbed by the thought that so many of the men who are paroled from prison or discharged from the penal system without a job, without a home, and without any community ties often revert rather quickly to crime and soon are led back to prison. Often the trip back to prison is within thirty to ninety days after release. They just couldn't cope with independence. Brown felt that not only was this pattern of criminality too much of a burden on society, but it really was unfair to these men, who for all purposes were practically helpless. He gathered together a group of friends, colleagues and citizens in 1964 to discuss this problem and what to do about it.

The result of these discussions was a decision to open a "halfway house" to help parolees surmount the big change from the complete security and control of prison life to a life of self-sufficiency. As almost any parolee from any prison in the United States can tell you, you come out of a prison with a suit, some money you have earned working in prison shops ($25 to $100), you find there's no place to go except Sally (the Salvation Army men's shelter) or the Volunteers of America, or maybe you find a room in a cheap hotel or boarding house. The money runs out fast, you can't find work, and pretty soon what little hope and expectation you may have had is washed away. Soon you're back with the old "has-beens" crowd, or doing dope or alcohol and headed back to prison.

Dr. Brown felt that ex-cons needed the security of a homelike atmosphere with a minimum of restrictions where easing into the mainstream of life could be accomplished. He also felt that they needed professional help in fitting themselves back into the community while coping with the problems that sent them to prison in the first place.

Community response to Brown's idea was supportive, which by the way is somewhat a rarity even in today's "open-minded" society. The Roman Catholic Archdiocese of Cincinnati donated the use of the vacant rectory of St. Anne's and St. Edward's Church in the west end of Cincinnati. Other civic and social organizations donated furniture. When the halfway house opened in August 1965, it was named Talbert House in honor of Dr. Ernest Talbert, University of Cincinnati professor emeritus of sociology, who in the twenties and thirties had been concerned with criminal rehabilitation.

In forming the board of directors, Talbert House founders legitimized the term "conartist," for in order for any group home to survive, it must have interested supporters who can get things done, who can get money, goods, services, other people. Talbert House board of directors from the beginning were composed of employment people, lawyers, physicians, psychologists, social workers, psychiatrists, business and government representatives, newspaper men, and representatives of political forces and major religions.

Funds were raised to hire a professional director. From Dr. Brown's founding efforts developed what perhaps today is an excellent example of an "alternative-system." John M. McCartt, who had been assistant superintendent of the Apalachee Correctional Institution in Florida, was hired in May 1966 to direct the Talbert House development. He brought with him as his assistant E.B. Henderson III, who had been the institution's psychologist. McCartt's first major project was to develop a practical rehabilitation program for Talbert House. Shortly after his arrival a federal grant, which was requested by the board of trustees, arrived. The initial grant request was $20,000 but the government experts tripled the budget, stating that it was too small for what was proposed. And so Talbert House became big business, with an initial supporting grant of $60,000. Today, most starting budgets for group homes housing twelve residents will range from $60,000 to $95,000. Dr. Brown's idea was now well on its way.

Initially the Talbert House treatment program was solely of professional design. To McCartt's background of criminology and corrections and Henderson's of psychology was added a weekly staff meeting which included a consultant psychiatrist, Ph.D. clinical psychologist, and social worker. These were the working sessions where treatment programs were shaped and reshaped for each resident before being carried out on a daily basis.

 As the program succeeded and expanded, two new houses and an out-client employment program were gradually added. After several years a relatively stable group of ex-residents was in the community. From these Talbert House employed first one, then another, for staff members. Today more than 20 percent of the more than fifty employees are ex-residents of the program.

 The basic theory of a halfway house is to help a person leaving an absolute controlled and total-care environment of an institution gradually make the transition to self-sufficiency outside the institution. McCartt sees it as a three-phase program, one phase consisting of a residency under a structured set of circumstances, a second phase part-time dependence on the home and its staff assistance, and a final phase in which the former resident is almost entirely on his own, using the home only to check with in time of crisis, special unanswered-need assistance, and the like.

Similar types of halfway houses are the Dismas houses in St. Louis, and Louisville. The structure of the programs within the halfway houses run from simply a place to sleep to severe encounter programs, such as at Synnanon in Los Angeles and Cenacore in Denver. While some group homes are established for particular clientele (drug addicts, alcoholics, etc.), most of the homes being established in recent years are for the general criminal. The extent of stay at the homes ranges from one or two days to several months or even a year or more.

Initially Talbert House accepted only parolees, but today it accepts parolees and probationers as well as federal and city work releasees. This differs from several other types of group home, some of which accept only convicts who have fully served their sentences and no longer have to answer to the law for their crimes. Talbert House does restrict applicants to persons from Hamilton County and the Greater Cincinnati area.

The basic criterion for admission to Talbert House is that the person is employable and wants to change. "If a man isn't interested in himself, I can't be interested in him," McCartt says. "I'd be wasting the staff's effort."

Once a month, one of the program directors sets out on a visit schedule to Ohio's five prisons and to the nearby federal institutions. This "selecting" aspect of a halfway house director's job is the toughest part. Each of the Talbert House halfway houses (there are two for men and one for women) can take a few of the many eligible parolees. In the past many deserving men have been turned down simply because of lack of space.

Usually the new resident arrives at a Talbert House the latter part of the week. It has been a customary practice for the state of Ohio to release prisoners that later part of the week, usually Thursday. He arrives with a prison-made suit, a handful of belongings, and a little bit of hope. During the first several days he is helped in establishing himself in the community. He is taken downtown to register at the police station as an ex-con, to meet with his assigned parole officer if he needs one, and whatever else needs to be done.

After a quiet weekend following his settling-in process, he begins looking for work. Most residents find work within a week or so, but there are a few who are hard to place, like sex offenders or ex-drug addicts whom nobody seems to want, or the ones who have such negative feelings about themselves that they are self-defeating. But even for the most difficult, there are many community resources available to Talbert House. In addition, Talbert House has its own employment program which has a staff and a budget to provide residents and nonresidents alike with job placements, job training, and educational programs. Much like a mini-Bureau of Vocational Rehabilitation, this program can pay for commercial schools, buy tools, grant stipends, and supplement salaries for deserving clients.

Talbert House also has been able to develop a bank of confidential resources in several of the community's largest and most conservative industries, who have hired some of the most difficult men. The Talbert House staff can generally find work for the residents, but they want them to make the effort themselves. The reality of job hunting with no significant experience, little education, and a prison record can be a devastating storm of rejection unless the man can build his aggressive effort, motivation, and interest in life. The job rejections can be handled better by men who at least have a place to sleep and eat. Talbert House's policy is to let them know "we care but don't coddle them."

That first week at Talbert House is a period of mutual appraisal, and of planning a program for the resident. Because these men come from a very structured society, the staff avoids too much organization and regulations. But, because they are basically loners, the staff tries, without pushing, to involve them in group activities like the house council and Monday bowling.

Graduate students and interns also come to the house to spend a few hours with the new resident and to develop his personal history. During this time, the house director has gotten to learn the new resident's mannerisms, his fears, his problems. Problems are talked about, not ignored. With the help of the consultants, the program director and his staff plan a program for each resident. By the time of the staff meeting for this purpose, the staff has analyzed the new resident's strengths and weaknesses and has tried to set up a realistic program, building upon the strengths and compensating for the weaknesses. The program includes short-term and long-term goals for a few months to a year. This idea of goal-setting differs from old patterns of immediate gratifications and letting tomorrow take care of itself.

Community resource agencies are asked to help, and contribute much to assist residents with family, financial, personal-emotional, educational, and training needs. Residents voluntarily attend alcoholic clinics and tattoo-removal laboratories. Groups of residents, with the aid of staff members as facilitators, work out many of their own problems. Absence of long-range goals is usual among parolees. They have led lives of frustration and have seen almost everything they tried go sour. Self-esteem is low and the staff work continuously at assisting residents to become more optimistic about themselves and their futures. Tasks like filling out a job application, making a long-distance phone call, or arranging for an interview at a potential employer's office are major crisis tasks for most of these men. They lack confidence in everything except how to pull a bank job, break into someplace, or steal a car. The job of the Talbert House staff is to help them to organize and build new attitudes toward themselves and toward the people they are now working with every day. Their social inadequacy is difficult for most people to understand or comprehend.

The typical resident doesn't know much about the real world, which he has been away from for several years. According to McCartt, for instance, some really don't know why they should wash their hands after going to the toilet, or why they should call the foreman at work when they are going to be absent from their job.

The residents live in Talbert House for an average stay of three months, though some stay considerably longer, and some would stay forever if allowed. The rooms are comfortable, with two and sometimes three to a room, which they are expected to keep clean. While at the house, they lead simple and uncomplicated lives.

A house council is encouraged, and consists of several residents who develop and decide on house policies for the residents. The council rather than the staff oversees housekeeping, meals, recreation, and most of the problems and small frictions that occur. Group dynamics and group functioning in any productive way is not comprehended by the resident. The program director and his assistants have to work closely with the councils to provide the prodding and guidance that helps the group to develop and grow. Examples of decisions the council may make include sending letters of welcome to men in prison who have been chosen to come to Talbert House, explaining curfews, visits, meal-serving systems, and handling of complaints. The council's group action is centered around the pivoting theme of a "concern for others," which is a milestone in human relations for these men so used to being self-centered loners.

Most residents come home for supper, but they are not required to. They are free to come and go as they please, with only one major restriction on their activities, other than their parole conditions; a 12:00 PM curfew on workdays (2:30 AM on weekends). The curfew means they must be in the house at this time, but not necessarily in bed. They are only asked to get the amount of sleep needed for them to be able to get up in the morning and go to work. The evenings at Talbert House are kept full with cards, ping-pong, and pool in a basement game room decorated by the residents. There is always someone to talk with, or there is television or hi-fi. Staff are on duty twenty-four hours a day.

There is an increasing amount of interaction with others now at Talbert House, including women and men students and others working with the residents, relatives, and "significant others" involved in helping the program in some way. When women are visiting many of the residents get awkward and self-conscious, like a boy on his first date, not knowing what to do.

Talbert House is now a very viable system of halfway houses in Cincinnati. At last count there were eight or nine units in the system, including two residential facilities for adult male ex-offenders, a home for adult female ex-offenders, a therapeutic community for adult drug addicts, a facility for youthful drug abusers, a twenty-four-hour switchboard and walk-in counseling center, and an out-client drug-counseling program and employment component.

How many persons receive care from the Talbert House conglomerate? In 1974, an average year, more than four hundred ex-offenders and drug users were assisted as residents. Another thousand were assisted by the out-client and walk-in programs. Each year more than fifty thousand receive some help by way of the twenty-four-hour switchboard system (whose telephone number is 621-CARE).

How successful is Talbert House? The odds are in favor of success. There are some built-in variables that help make this so. Those chosen show the greatest potential for rehabilitation. Incorrigibles, those with severe mental disorders, or those who just don't show interest aren't invited to live there. People who can be helped and appear to be good risks often give up too soon after release from prison simply because there is no help. Talbert House does affect these types, and thus affects the recidivism statistics. Talbert House is structural freedom. Residents of Talbert House are not spoon fed, however. They are loaned some clothing if needed until they begin to receive wages. They are charged a fee of $21.00 per week for room and board from the day they enter. (If they are not working, the fee is one-third that amount.) It isn't the amount of money for services that counts, but the sense of dignity it gives the men of paying their own way.

Inexperienced in handling money and without any real sense of money values and long-term needs, money crises do occur with some of the men. Recently, one, without telling anyone, bought a used car and committed himself to payments of twenty-five dollars a week, even though he was only making sixty-five clear. Naturally the car needed a lot of repairs, and when the going got real tough he wanted to just take it back to the used car lot and leave it, and just forget the whole thing. McCartt talked him out of that, pointing out that he made the commitment and must live up to it. "What seemed an insurmountable crisis probably turned out to be a blessing," McCartt said. "We have been spending a lot of time with him, helping him budget, and now he has to tread the straight and narrow, because he has no money left over. He has learned something about financial responsibility and planning ahead. He spends a lot of time working on the car instead of drinking, and one of the night counselors who also likes to tinker with cars, has been able to get pretty close to him and lead him into a new kind of inter-personal relationship. Most of the cases are less dramatic; the routines of Talbert House are normally mundane. Talbert House is not a panacea for all the problems of criminal rehabilitation. There are no rescue fantasies among the Talbert House staff.[4]

Evaluation is part and parcel of the program to answer such questions as how to handle the transfer from Talbert House to the outside of residents who need long-term relationships with a substitute parent such as they found in McCartt and Henderson. There are scales for evaluating the men when they come into Talbert House and when they leave, and follow-up checks; scales to indicate ratings of adjustment in Talbert House, in their jobs, in their relations with others, and their degree of identification with others.

The surface evidence indicates that halfway houses work, and with a lot of educated guessing, the psychologists, psychiatrists, sociologists, and penologists can fairly accurately pick out the parolees who will most likely benefit from a halfway house.

The need is far greater than any single Talbert House can hope to fulfill. Many people in the field believe that most of the parolees and full-termers getting out of prison can be helped by halfway houses. The Federal Bureau of Prisons, which contracts with private agencies and maintains several of their own pre-release and work-release programs based on the halfway house concept, has declared its future intention of releasing all federal inmates, except those convicted of violent crimes or organizational crimes, through community-based treatment programs.

The halfway house or community-based group home movement will undoubtedly gain more momentum, as it has from 1967 when the 97th Congress of Corrections met in Miami and declared its intention of focusing corrections away from institutional settings and toward the community, where the problems originated and where the treatment should occur. It would appear that government, particularly state and local government, is learning what the private agency has known for a long time; that is, that manipulation of environment is not the answer for effective change. We must treat social disorder in a more personalized manner within the community.

When Talbert House was getting started, there were about seventy halfway houses in the United States. Today there are hundreds. There are upwards of 200,000 persons behind bars, and about 35,000 go out on parole each year. Halfway houses reach about one-fourth of these ex-convicts. The typical halfway house resident is thirty-two or younger, was first arrested around age sixteen, and has gone through a wide variety of care or correctional environments like foster homes, jails, probation, juvenile institutions, older youth reformatories, adult prisons, and parole; he has an eighth-grade education, a spotty employment history, and few or no work skills.

If we have to use only one variable for the criteria to determine the success of halfway houses, it would be whether or not a resident stays out of jail for at least two years after he is paroled. Chances are he'll make it outside of prison if this happens. Using this criterion for evaluation, we can say that the halfway house, the community-based group home, is a successful venture in alternatives to incarceration. But recidivism as the criterion doesn't tell the entire statistical story. There are other variables, of course, long-term gains in terms of preparing people for jobs, for marriage, for life. Budget is another important variable. It costs about $4000 to $7000 per year per prisoner to maintain prisons. Although the cost of providing quality community-based treatment services to the offender is quickly approaching the cost of keeping him in the institution, there are considerations other than the much more personal service which contributes to the lowered recidivism rate.

By removing the offender from the institution and placing him in the community where he can acquire a job, we save untold tax dollars which would otherwise go to maintain him in prison. Instead of a tax liability, he becomes a tax asset, because he works, pays taxes, contributes to his own upkeep, and in many instances supports a family that otherwise would be receiving welfare and Aid for Dependent Children.

The federal government and many cities and states now support halfway houses or community treatment centers which contain programs for furloughed prisoners or work-releasees. These offenders are hand picked by the institutions as "low risks" and returned to the community in a supervised residential setting. In most instances, they are allowed away from their local treatment program only to work, and must return immediately after work. More states are getting on the bandwagon and are operating themselves or contracting with private agencies to provide these local treatment services. Presently there is a great need for trained staffs, better organization and management, and increased community awareness and support, and finally supportive legislation, reduction of red tape in selection and placement of residents into homes, and more liberal attitudes by business and industry in its ex-convict-hiring policies.

While research is sparse, some can be discussed here. Cowden and Monson (1969) compared three groups of delinquent youth in terms of adjustment in different environments. These environments included community-based juvenile corrections, juvenile foster homes, and juvenile group homes. It was found that boys who are more disturbed and, according to prognostic tests, more likely to get into trouble, tend to be placed in group homes rather than boarding homes. Boys placed in group homes showed greater adjustment after release from institutions than the two other groups. While Cowden and Monson are not sure of the reason for this, they suggest that being away from the home environment is a positive rehabilitative factor.

In terms of differential placement in group homes, Palmer (1972) found that the group home environment for lower-maturity delinquents appeared to be unsatisfactory in terms of their adjustment to society when released. Temporary placement in group homes of higher maturity delinquents was successful.

Wilgosh (1973) studied the effectiveness of group home placements for juvenile delinquents in the Toronto area. The results of his research indicated that group homes may be beneficial in the control of delinquent behavior, provided that the placement lasts longer than six months. The positive and negative outcome of adolescents did not differ in terms of number and nature of legal charges, or in an age at placement. However, there was a difference in parental attitude. Where that attitude was positive and supportive, the outcome was generally positive.

Palmer (1972) in a final report of a research project concerned with differential placement of delinquents in group homes is summarized as follows. The California Youth Authority and National Institute of Mental Health sponsored homes for long-term care and facilities for temporary care. These homes were operated within the structure of California's community-based program for court commitments. Two additional homes, one designed to accommodate up to six higher-maturity youths, and a group home for girls, were also studied. From an overall operational standpoint, there appeared to be two quite successful boys' group homes—the boarding home for higher-maturity youths and the temporary care home for all types of youth. The girls' group home was also found to be successful—the containment home for manipulators, and the home for those labeled cultural conformists, proved unsuccessful. It appears that increased emphasis should be given to the issue of matching the maturity levels of the staffs of group homes in such a way as to be beneficial to the furtherance of the maturity levels of the residents.

Kirby (1970) researched adult halfway houses in San Diego, specifically Crofton House, using an experimental and control group. The success-failure rates of men in the program were compared to the control groups in work camps and jails. Results indicated little or no significant difference between outcomes of experimental and control groups in terms of social adjustment and recidivism rates.

Gilliam (1969) reported on Project "First-Chance," a three-year experimental and demonstration project using vocational training, basic adult education, and halfway house applications. While the experiment was a model in joint efforts to assist the law-offender, no significant results were reported.

Deehy (1969) did a case study of the halfway house as a part of the correctional sequence, and suggests that organizational structure and staff must be appropriately developed in order for such programs as group therapy to work within the halfway house environment. Part of the success of a halfway house will be dependent upon the interaction of staff members and residents; they cannot remain aloof of each other and still expect success.

Elder (1972) reports on the closing of a halfway house that was designed for ex-Borstal girls. He lists several factors for the failure, including the tendency of the girls to be loners rather than relying on groups for support and developing too much dependency on the security offered by the home.

Aledort and Jones (1973) described early results of their research at Euclid House in Washington, D.C. Euclid House is a therapeutic community-based halfway house for prisoners. The house was staffed almost entirely by black mental-health personnel, four of them ex-offenders. Early statistics showed a marked decrease in the number of escapees and amount of recidivistic activity.

While these examples of research are indicative of trends, none of them tells us why some halfway houses are successful and some fail. The combinations of staff, program, budget, selection, and length of stay are all very important variables, and much more objective research is needed to establish more definitive "recipes" for their success. While the Talbert House system appears successful in Cincinnati, there are no research statistics indicating how successful it is or what combinations—length of stay, type of program of staff-resident, interactions between staff-staff, resident-resident, staff-client, and staff-resident-community—are most successful and could easily stand the test of replication, which in the long run is the key to usefulness of any program designed to improve society on a more universal basis.

Rubinton (1970) found that length of stay is a critical factor in the success of an alcoholism halfway house. The long-term member will more likely change his attitudes and achieve stable residence, increased abstinence, and regular employment. In this particular study the median length of stay in a halfway house was 28 days and the range was from 1 day to 184. Of the 72 men referred to the house from prisons, 62 percent stayed less than 28 days, compared with 43 percent of the 107 men referred from sources such as alcoholism clinics and hospitals. The findings indicate that those who stayed 28 days or longer are exposed to fewer negative and inconsistent societal reactions than the short-term members. Many of these longer-time members of the halfway house environment develop more normal aspirations to conformity and a more normal self-image and thus tend to adjust to noninstitutionalized environments without excessive drinking habits.

Ackerman (1971) describes research that carries the halfway house idea to some dangerous outer limits, suggesting that treatment in halfway houses can become as threatening as treatment within the most closed and secluded prison. This study deals with halfway houses in Germany, and describes treatment programs consisting of environmental therapy, conversation, group therapy, contacts with the outside community, direct social integration through family and halfway houses, surgical or pharmacological castration of sex-offenders, and counseling after discharge.

With increased emphasis on the discovery of alternatives to prisons during the seventies and eighties, much energy will be used in the development of community-based correctional facilities such as the halfway house. It appears that much greater effort should be made toward discovering some organizational and operational criteria through objective research. Without these data, our nation will continue to start and stop halfway houses and group homes in a costly manner in terms of staff, residents, budgets, and public support.

References

1. O.W. Mueller Gerhard, "Imprisonment and Its Alternatives," unpublished paper, New York University, 1973, p. 13. By permission of the author.
2. Ibid., p. 14.
3. Ibid.
4. *The Frightening Step to Freedom for the Ex-Con*, Cincinnati Alumnus, University of Cincinnati, October 1967, p. 26. By permission of the editors.

Additional References

Ackerman, Edwin, "Two Years' Experience at the Special Penal Institution," Hamburg-Bergedorf, Germany, Monatsschrift fur Kriminologie und Strafrechtsreform, KDLN, 54(8): pp. 367-71, 1971.

Alper, Benedict S., "Community Residential Treatment Centers," National Parole Institute, *National Council on Crime and Delinquency* (1966).

Benson, Margaret, "A Whole-Hearted Look at Halfway Houses," *Canadian Journal of Corrections* (July 1967).

Bradley, H.B., "Community-Based Treatment for Young Adult Offenders," *Crime and Delinquency*, Vol. 15, No. 3 (July 1969).

_____ , "Designing for Change: Problems of Planned Innovation in Corrections," *Annals of the American Academy of Political and Social Science* (January 1969).

Breslin, Maurice A., and Robert G. Crosswhite, "Residential Aftercare: An Intermediate Step in the Correctional Process," *Federal Probation*, Vol. XXVII (March 1963).

Carlson, Norman, "Pre-Release Guidance Center Demonstration Projects," *American Correctional Association Proceedings* (1962).

Crime and Delinquency, Vol. 17, No. 1 (January 1971).

Denton, George F., "The Halfway House," *American Correctional Association Proceedings* (1962).

Grygier, Tadeusz, Barbara Nease, and Carol Staples Anderson, "An Exploratory Study of Halfway Houses," *Crime and Delinquency*, Vol. 16, No. 3 (July 1970).

Haskell, Martin R., and Bert Madison, "A Group Home for Parolees," *California Youth Authority Quarterly* (Winter 1966).

Hughes, Clay, "Halfway House," *Presidio*, 32 (Iowa State Penitentiary, 1965).

James, J.T.L., "The Halfway House Movement," *Canadian Journal of Corrections* (October 1968).

Kehrberg, John H., "Halfway Houses: Good or Bad," *American Journal of Corrections* (January-February 1968).

Keller, Oliver J., and Benedict S. Alper, *"Halfway Houses: Community Center Corrections and Treatment,"* (Lexington, Mass.: Lexington Books, D.C. Heath, 1970).

Kennedy, Robert F., "Halfway Houses Pay Off," *Crime and Delinquency* (January 1964).

Kirby, Bernard C., "Crofton House: An Experiment with a County Halfway House," *Federal Probation* (March 1969).

Libis, Claude, "Helping an Adolescent Boy in His Movement from the Training School to the Community," *Journal of Social Work Process*, VII (1956).

McCartt, John M., and Thomas J. Mangogna, "Guidelines and Standards for Halfway Houses and Community Treatment Centers," *LEAA Document*, U.S. Department of Justice, Washington, D.C. (May 1973).

McNeil, Frances, "A Halfway House Program for Delinquents," *Crime and Delinquency* (October 1967).

Mandell, Wallace, "Making Corrections a Community Agency," *Crime and Delinquency*, Vol. 17, No. 3 (July 1971).

Meiners, Robert G., "A Halfway House for Parolees," *Federal Probation* (June 1965).

Moeller, H.B., "The Continuum of Corrections," *Annals of the American Academy of Political and Social Science* (January 1969).

Nelson, E.K., "Community-Based Correctional Treatment: Rationale and Problems," *Annals of the American Academy of Political and Social Science*, Vol. CCCLXXIV (November 1967).

Nice, Richard W., "Halfway House Aftercare for the Released Offender," *Crime and Delinquency* (January 1964).

Nishinaka, George M., "A Part-Way Home Program," *California Youth Authority Quarterly* (Fall 1966).

Ohio Adult Parole Authority, "Halfway House Specifications" (Columbus, Ohio, 1969).

O'Leary, Vincent, "Some Directions for Citizen Involvement in Corrections," *Annals of the American Academy of Political and Social Science* (January 1969).

Powers, Edwin, "Halfway Houses: An Historical Perspective," *American Journal of Corrections* (July-August 1959).

Presidio, "Ex-Convicts Halfway Home," Vol. 31 (1964).

Richmond, M.S., "The Practicalities of Community-Based Corrections," *American Journal of Corrections* (November-December, 1968).

Rieff, Robert, and Frank Riesman, "The Indigenous Nonprofessional—A Strategy of Change in Community Action and Mental Health Programs,"

Monograph #1, *Community Mental Health Journal*, Behavioral Publications, Inc. (Morningside Heights, N.Y., 1965).

Rubington, Earl, "Post Treatment Contacts and Length of Stay in a Halfway House; Notes on Consistency of Societal Reactions to Chronic Drunkenness Offenders," *Quarterly Journal of Studies on Alcohol*, 31(3): (1970).

Russo, Robert J., "Alternatives to Institutionalization: Halfway Houses," Proceedings: *Institute on Youth Correctional Program and Facilities* (Honolulu, 1966).

Scheier, Ivan, and Judith Lake Berry, "Guidelines and Standards for the Use of Volunteers in Correctional Programs," Contract #J-LEAA-003-71, LEAA, Department of Justice (Washington, D.C., 1972).

"The Frightening Step To Freedom For the Ex-Con," *Cincinnati Alumnus*, University of Cincinnati Press (October 1967).

Turner, Merfyn, "The Lessons of Norman House," *Annals of the American Academy of Political and Social Science* (January 1969).

United States Bureau of Prisons, *"Treating Youth Offenders in the Community: A Report on Four Years Experience with Pre-Release Guidance Center,"* (1966).

United States Bureau of Prisons, *"Residential Center: Corrections in the Community,"* Department of Justice, Washington, D.C.

United States Children's Bureau, *"Halfway House Programs for Delinquent Youth"* (1965).

Vasoli, Robert H., and Frank J. Fahey, "Halfway House for Reformatory Releasees," *Crime and Delinquency*, Vol. 16, No. 3 (July 1970).

Yablonsky, Lewis, *Synnanon*, Penguin Books, Inc. (1965).

Computer Search and Retrieval
Abstracts Cited

Cowden, J.E., and L. Monson, "Analysis of Some Relationships Between Personality Adjustment, Placement, and Post-Release Adjustment of Delinquent Boys," *Journal of Research in Crime and Delinquency*, VI (January 1969).

Deehy, P.T., "Halfway House in the Correctional Sequence—A Case Study of a Transitional Residence for Inmates of a State Reformatory," unpublished dissertation, University Microfilms, Ann Arbor, Michigan, 1969.

Gilliam, J.L., *Project First Chance—An Experimental and Demonstration Manpower Project—Final Report*, search and retrieval abstract, United States Department of Justice, South Carolina Department of Corrections, 1969.

Kirby, B.C., *Crofton House Final Report*, search and retrieval abstract, United States Department of Justice, San Diego State College, California, 1970.

Palmer, T.B., *Differential Placement of Delinquents in Group Homes—Final*

Report, search and retrieval abstract, United States Department of Justice, California Youth Authority, 1972.

Rothman, Fred B., "House for Ex-Borstal Girls—An Exploratory Project," *British Journal of Criminology*, XII (October 1972).

Wilgosh, L., "Study of Group Home Placements as a Possible Correction of Delinquent Behavior," *Canadian Journal of Criminology and Corrections*, XV (January 1973).

11

The How and Why of Partners

Robert Moffitt[a]

Overview

Started in 1968 by eleven seminary students who were challenged by a Denver businessman to make themselves useful in the community, Partners has grown to become a nationally recognized youthful offender program. Over the past six years, Partners has attracted more than two thousand volunteers. These volunteers are supported by a full-time staff of twenty-five, in anticipation of Partners' plan to increase its number of active volunteers to six hundred by January 1975. Established as an arm of Young Life, a National Christian youth organization, Partners achieved independent status in January 1972 and took a nonsectarian stance twelve months later.

Originally designed to be a service agency to the Denver Juvenile Court, Partners recently received a grant from the federal government to work with youngsters referred directly from the Denver Police Department. Partners will continue to work with the court, but in addition receives referrals of youngsters who have been arrested, but not yet sent to juvenile court.

Primarily through the local media and by word of mouth, Partners seeks to attract concerned and capable citizens as volunteers. After successfully completing an intensive nine-hour training program, prospective volunteers are matched on a one-to-one basis with ten-to-eighteen-year-old juvenile-court- or police-referred youngsters. Once matched, the adult volunteer becomes a "Senior" Partner; the youngster a "Junior" Partner. Both Partners enter the program voluntarily and agree to spend a minimum of three hours a week with each other for one year.

While encouraging the partners to develop the types of relationships they find most comfortable, Partners has developed a number of objectives that are presented to the volunteers at training:

To develop a close relationship between partners, the main function of such a relationship being the development of love, mutual trust, honesty, open communication, and sharing of values.

To increase the conditions in which an improved sense of self or self-concept is possible for the Junior Partner.

aPartners, Inc., Denver, Colorado, reprinted by permission. Robert Moffitt is the Director of Partners, a former Peace Corps member who served in the Corps in Africa.

To increase the Junior Partner's sense of self-worth and effectiveness, and his general state of happiness.

To seek to develop a level of moral judgment for Junior Partners that takes into account the effects of one's decisions and actions for other people as well as for oneself.

To develop an awareness for Junior Partners of the way in which social values and institutions affect one's life and to learn more effective and appropriate ways of relating to these, whether this be conformity or nonconformity.

To facilitate a reduction in delinquent behavior on the part of the youth that is clearly harmful to the youth and to society.

To develop an increased awareness among Senior Partners of the problems within the area of juvenile delinquency in this society, and also to develop a willingness and commitment that leads to action among volunteers to continue to make a contribution to the solution of these problems.

The bi-weekly telephone contacts Partners counselors have with the Senior Partners reveal almost as many different types of partnerships as there are people in the program. A well-developed support system helps to meet the unique needs of these different relationships. For those who wish to participate in group activities, Partners sponsors water skiing, river rafting trips, camping, and fishing in the summer; snow skiing and snow tubing in the winter. Various field trips, minibike riding, hiking, and climbing are among Partners's fall and spring activities. In addition to group activities, Partners also is able to obtain free tickets from several of the local sports teams and movie theaters. A wide variety of local business and individuals have come to Partners's aid over the years, offering services ranging from free plane rides over Denver to free use of Celebrity Sports Center and the YMCA.

In summary, the Partners philosophy stresses the conviction that "in-trouble" youth deserve, but are often denied, the right to understand and successfully operate within the systems of mainstream society. Partners's answer to this dilemma is to give community volunteers the support they need to share their knowledge and coping styles as a model for their Junior Partner. In the process a beautiful by-product is born: Two human beings develop a warm friendship and an appreciation for one another's backgrounds that spreads. To both families. To both circles of friends. To both communities.

For a closer and much more detailed look at the Partners program, we will take a tour through the various "departments" of the Partners operation: recruitment, training, screening, contracts, interviews, counseling, activities, staffing, evaluation, and funding.

Recruitment

The Buck Begins Here

Adapting Harry Truman's famous phrase about the presidency—"The buck stops here"—one has an apt description of the Partners's recruitment campaign—"The buck begins here." Recruitment is the first step in a process that culminates in the building of a relationship between an alienated youth and a caring and capable adult.

Each month, Partners opens its doors to as many as sixty new youngsters. For each of these youngsters to have a Partner, nearly three hundred potential volunteers must inquire about the program, as only a small percentage of those who request information from Partners actually become Senior Partners. To inform the public about the program, Partners makes extensive use of the mass media, and at the same time is constantly searching for new and creative means of attracting potential volunteers.

If you happen to be driving south on Colfax near Colorado Boulevard you will probably see a billboard that tells the reader how he can get involved with one of Denver's troubled youngsters. This is one of twenty-five spaces that has been donated to Partners by Eller Outdoor Advertising. You may be aboard a Denver Metro Transit bus or following a Yellow Cab, and notice the same message—"Help a Kid. Call Partners, 893-1400."

One of the best ways to get word out about Partners is by distributing literature about the program. Last spring, the Colorado National Guard gave out close to 15,000 brochures at homes and shopping centers throughout the Denver area. Since that time, a variety of groups has undertaken similar projects.

Several entertainers, including Academy Award winner Patty Duke, actor John Astin, and recording artist O.C. Smith, have freely given of their time to do television commercials for Partners.

A Denver resident can find himself eating lunch from a Partners placemat at a favorite restaurant, or opening his bank statement to find another reminder that there is a kid in Denver who needs him.

Active volunteers are the best advertisers, recruiters, and public relations representatives that Partner has. People talking to people does more than any widespread campaign ever could do. If each volunteer were to recruit two more volunteers, its needs would be met for a long time to come—not only its needs, but more important, the needs of the thousands of youngsters who come before the court each year.

Training

Most volunteer efforts in the social services face a continual problem of credibility for the task at hand. This is, of course, largely due to the lack of sanctions available to the sponsoring agencies. Perhaps the most effective tool in overcoming this inherent difficulty is a training program. Training at Partners serves as the primary means of achieving "legitimacy" for the volunteers when they begin their assignments.

Although this objective may seem superficial, its importance to the status of the organization and to the volunteers must be appreciated. However, it is not enough just to conduct training sessions without regard to their substance and relevance. Every attempt must be made to continually upgrade and update the training program.

The operational objectives of our preservice training are limited. (It is probably not reasonable to expect volunteers to attend more than three or four nights of sessions, and in most cases training must be conducted at night.) Partners conducts one training program per month, which fifty to one hundred volunteers attend.

The program does not attempt to make people experts in juvenile corrections. At best, training can offer the proper perceptual framework for the volunteer and provide some insight into the inevitable problems in the future relationship. *Experience has illustrated that the real nitty-gritty training can only come from the blunders and fumbles involved with actually performing the task.* Thus, Partners relies on in-service training to focus on specific problems.

The Partners Training Program attempts to realize three substantive objectives in the course of the curriculum:

1. A thorough explanation of the program. It is mandatory that the volunteers fully understand the philosophy, goals, requirements, and operation of the project. We usually devote most of the first night of training to this objective. This session can be more than a series of speakers—a movie or slide show can give an overview of the project, and group discussions can take place concerning the philosophy and goals of the program. This session is presented by the director and the staff of Partners.

2. A complete description of the court process. It is imperative that the participants have a basic knowledge of the usually complex structure and process of the court system with which kids in trouble with the law must cope. This presentation is given by a probation officer of the Denver Juvenile Court. This official also performs the extremely important function of making the volunteers feel welcome in their new roles as part of the criminal-justice system. (This function is also served by a brief welcome speech from the director of Juvenile Court Services.) The trainees hear that they are not a threat to the court system, but rather an asset. Also, the trainees attend court hearings and visit detention facilities wherever possible.

3. Exposure and possible approaches to situations in the field. Of course, it is impossible to anticipate the infinite and varied number of situations that will confront the volunteers. However, experience indicates that it is important for the trainees to at least learn something of counseling techniques and gain an appreciation for the conditions that spawn crime. Because of the time limitation, the staff must decide what is most crucial for the participants to know. This means establishing a system of priorities. Traditionally we have provided lecture-discussions on counseling, adolescent psychology, and the drug scene. Because of the incredible myths and misinformation concerning drugs today, we feel it is wise to include a lecture from an authoritative person who really knows drugs, followed by a discussion. There is always a danger of relying too much on

academicians. We've been utilizing ex-convicts, young men from the streets, and other people who have had the experience. Employing outsiders (nonstaff) helps the project's credibility, and can broaden the base of support for the program. It seems best to avoid lectures whenever possible; an effective workshop almost always involves the group in the learning process. Training techniques like role playing, sociodrama, communication games, and group discussions are used to achieve this third goal.

Our role plays are about situations that the Partners staff feels certain the Senior Partners will most probably encounter in the field. These include a kid missing an appointment, an extremely shy or silent Junior Partner, a kid who is constantly missing school, or a runaway case. We have the staff or actual Junior Partners play the Junior Partners and the trainees play the Senior Partners, the role they will soon be playing in real life. After each role play, lasting five to ten minutes, we stop for discussion. We may allow two or three people to try the same role play. We attempt to avoid too much criticism of the trainees, and emphasize the important points the role play and discussion produced. (We have utilized this method with much success.)

Good documentaries and movies concerning juvenile crime are available to court programs (e.g., "This Child Rated X"). If at all possible, it is desirable to conduct some field training, which seems to appeal more to the trainees than "classroom" material, using kids to teach the participant (one-to-one) about their community and activities.

The trainees are provided with notebooks that serve as training textbooks. In the notebook is information about the program and the court, and also forms the volunteers will be using during their assignment as Senior Partners. The notebook also serves as a future resource book. The staff must decide what literature they consider most important for the group to read—it is possible to get so much in the notebook that it won't be read.

It is doubtful that a training program can be evaluated in and of itself. The only test of the training is in its relevance and meaning to the volunteer. The staff at Partners gives considerable attention to the perceptions and reflections of the volunteers who have been through training and worked in the field. It also consistently seeks the opinions of the kids with whom the project works.

The most effective training is in-service training, because it deals with concrete, real problems. Groups of volunteers come together to share their varied experiences and different techniques. If a volunteer is having a difficult time with his kid, he can talk to the group about it and get suggestions or alternative approaches. These in-service sessions, on occasion, also utilize speakers, films, etc.

We require the Senior Partners to come to at least four in-service training sessions. The unit counselor conducts these meetings and serves as a resource person. This training occurs every other week with groups of about twelve volunteers. The required sessions are directed to the new Senior Partners at the early stages of their assignment. We believe it is at this time that the volunteer needs the most feedback, criticism, and support.

Though we do not lay pedantic stress on philosophy, we believe that the philosophical base from which the program administration operates is important. Consequently, we share our philosophy with the new trainees as follows:

The formula—One-to-one relationship + unique experiences + shared activity + weekly contacts X unconditional warmth = new habits.

The *one-to-one relationship* is the basis for approach to rehabilitation. The volunteer is the model against which the Junior Partner compares his own life-coping patterns. The *unique experiences* are provided by the program in order to give the volunteer a chance to win the right to be a model. Many volunteer/court-child units are composed of children who would not normally accept a one-to-one relationship without some outside reason. Partners has discovered that court-referred children will almost always accept an invitation to participate in exciting activities. Consequently it has developed the unique experience and exclusive-club idea in order to draw court-referred youths in a position where they will want to participate in the program. The *shared activities* are the tools the volunteer uses to develop a relationship. Neither the volunteer nor the youth is allowed to participate in Partners activities alone. They must be together to take advantage of any Partners activity. These shared activities give the Junior Partner a chance to observe the volunteer in a number of stress situations. The objective here is that the youngster will be able to compare his life style with that of the volunteer as he sees the volunteer in real life.

Weekly contacts are required so that a consistent vehicle for interaction between volunteer and child is established. Many volunteers now actually make more than one contact a week. If volunteers are not in the community, they will still be required to make contacts by telephone or letter.

Volunteers are encouraged to give *unconditional warmth* to the child; they are told that this does not necessarily mean they are to accept the child's behavior, but that they are to accept the child for who he is. The Partners staff feels this is one of the key factors in developing a positive relationship with a probationer.

The Partners staff believes that the above conditions will generate *new habits* in the referred child as long as the volunteer, in seeking to establish himself as a model, shares his life for what it is without either hiding his value system or attempting coercively to force his value system on the child.

The establishment of new habits, communication, and a new friendship with a volunteer is only the *beginning of rehabilitation.* Volunteers are encouraged to continue their relationships with the child beyond the one-year contract, either within the Partners structure or on an informal basis. More than half of the volunteers in the program who have completed their contract have continued their relationship with the Junior Partner in order to reaffirm and strengthen the initial Partners relationship step and to move toward meaningful rehabilitation.

Screening

Screening is a must for any volunteer program, and Partners attempts to make every potential volunteer fully realize the responsibility of the Senior Partner role. In this way we strive to achieve self-deselection from the program. We feel that this method is preferable to an arbitrary set of standards for entrance into Partners. However, we do demand that several requirements be met before one can become a Senior Partner. This process in itself is a strong deterrent against any "kooks" who have applied to the program. (The "kook" problem is generally overemphasized for they're almost always easy to identify. Then again, they don't often apply.) The more difficult problem is to screen out those who are well-meaning and really want to be involved, but have overestimated their ability to fulfill the program's commitment in terms of time and energy. These people, it is to be hoped, will deselect themselves. Experience has shown us that this process can be achieved if we will simply "tell it like it is." For example, the introductory brochure or letter should spell out the commitment. Training should, as much as possible, let the potential volunteer know how difficult, as well as how rewarding, the experience can be. Volunteer trainees should be encouraged to step out if they don't feel they can meet the responsibilities of the assignment. On the other hand, we are careful not to scare away a potentially effective volunteer who might be overapprehensive—we avoid the "war stories." Also training time should be a test of dependability (punctuality at sessions and interviews, meeting requirements, etc.) These indicators generally tell as much about the reliability of the volunteer as background reference material. By the time the volunteer gets to the stage where he is being considered for a match with a client, you should be able to at least be confident of his sincere desire to give it a good try.

In short, volunteer self-screening should essentially be the only screening until the interview preceding the match with the client. After the self-screening process is complete, a program should have to formally deselect very few applicants.

Volunteer Contract and
Trial Relationship

It is obviously important for a court volunteer program to stress the significance of the volunteer's commitment to a troubled youth. However, we also must emphasize the commitment that the Junior Partner must share. A relationship is a two-way street, and makes demands on both Partners. Of course, the volunteer will inevitably carry the major burden of responsibility for the relationship, especially in the intial stages of the relationship. To accomplish these two objectives we use a contract in which all the parties commit themselves to the support of the relationship,—the Junior and Senior Partners, the parents of the Junior Partner, and the Partners counselor who is responsible for supervising the specific Junior and Senior Partner unit.

This contract is not signed until the new Junior and Senior Partners have successfully completed a six-week trial relationship in which both are given a chance to test the partnership.

Interviews

Interviews are crucial to the development of a Partnership. It is mandatory that the same counselor interview both the volunteer and the client. The interview is probably the most effective tool in facilitating a successful match. Interviews are conducted by Partners staff members called Unit Counselors. The Unit Counselor who interviews the kids and matches them with volunteers then assumes this Partners "unit" on his caseload.

The Junior Partner or Youth
Client Interview

Interviews with the youth generally take longer than those with the volunteer. The youth's only knowledge of the program may have come from a brief introduction during a police or court interview. The volunteer, on the other hand, will have spent up to twelve hours in training before his interview. In addition, the youth's maturity level generally dictates a more thorough explanation and preparation of and for the future relationship.

Interviews with the youth are best held in his home. First, the home is the youth's own territory and the place where he probably feels most comfortable. Second, parents and siblings generally have very limited or no knowledge of the program and how it works. They usually want to sit in on the interview, and that is good because their new acquaintance with the program will often mean their support. Third, since parental permission is necessary for participation in the program, it is logistically easier to get that permission if the interviewer goes to the home than if the parent and client are asked to come to the Partners office.

The interview of the youth client consists of three parts:

1. Sell the program. In our approach to the youth, we bill Partners as "An exclusive club for kids who want to make Denver a better place to live." Membership benefits include a lot of great activities plus a big brother or big sister type of person, called a Senior Partner, who will participate in these activities with the client at least once a week for a year. Members are admitted by invitation only. Many more kids want to get into the program than there are places for them. Therefore, acceptance is a privilege. Before one can apply for

membership he must: (1) want to be in the program; (2) be willing to meet with his Partner once a week for at least a year; and (3) be willing to try to be a good citizen of Denver. Parental permission is also required. After the program and application requirements are explained, the youth is asked if he wants to participate. If, on the basis of the interview, the client doesn't want to be a member of Partners, we will not accept or push him into the program. If the youth is interested, he is assisted at this point in filling out the Junior Partner Application.

2. Obtain parental permission. The role of the volunteer is explained. He is not a substitute parent, but a stable community person who wants to be a friend to the youth and support to the parent(s) in building stronger home relationships. It is also explained that since there are a limited number of memberships available, Partners must be sure that the parent or parents want their child to be in Partners and that they are willing to help the child meet the requirements of membership. If the parent agrees, he signs his statement of agreement on the back of the youth's application.

3. Obtain firsthand information regarding the youth's background and interests. Background information may come from the referral agency. Even when it does, there are often gaps. These can be filled in during this interview. It is extremely important at this point for the interviewer to assess the youth's family, likes, dislikes, interests, and personality with the view of matching him with a volunteer who will be able to build a relationship with a minimum amount of frustration.

After these three steps, the interviewer takes a picture of the client to attach to the file to ease reference when making the match. Before leaving the interviewer lets the client and parent know about how long it will be before the match and introduction of the client to his Senior Partner will be.

The Senior Partner or Adult
Client Interview

The interview of the Senior Partner is conducted after training by a Unit Counselor. It is a basic assumption of Partners that after a volunteer reaches this stage he wants at least to try to be a good volunteer, and that if he would not be able to do a good job, he will have already screened himself out of the program—perhaps by not showing up for the interview. One final indicator of volunteer sincerity is the book report (covering at least five hundred pages of material and at least five pages long), which he brings with him to the interview. If the volunteer does not bring in the book report, he will be interviewed but not matched until it is in. Occasionally, however, a volunteer who will not make a good Senior Partner does make it to the interview with his book report. It is then the counselor's difficult duty to tell him so and tell him why. This interview is the last point at which a volunteer would be potentially screened out before assignment to a Junior Partner.

However, the central purpose of the volunteer interview is not screening. It is simply to gain an understanding of the volunteer's preferences and interests. The forms that follow illustrate the rather uncomplicated method that Partners utilizes in the interview process. It is really the counselor's information and feelings that eventually determine the pairing of the partners. One should examine closely the questions on the volunteer interview form, for they are the fundamental facts that dictate the counselor's decision. The personality charts are quite subjective, but helpful for a reference point. A third objective of the interview is to provide the volunteer with the opportunity to become acquainted with the counselor. The counselor must attempt to establish rapport with the people with whom he will relate during the course of their partnership. This rapport should be developed and sustained throughout the course of the assignment.

Counseling

If there is a "most important job" in our organization, it is that of the Unit Counselor. Our counselors are closer to the partners and the pulse of the program than any other members of our staff. The counselors maintain separate caseloads, and the Senior and Junior Partners are immediately responsible to them. The entire operation of the project is greatly simplified both in personal and records terms by this division of the workload. The Unit Counselor is responsible for assisting in preservice training, interviewing the Senior and Junior Partners, matching and introducing the volunteers and the kids, conducting the in-service training sessions, securing the weekly reports, and counseling the partners. The counselors are also responsible for filing both a weekly production report and a monthly report which reflects significant statistics about their caseloads.

We have learned that the requirement of a weekly report can have considerable impact on the partnership. The Senior Partner is consistently reminded of his commitment to the youngster by the knowledge that he must submit a weekly report. This does not mean that we want people to stay together as a matter of duty; rather, it is a matter of accountability. The weekly report keeps the counselor continually informed about the relationship, and it provides a guarantee against a partnership "getting lost."

The Unit Counselor rarely talks with a Junior Partner without the presence or knowledge of his Senior Partner. The guiding principle is to do all that is possible to bolster the partnership through helping the Senior Partner. We do not want to interfere or compete with the volunteer. Sometimes both parties want to visit with the counselor, and this is done most willingly. The more common case is a

Senior Partner wanting some advice or a good ear, either on the telephone or face to face. The counselor slowly develops relationships with the people on his caseload through training, interviews, the introduction, in-service training, and Partners activities to facilitate these counseling sessions.

The questions and concerns of the Senior Partner run the gamut from trivia to tragedy, and the counselor must respond accordingly. Obviously some people require much more attention and feedback than others, and the counselor must pace himself to these varying needs. We urge people to call their counselors even if they feel their problems are trivial. We much prefer an overload of calls to an undetected crisis. Because we believe the counselors should be available beyond the nine-to-five working day, their schedules are quite flexible. They maintain office hours when one can be certain of contacting them, but the bulk of their work is done on the weekends and in the evenings and away from the office. We believe the counselor's role in working with the volunteers is to assist in problem-solving. Many people want the counselor to make decisions for them; this must be avoided. We have learned that the volunteers will be as responsible to the counselor as he is responsive to them. The counselor should continually demonstrate his concern for the volunteers through phone calls, postcards, or personal visits. If the counselor really enjoys his work, he will be involved in the caseload far beyond the dictates of the job description.

In Partners, we do not espouse a particular theory of counseling with which we attempt to inculcate our staff or volunteers. Rather the primary job of the counselor, aside from the mechanics of interviews, matching, and reports, is to act as a catalyst for the developing relationship between the Junior and Senior Partner. He encourages and insists that the Senior Partners do as much as possible on their own. After we have set limits in training and accepted a volunteer, we let the volunteer write and carry out his own program rehabilitative theory and practice.

The counselor steps into the relationship directly only as a last resort. If a counselor allows himself to assume tasks that should be handled by the Senior or Junior Partner, he cuts down on the time and energy he could be spending helping others on his caseload. Said another way, a counselor can effectively work directly with only two to three dozen Junior Partners. If he acts as a catalyst and lets the volunteers do the direct work, he can multiply his effectiveness many times. The reason we stress this concept is that a good counselor loves kids and has many temptations to become directly involved when he knows that he can "do it better" than the volunteer.

Activities

Partners operates on the thesis that two people who share in activities or common experiences build a foundation through those activities on which to build a relationship. We have found that it helps if these experiences are unusual; if they stand out in the youth's memory and are positive in nature, they generally guarantee success. Partners therefore places a lot of effort in supplying unused activities such as airplane rides, river rafting, pack trips, snow and water skiing, rappelling, fishing, snow tubing, etc.

Our program also depends heavily upon community support for activities. These are generally less unusual but more readily available community-operated activities, such as ice skating, swimming, bowling, horseback riding and billiards.

One reason Partners uses activities so extensively is that the age group with which we work is primarily young adolescence. This group seems to respond better to activities than counseling, job, or educational experiences per se. This is not to discount the usefulness of counseling, job, or educational involvement as important and necessary ingredients to a helping relationship. Rather, they are areas to move into after a relationship is established.

We therefore find activities the best initial tool for relationship development for this particular age group. We also feel that activities broaden the Junior Partners' frame of reference by giving them exposure to new experiences—new constructive ways to use time.

Pictures

As Partners, we use photographs to reinforce the ground gained during the activities which our program sponsors. The time that a volunteer spends with his Junior Partner is short when compared to the total hours of the entire week. We therefore operate on the theory that the more significant and important the Junior Partner finds the short time he spends with his Senior Partner, the more of an impact it will have in the development of the relationship between them. The type of activities that we sponsor as a program, like river rafting and plane rides are designed to be "highly significant" to the Junior Partner. To reinforce the good time that the Junior Partner had with his Senior Partner, we take pictures of each Junior-Senior partner pair on all of our sponsored trips. (We would do this for every contact if it were possible.)

It takes about two weeks before we can process and get the pictures to the individual partners. Both the Senior and Junior Partners get one or two pictures of themselves on the trip. The pictures always are of the Junior and Senior Partner doing something *together.* After a period of time, each of the partners begins to collect a mini-album of great memories. It is hard to find a better or more economic reinforcement tool than pictures.

Soliciting Community Facilities

We have had a lot of experience at developing our own activities that are sophisticated and tailored exclusively for volunteers and kids. Our camping and river-rafting programs are examples. Though these activities are very helpful, they demand a great deal of energy and money. For starting programs we suggest taking advantage of the recreational opportunities already available. Many communities have quite a varied selection of entertainment and recreational facilities—for hire. However, a good salesmanship and community spirit, has enabled Partners to extensively expand its activity program at little or no cost to our Junior and Senior Partners. At first, profit-oriented recreational centers were reluctant to open their doors to Partners units on a no-charge basis. However, we seldom accepted No for an answer, by always trying to leave the door open for another visit. One by one reluctantly gave in; and some facilities were readily opened to us on the basis of a phone call. Yearly Partners has approximately one-half million dollars' worth of recreational opportunities available to our Junior and Senior Partners. We are not able to take advantage of anywhere near all the opportunities open to us.

Logistically, arrangements with cooperating centers work as follows: Junior and Senior Partners are able to go to Celebrity Sports Center where they can swim, bowl, or play the slot cars. They can go only during the times when the Center is usually not booked full. These times are arranged with Partners on a seasonal basis. The Partners are admitted on the basis of their membership cards, but they must be together. In other words, neither the Junior or Senior Partner can use his card to get into the facility alone. Some recreational facilities that are not able to give us free entrance charge whatever they need to cover their costs. These charges are far below the regular entrance fees.

We have found that a straightforward method of presenting our program and our needs is best. It is important to be aware of the value of the time of the man you are approaching. Be direct, to the point, and friendly. The use of words like "court-related" or "disadvantaged" more often than not open doors that might otherwise stay closed. It is important to leave appropriate materials of the program. These materials should visually reinforce what has been said in narrative and photographs. Make sure you put together a small packet of information on your program to leave with the person to whom you speak. This packet could include a brochure, a poster, a recent newspaper article on your program, and a letter of endorsement from your juvenile court judge.

Remember to make the individual or organization to which you make your request feel he or it is getting something in return, i.e., involvement in something very important—helping kids.

Make sure you talk about specific arrangements. For example, talk about the schedule for using the facilities and the use of membership cards. Will there be any charges, and if so, who will pay them? Make it clear that you are asking for very limited privileges under controlled situations. There would be one volunteer to supervise each youth. In other words, the facility will not be overrun with uncontrolled delinquent kids. Also, make sure to mention the other facilities that have agreed to or are cooperating with you.

Funding

Whole books are written on budget planning, on soliciting community support, and on how to approach foundations, government granting sources, and corporations for support. Partners, like many of its sister agencies, has had difficulty obtaining support. So we don't pretend to be experts. What we share here are some basic guidelines which have been helpful to us.

Philosophy

One of the first steps in obtaining fiscal help is to decide from where and in what combinations you ultimately want your support to come—publicly, privately, or a combination of both. There are advantages and disadvantages to each. Public funding is usually easier to obtain but almost requires the creation of special bureaucracy in your program to administer it.

Government sources differ in the amount of red tape required. Of the three government agencies we have worked with, LEAA has been the best, and HUD funds administered by city government the worst. Also with public funding accountability is often extremely cumbersome, requiring detailed records and reports that we feel are filed and seldom read.

Private funding has been more difficult to obtain at Partners, but it has been much cleaner. It comes in one check per year. There are no vouchers. Reporting is done on your own format rather than the complicated quadruplicate forms of a government bureaucracy. Accountability to private funding sources must be good if funding is to continue, but it can be in a realistic, concise style in *your* format. Most important, you can be sure that the reader cares more about how his money is affecting kids than whether a certain requisition is properly filled out, or too much has been spent for a box of pencils. Tragically, such accounting concerns seem to be more important than kids with government funding sources.

Making this decision allows you to begin to plan where you want to put your solicitation efforts. It does not, however, mean that your decision is immediately or ultimately possible. In our program, we have decided that we would ultimately like to have public and private funding on about a 25 to 75 percent ratio. At present that ratio is reversed, because we needed and were able to obtain public funding for rapid growth. However, we were able to rely, much more, on private funding for the 1973 and 1974 court-related program. We are planning a further expansion into a new area, Police Diversion, for which we applied for government help. In other words, we have a long-range plan toward which we are constantly working, but in the meantime we are taking advantage of any funding resources available to maintain and expand the program.

Soliciting Community In-Kind Support

A good salesman once said that if you knock on twenty doors, one will open. That statement has two important points. First, if you want something you will get it if you work hard enough. Second, realize that there are going to be refusals. Anticipate them and don't be disappointed when they come.

Our record at Partners has been much better than 20 to 1—it has been more like 3 or 2 to 1. There is almost no end to what the community will provide for your program if it is approached properly. We have received use of gasoline credit cards, vehicles, office and audiovisual equipment, advertising, printing, and mailing services, pilot and plane services, recreational facilities, medical services, clothing, furniture, and a number of other free in-kind donations. Some have come without our asking. Most of these donations came because we let the community know that we had needs that required the above. It took six tries to get into the YMCA on a free-membership basis, but it finally did open its facilities to our kids and volunteers.

When soliciting services or in-kind goods there are a few important things to remember.

1. If you have a heavy need for one kind of service, such as printing, spread it around. Don't ask one printer to do it all.

2. Treat your in-kind donors with the same respect and importance as a cash donor. If the in-kind donor didn't provide his services or goods, you would have to pay cash for it.

3. Remind the donor that he is part of an army of people who are making similar contributions.

4. Ask a potential donor to try this on a temporary basis, say for three months, and then evaluate whether it is something he can handle on a longer basis. Once a donor gets started he will usually become happily involved. In other words, stress that you are "not asking for much" or "asking for forever."

Earning Moral Support from the Agency

"The Agency" is the organizations or institutions with which your program works or provides services. For Partners, the most important agency is the juvenile court, but it also includes welfare, the police department, and the schools. Because Partners is a private nongovernment-allied program and because it has a Christian orientation, acceptance was not easy to come by and had to be earned.

A few rules of thumb we have discovered that might be helpful in earning acceptance for your program follow.

1. Don't assume that you have the right "to be there." Earn it.

2. Involve relevant people in the initial and further developmental planning stages of your program.

3. Invite agency personnel to serve on your advisory board. Our presiding judge is president of our board of directors.

4. Find out what some of the needs are of the "hard to convince" people and, if you can, try to meet them. We have taken probation officers and some of the kids with whom they wanted to develop better relationships on water-skiing and camping trips at our expense.

5. Be accountable to the agencies. We regularly report back to the agency, sometimes sending copies of the volunteer weekly reports.

6. If you say you will do something, do it whether or not the agency holds up its end of the bargain.

7. Be patient!

Keeping Your Supporters Happy

Assuming that your program is going well, keeping your supporters happy means being accountable to them. There are several ways to do this. One is through meeting them personally for lunch or coffee and bringing them up to date on recent program developments. This is possible only with a limited number of people. So if your base of donors gets large, you will have to be selective. But do it at least once every three or four months for the larger donors.

The regular way we keep our supporters informed is with the VIP notebook. This publication takes a lot of effort to put together and keep up to date, but it is worth it. You will need to put together regular comprehensive reports for your larger donors, and it is not that much more work to put them together for the smaller but usually larger group of donors. VIP membership is open to all who give over $100 per year.

Basically, keeping your supporters happy means:

1. Regularly let them know you appreciate them.

2. Do a good job with their investment.

3. Keep them informed.

Preparing Your Budget

Unless you are an expert you will probably not be able to anticipate or project all the hidden costs of the program, particularly when the project is new and growing. We have consistently underprojected for the next year's budget, from 20 to 40 percent. It is only recently that we have stabilized the current court-related program (this does not count our planned police diversion project) to the point where we feel we know what it will cost us to run the program next year. This doesn't mean that you shouldn't plan. If you don't, you invite disaster!

Here is a simple outline for budget preparation.

1. Study as many similar program budgets as possible.

2. Look at your resources.

3. Decide how much you want to accomplish during the next year and have someone who knows help you project what it will cost to do what you want.

4. Match, as realistically as possible, your plans to your estimated resources.

5. Finally, add at least 20 percent of your total to the budget for unplanned contingencies, but if your program is growing healthily don't be surprised toward the middle of the year if you have to revise your budget.

Preparing Government Grant Requests

Every government grant source has a complete set of instructions for preparing requests. However, two things they usually don't emphasize enough are:

1. Answer every question in the narrative that is asked, and do it in the outline form suggested. When you do so, you will be repetitive. That is OK. Do it and do it again. It will pay off.

2. Add as much supportive material as you can. Letters of recommendation. Your training manual. Your brochures, etc. These will help the government agency know that you are not a fly-by-night or flash-in-the-pan organization. In our government grant proposals we use our entire *Administrative Seminar Manual* as one of the appendices. It takes a lot of work to be so thorough, but it has paid handsomely.

Part III: Conclusions

12 A Nation Without Prisons: Dream or Reality?

Calvert R. Dodge

Few persons familiar with America's prison system would argue that the system is operating efficiently at present. Evidence to the contrary abounds—rates of recidivism are overwhelmingly high; inmate behavior problems seem to have multiplied; the incidence of riots and disorders is alarming; the suicide rate among prisoners is far greater than that of the general population; and the courts are jammed with writs and lawsuits filed by or on the behalf of prisoners. Historically, such grave problems have been forces for change; and so it seems inevitable that the nation's system of incarceration will change.

Perhaps these changes will help to create a more viable, more adaptable, more mature corrections system in America. Experience tells us, however, that institutions change only slowly. Throughout our history, the prison system has been continually changing, but changing cautiously, ponderously. And after centuries of such gradual change, we have a system which, in the judgment of many, has utterly failed. As evidence of that failure mounts, perhaps it is time that we take a long, hard look at our nation's system of prisons and decide how best to cope with the future.

Perhaps a very drastic and dramatic change is in order—the elimination of prisons in America.

It would be foolish to pretend that such a suggestion doesn't give rise to great insecurity. None of us knows what would happen in an America without prisons. But those who provide leadership for the social systems of man are faced with momentous decisions and challenges, and it would be foolish for them to allow undue caution and respect for tradition to limit the scope of their search for answers. Especially when the current system is so manifestly defective.

This book discusses only a sample of alternatives, some more radical than others. However, they all seem to relate to the ultimate question: Should prisons be abolished in America?

Our most immediate choice is clear. We can take advantage of the ideas postulated herein, and thus perhaps anticipate some of the needs and problems of the future (and ameliorate our current problems); or we can merely sit tight until those problems force us to make immediate, instinctive decisions. The latter has always been a losing game.

In this chapter we shall discuss some aspects of the current penal system in America, some alternatives for changing that system, and the concept of reformation. We will also discuss whether or not prisons ought to be eliminated.

233

No matter how weighty the evidence to the contrary, members of the general public seem convinced that prison staffs do make an effort to rehabilitate prisoners. In actual practice, prisons do little except punish those who have been found guilty of breaking the law. As they are managed today, prisons almost certainly do more harm than good. Most convicts leave prison far worse off than they entered them. The system neither corrects, retrains, nor rehabilitates criminals in any meaningful way. Recently several authorities have suggested there is a direct link between our prison system and the rising national crime rate.[1] Our prisons serve as sophisticated training centers for the criminals among us.

Most prison superintendents will acknowledge that their primary functions are not to correct and rehabilitate but to punish and confine. Their job, as they see it, is to keep large numbers of convicts securely penned up until the parole board allows some of them a restricted freedom. The final report of the forty-second American Assembly, consisting of seventy Americans from twenty states and the District of Columbia—leaders in all walks of life—underlines this dismal judgment of prisons in America today.[2] The report, like numerous others, suggests that it is urgent that we solve the "prison problem," and that we can no longer afford delay in dealing with the chaos of our correctional system. These reports agree that criminal sanctions have lost impact because the apprehension of lawbreakers is not certain; trials and dispositions are absurdly delayed; and sentences are often meted out in such a way as to make logic seem uninvolved. Cynicism and public mistrust permeate the criminal-justice system today.

The American prison system is actually composed of 53 different subsystems. Apart from the nationwide complex of federal institutions, there are systems in the 50 states, Puerto Rico, and the District of Columbia. Other elements of the total justice system are similarly fragmented. Execution of the laws is not at all standardized. Differences between jurisdictions are so extreme that they often seem ludicrous. From time of arrest to incarceration, the justice system sometimes seems a comedy of errors protected by a judicial system that is itself in need of total overhauling. A judge in New Orleans sentences a person caught with a matchbox full of marijuana to fifty years in prison; in the same year in Louisville, fourteen persons in possession of varying amounts of marijuana are taken to the station, relieved of the weed, and sent home without so much as a record of arrest. A prison in Arizona only recently abolished cat-o'-nine-tail whippings. Chain-gang "rehabilitation" still goes on in this country.

And most so-called changes in the prison system are not changes of substance, but of method. High walls have merely been replaced by more efficient means of restraint, like closed circuit television and behavior-altering drugs.

Our judiciary have virtually no guidelines concerning the purpose of confinement or criteria for sentencing. In classical punishment-oriented penology, each crime carried its own specific punishment; such is not the case in America.

Instead of specific standards, judges have had slogans: "gravity of deed," "protection of society," "sound exercise of judicial discretion," etc.

Professor Gerhard O.W. Mueller, Director of the Criminal Law Education and Research Center, New York University, made a study of retribution in foreign and domestic courts and found that American statutory sentences are generally twice or three times as long as those of other nations, even authoritarian states.[3]

Many of our current legal alternatives may be worse than imprisonment. A six-year, limited-detention program for treatment of a petty thief (as opposed to a maximum prison sentence of one year) is totally at odds with traditional considerations of retributive justice, according to Mueller.[4] He states:

It is my contention that we have reached the point at which we can speak of an old and a new American penology. The old penology, centering around the hanging tree, the gallows and the maximum security prison, is a matter of the past. A new penology has come and it is visible everywhere—in a physical sense, i.e. buildings and grounds; in a statistical sense; in a legal sense; and in terms of attitudes and philosophies. Whether even the new penology is good enough for America today remains to be examined.[5]

Mueller's ten recommendations for changes in correctional practice deserve consideration.[6] The first is that the constitutionality of "caging" human beings be attacked.

For all practical purposes, imprisonment means the caging of human beings either singly or in pairs or groups. Half a century ago, Hagenbeck, the Hamburg zoo specialist, realized that caging was detrimental to the health and well-being of animals accustomed to roaming, and he introduced his zoo design which provided for relatively wide spaces for his animals resembling their natural habitat. Brookfield's zoo in Chicago became the first American zoo with habitat design. With respect to human beings, however, we have not quite reached the same stage of development. If there were the slightest scientific proof that the placement of human beings into boxes or cages for any length of time, even over night, had the slightest beneficial effect, perhaps such a system might be justifiable.

There is no such proof; consequently, I should think that a massive attack on the constitutionality of the caging of human beings is in order. Who could doubt that a sentence of strapping an acrophobic human being on top of a 300-foot radio antenna would be cruel and unusual punishment? Who would doubt that the sentence of caging a claustrophobic human being in a seven-by-seven-by-seven-foot grilled cage is cruel and unusual punishment? But by definition, all human beings are claustrophobic, since ranging and roaming are natural instincts of the human being, requiring satisfaction as much as the hunger drive and the sex urge.

Mueller concludes:

Caging is in violation of the Eighth Amendment to the Constitution. It should not be too difficult for designers, architects and corrections personnel to design alternatives to cages, e.g., landscaped grounds firmly protected if need be, which permit rehabilitative effort, including self-effort, without mentally or emotionally harming those institutionalized.

Mueller's second recommendation is that American penal codes be rewritten to incorporate the requirement of rehabilitation.

All offenders are entitled to a disposition envisaging treatment adequate for their social habilitation or rehabilitation. It is incumbent upon the Bar to incorporate the requirement of social habilitation or rehabilitation into penal codes to enforce these requirements which are in the nature of rights of prisoners, and to police the administrators of the system in effectuating that right, but not duty. . . .

A person detained under order envisaging treatment is entitled to release on habeas corpus unless a reasonable effort is made to provide such treatment to him.

Thus [we must] . . . introduce into legislation and enforce through litigation, the right of every prisoner to be treated or to have reasonable efforts made toward his correction.

If such legislation were passed tomorrow, nearly every prisoner in the United States would be entitled to release on habeas corpus.

The third of Mueller's postulates is that whoever wants a convict to be imprisoned should have the burden of proof that imprisonment is necessary for obtaining the legal purposes of the statute.

In the Anglo-American legal system, it is a fundamental premise that a petitioner at the Bar who wishes to obtain a judicial disposition has the burden of proof with respect to the desired disposition.

But when it comes to imprisonment we find the astounding situation that no one is required to prove the need for imprisonment. A sentence of imprisonment may follow automatically upon proof of a past event—the commission of a crime.

I would suggest that we had better get out of the rut of the virtual inevitability of imprisonment upon conviction of crime and that we require a meaningful sentencing hearing in which the prosecutor has the burden of proving that imprisonment is required. . . . I would couple this proposition with the presumption—based on the vast experience data of our society—that imprisonment as such entails such enormous negative consequences that it is not a desirable disposition upon conviction.

As Mueller notes, the draft of the Federal Criminal Code has moved in the right direction by providing in 3101 (2) that:

The court shall not impose a sentence of imprisonment upon a person unless, having regard to the nature and circumstances of the offense and to the history and character of the defendant, it is satisfied that imprisonment is the more appropriate sentence for the protection of the public.

"The Code then lists a number of criteria for imposition of either imprisonment or probation," Mueller adds, "with the unhappy proviso that the Court is not required to refer to these factors at sentencing."

Mueller's fourth postulate is that our penal code is vague and unconstitutional as it relates to the imposition of sentences.

"Consequently," he suggests, "legislation is required which will save our codes from unconstitutionality by insertion of enforceable provisions indicating the sanctioning purposes and the criteria for imposition of sentences."

Mueller cites as an example a provision of the new penal code of the German Federal Republic, which provides:

1. The culpability of the perpetrator is the basis for the composition of the sentence. The potential effects of the sanction upon the life of the perpetrator within society must be considered.

2. In sentencing, the court weighs the circumstances for and against the perpetrator, especially the following: The motivations and goals of the perpetrators, the attitude which speaks from the deed and efforts made toward perpetration of the deed, the background of the perpetrator, his personal and economic conditions, and his behavior after the deed, especially his efforts to make up for the harm caused.

3. Circumstances which already are definitional elements of the offense may not be considered.

Mueller's fifth postulate calls for a meaningful sentencing hearing.

Our system of criminal proceedings has the advantage over some foreign systems of the bi-partition into trial proper—ending in verdict or judgment of guilt—and sentencing hearing, which is meant to focus on disposition. Unhappily, a paradox has resulted. Trial proper, which, in view of the many guilty pleas, has become a statistical rarity, not to say anomaly, is procedurally highly developed, while the dispositional part of the process, which occurs in every case of a guilty verdict or judgment, is totally underdeveloped as to both procedure and substance.

I will not concentrate here on the procedural aspects. Constitutional problems loom large. The Bar must do its share toward the process of regularizing and institutionalizing the procedure of the sentencing hearing. I want to concentrate here on the substance of sentencing.

Working in decent procedural settings with acceptable evidentiary standards, the Bench and Bar could concentrate upon working out a correctional program which is designed in terms of the impact of a sanction upon the life of the defendant within the community. If defense counsel and prosecutor were forced to do their homework on the question of changing human behavior, we might wind up with a criminal justice system that does correct. It will not do to say that judges and lawyers are not behavior specialists. They have assumed that function long ago. They are stuck with it. The criminal law game is a behavior simulation game. Judges and lawyers are playing that game, albeit by rules developed through hunch and superstition. It is time, then, that the game be adjusted to the real rules. That judges and lawyers need help from other behavior specialists—no one can doubt.

Mueller's sixth postulate calls for appellate review of sentences.

I doubt whether anybody would regard this point as controversial. The Report of the National Commission on Reform of Federal Criminal Laws recommends an amendment of 28 U.S. Code 1291 by clearly giving courts of appeals the power to review sentences and to modify them, or to set them aside for further proceedings. This recommendation is in accordance with the recommendations of the ABA and IJA Minimum Standards of Criminal Justice Project.

Mueller also proposes that the execution of all prison sentences be monitored by representatives of the judiciary. "If a prison sentence calling for rehabilitation is executed either by refusing to extend rehabilitative services or by denying human rights, contempt has been committed and a judicial remedy should be available," he claims.

Current prisoners' rights suits are gradually developing some badly needed remedies. More effective methods are needed. Ideally, sentencing judges should constantly monitor the execution of sentences they have imposed. If that cannot be done, special judges may have to be appointed and specially assigned to individual penal institutions, where they would be physically present to monitor the lawful execution of the court orders which sentences constitute.

European countries have precisely this kind of an institution in the person of the Surveillance Judge (Article 144, Italian Penal Code; Articles 585, 634-654, Italian Code of Criminal Procedure; see Seewald, The Italian Surveillance Judge, 45 Nebs. L. Rev. 96, 1966).

In some countries, this institution has been beneficial, in others not. The idea, however, is excellent. It just might have the consequence of preventing future Atticas, by protection of the human rights of prisoners; including those which are postulated by the United Nations Standard Minimum Rules for the Treatment of Prisoners.

Mueller's eighth postulate has it that no extraneous disabilities should attach upon conviction, and that all rights must be restored to prisoners when the need for their deprivation has ceased.

Just as loss of personal liberty through imprisonment has long been regarded as the automatic and inevitable consequence of criminal conviction, there is a collateral and equally automatic loss of all other adjuncts of individuality and personality, including the whole slate of human and constitutional rights.

Why? There may be justification for automatically stripping a prisoner of his constitutional right to bear arms, but why strip him of his right to read, to have normal sexual relations, to communicate, to work, to earn, to walk, to contribute financially and economically to his family and his nation? If we are committed to a Government of laws, we are obligated to provide for a legal system of deprivation of rights only upon proof that loss of that right is necessary for a legitimate reason. . . . I am calling for a reassessment of the system of automatic loss of rights upon imprisonment and its replacement by a system under which no right can be lost unless there is proof by the moving party that this loss of right is a necessity.

Mueller's ninth contention is that American social planners must make an effort to develop alternatives to imprisonment for dealing with those convicted of crime.

While in the Nineteenth Century the U.S.A. was regarded as the innovator in corrections through the development of penitentiaries, probation systems, workhouses and juvenile courts, we have long lost that reputation, particularly to the Scandinavian countries. It behooves us well, therefore, that we explore the range of alternative sanctioning methods available in foreign legal systems. Even the most obnoxious penal code may have innovative provisions, which can be applied to United States conditions, particularly if they are adjusted to our own due process model.

What permeates foreign sentencing systems is an insistence on the performance of useful labor, the habituation to regular work, participation in the economic life of the community or nation, economic incentives, including the provision of sustenance for one's self, one's family, and the financial restoration of harm caused.

Many countries are experimenting with non-institutional care for prisoners.

Countries in which every citizen has the opportunity to obtain gainful employment have experimented with the day-fine system which has gained great significance. Under that system, fines are graduated as to their severity in terms of day's earnings, e.g., two days' earnings for a minor offense, thirty days' earnings for a more severe offense. But since a day's earnings vary with the job or profession of the defendant, they are calculated to have an equalized impact on offenders of different economic status. This system, invented in the Scandinavian countries, has now been incorporated in the Latin American Model Penal Code. But even when the day-fine system does not exist, fines are always adjusted to the ability to pay and the modern codes never threaten imprisonment as a substitute when there is inability to pay, not due to the fault of the offender.

Some nations have become more careful with respect to loss of rights of offenders. Japan deprives civil rights only for the duration of imprisonment. Most importantly, some nations remind us that punishments need not be drastic to be effective—although a scaling down to less drastic levels may have to be done gradually. Human beings can be goaded into action, shamed into inaction, praised or reprimanded, helped and guided, ridiculed and held out to contempt, love may be extended and withheld, causes of crime may be removed by arbitration, counseling and settlement. Those were the sanctions used by our supposedly less civilized forebears—including the American Indians.

Might it not be time to start de-escalating our drastic prison sentences in terms of the alternatives we once knew and still, or again, know in other systems and nations?

Mueller's tenth and last postulate is simple: that we take care that our current concern for correctional reform will not be a passing fancy, but a sincere, permanent, dynamic and human commitment.

Commenting on his proposed reforms for "Correctional Research," Dr. Mueller writes:

I do not think that any of the reforms I proposed will significantly help reduce recidivism. I have no answers on the recidivism question and I distrust anybody who claims he does have answers.

I think the trend of developments is such that we can expect the reforms which are indicated in my paper to be realized within about eight to 12 years. The obstacles are primarily to be found in the conditioning of those who run the system. Reconditioning, education and sensitizing seem to be the answer there.[7]

We have presented a lengthy description of Mueller's recommendations, not because we believe his are necessarily the best and only answers, nor because we endorse each of his ideas without reservation; but because we believe his recommendations are illustrative of the kind of thinking that needs to be done.

His projection that the recommendations will be realized within eight to twelve years seems optimistic. But perhaps if his tenth postulate, which calls for honest and immediate inquiry, is taken to heart, the American correctional system may be moved significantly in a constructive direction.

Time for Change

The time is here for planning a nation without prisons. Our major prison facilities for adults in America are ancient, having been designed for purposes better suited to a much earlier period of our history. Most are not adaptable to current correctional concepts and programs. Sixty-one of the American adult prisons now in use were opened before 1900, and twenty-eight of these are now more than one-hundred years old. Of the housing units currently utilized, over 30 percent were first occupied before World War I. Another 30 percent were built between the two world wars.[8]

American prisons were built to last, and they certainly have. At the Kentucky State Prison at Eddyville, the walls are built of stone measuring about three feet thick. Visits to Canyon City, Colorado, Joliet, Illinois, and other locations indicate that the Kentucky facility is no exceptional institution in this respect. The old Eastern State Penitentiary in Philadelphia was built in 1829 and closed in 1970. It still stands in all its grimness because its thick walls and solid steel and masonry construction defy demolition. It would cost $3 million to tear it down.

American jails aren't much different. Twenty-five thousand of the nation's jails were built before 1920. One-fifth of them are more than one-hundred years old. In 86 percent of our jails there are no facilities for exercise or recreation; 90 percent have no educational facilities; 25 percent have no visiting rooms; and forty-seven American jails are without flush toilets. Most jails are so primitive as to offend the sensibilities of the American people, and should be demolished.[9]

Practically all the nation's prisons, including recently constructed facilities, are located in rural settings, far from universities, large cities, public transportation, and industry. They seem to have been designed in such a way as to discourage citizen and community involvement. They are generally staffed by rural persons who are generally unsympathetic, even antipathetic, to the hopes, life styles, and ethnic values of the prisoners, who are mostly black, brown, and urban.[10]

The argument that we should construct smaller modern prisons near centers of population doesn't address the real problem. Until we decide whether prisons are worthwhile at all, no further plans should be developed for the construction of new prisons.

In two-hundred years of correctional practice in America, one treatment concept after another has evolved and been absorbed into the system. None has seriously challenged the worth of confinement, or overcome its inherent weaknesses.

Wolfgang, Wilkins, and more recently Martinson have reported few, if any, correctional programs have noticeably affected the recidivist rate. Martinson, in fact, reviewed 231 accepted studies of correctional treatment published since 1945. The evidence from his survey indicates that the present array of correctional treatments have no appreciable effect, positive or negative, on the rate of recidivism.[11]

John B. Martin, in his book *Break Down the Walls* (written after American prison riots during the 1950s), charged that professional people in corrections had devised a dangerous muth—that of institutional treatment itself. He said rehabilitation is nothing but a pie-in-the-sky notion. "We appear to believe," he wrote, "that if we provide the stainless steel kitchen, the schools and shops and toilets, one day rehabilitation will descend upon the inmate, like manna."[12]

Ben Bagdikian came to the same conclusions twenty years later in *Shame of the Prisons*, written in 1972 after another series of riots at Attica, Holmsburg, and Rahway.[13]

More recently, Norman Carlson, director of the federal prison system, notified the public that special experimental "behavior modification" programs in federal prisons would be curtailed. Donald Santarelli, former director of the Law Enforcement Assistance Administration under President Richard M. Nixon, also disclosed that funds for such programs would no longer be available. Increasing public pressure, resulting from closer scrutiny of prison systems by journalists, has seen to it that treatment programs in prisons are being carefully examined and evaluated.

There are some meritorious theories to explain why prisons don't work. Haynes, in 1948, found the inmate community to be distinctly antisocial, working against the goals of the larger society and thereby frustrating efforts at rehabilitation.[14] Reimer, even earlier, had noted that inmates acquire status in terms of their reactions against authority, and that therefore the behavior of convicts is largely determined by convicts themselves.[15] Clemmer observed that the prisoner, through assimilation and acculturation, takes on the delinquent values, norms, customs, and the general culture of the prison.[16] McCorkle and

Korn concluded that the prison represents—in fact is—the ultimate in social rejection, and that inmates develop increased antisocial values in order to "reject the rejectors."[17] Other serious investigators, including Sykes, Goffman, Cloward, and Schrag, have noted that prison subcultures work powerfully to subvert even the most conscientious of treatment efforts.[18]

Counterproductive pressures are created whenever large numbers of human beings are placed in a closed society in which they are controlled by a few officials (as in prisons), according to Gaylin, Weber, and others.[19] The values of an open society are not the values of a closed society. In prisons leadership is blunted, assertiveness is equated with aggression and is repressed, and docility is rewarded.

Each time a new prison is built the ambitions of people interested in alternatives to confinement is squelched. Each time another cell is built, those with innovative ideas, with programs that offer something new, are defeated.

Why have we as a society become addicted to prisons?

Our reliance on imprisonment is somewhat counter to America's ordinary utilization of invention and innovation for progressive change. It is even more surprising when we consider that the prison concept was inherited as an institution from medieval highway robbers, who used imprisonment as a means of making cities pay ransom for captured merchants.[20] The only alternative that has been developed is a withholding of imprisonment, the primary sanction, by a secondary sanction, probation.

Mueller and many others would deem the alternatives suggested in this book—the halfway house, work release, etc.—inadequate. They would judge that these alternatives are merely diversions from the mainstream of imprisonment, rather than true alternatives.

It is astounding that so little imagination has been exercised in the field of corrections. It seems as if people with creativity have more or less abandoned the field of corrections in favor of more productive enterprises. The inventive people, the reputable scientists in our criminal-justice system, have chosen careers as attorneys or judges. Thus, the uninventive but hard-working persons have been given responsibility for the sanctions system, while those who have sentenced the criminal or supervised his journey down the road toward conviction are left to more profitable pursuits. Corrections personnel have a long record of unimaginative management. And promoters of innovation involve themselves in risks that only the most confident and courageous staff persons would ordinarily dare to face.[21]

Prisons exist. Cells await tenants. Experience tells us that prison cells are almost automatically filled with men and women. Yet no one is required to prove the need for imprisonment. We know that imprisonment does most people no good, yet it and its sister-sanction, probation, are the only services our ostensibly modern prison system offers.

To summarize:

We have a firmly established complex of correctional institutions in this country. They clearly do not correct. There is evidence, on the other hand, that they actually promote antisocial attitudes and behaviors and foster social pathology. And creativity in the field of corrections has been generally rebuffed.

Yet the call for elimination of prisons receives little support from many leaders in the correctional profession, even those noted for progressiveness and for devotion to the notion of reform.

Federal Bureau of Prisons Director Norman Carlson, for example, is considered a leader of the prison reform movement, a proponent of change. Yet, under his direction, the Bureau of Prisons has begun a major construction program.

In a speech delivered to the Houston Rotary Club early in 1974, Carlson said that, in all fairness, one must note that the breakdown of communications between citizens and criminal-justice agencies has been a two-sided problem. He noted that government agencies have often been "defensive, secretive and unresponsive."[22] On the other hand, citizens have largely failed to accept their own responsibility for improving the system, "at least so long as they perceived the threat of crime as a problem in someone else's neighborhood."[23] He reiterated a position he has taken on numerous occasions during his career: "The only thing we can say with certainty is that we still know comparatively little about how to deal with offenders."[24] Despite the "many minds" of society as to the reasons people are imprisoned—for retribution, deterrence, or rehabilitation—it is Carlson's position that offenders are sentenced *as* punishment, not *for* punishment. He wants to see changes brought about in the prison system.

The Bureau of Prisons' construction program, which began in the spring of 1974, has been under fire from several organizations. In undertaking the program, Carlson said, the bureau has three objectives in mind: to reduce the critical overcrowding in existing institutions resulting from the "substantial increase in commitments from federal courts"; to provide smaller institutions with environments designed to facilitate treatment and to "meet the human needs for privacy and dignity"; and to eventually replace all large, antiquated federal penitentiaries, three of which were built before 1900.[25] Carlson has expressed a lack of faith in programs like those described in this book; he claims that "experience has clearly indicated that they will not solve all the complex problems we face."[26] As a general rule, Carlson has acknowledged, persons who will respond positively to some form of community treatment without posing a threat to their fellow citizens should not be imprisoned. "It is a terrible mistake, however," he warns, "to conclude that all offenders can be handled under such supervision."[27]

In a white paper dated February 1, 1974, the federal Bureau of Prisons indicated its major commitments:

The Bureau of Prisons has made a commitment to carry out the directive of the

President and especially to develop a comprehensive correctional program which will hopefully serve as a model for the entire nation. Briefly stated, the Bureau's primary objectives are:

To provide a level of inmate supervision that is consistent with human dignity and capable of carrying out the judgments of the United States Courts and proving maximum protection to the community, staff and inmates;

To significantly increase the number of federal offenders achieving a successful adjustment upon their return to the community;

And to increase program alternatives for offenders who do not require institutional confinement.

Our long range plan places emphasis on the increased development of a professional trained staff; development of correctional programs designed to meet the needs of changing offender groups; increased development and utilization of research and evaluation capabilities; provision of facilities to meet present and future requirements; and expansion of the Bureau's technical assistance to state and local correctional systems.[28]

Also mentioned in this white paper were the bureau's achievements: an increase in the number of inmates enrolled in educational programs; an increase in the number awarded high-school diplomas or equivalency certificates; an increase in the number enrolled in vocational training programs; an increase in the number earning college credits. Also cited were the bureau's greater use of outside resources for education and training, and the development of an automatic data-processing system to facilitate the educational offerings. The report also claimed that progress has been made in such programs as prison industries, drug-abuse programs, mental-health programs, community-based programs, legal-aid programs, staff-training programs, and construction programs.

The goals of the bureau include the following: improvement of correctional programs and facilities, to meet a wider variety of inmate needs; amelioration of congestion in existing facilities; elimination of outdated facilities; reduction of the capacity of all prisons in the system to five hundred or fewer men; and the implementation of innovative correctional concepts.

Such concepts are to be evaluated carefully, and expertise thus gained is to be widely disseminated. Facilities are to be designed to accommodate discrete groups of offender types. Institutions are to be built near population centers, so as to be more accessible to university facilities and other community resources. Institutions are to be created to serve specific populations, such as psychiatric patients, drug addicts, alcoholics, and persons who are excessively violent. The final goal is to develop community ties and make wider use of community resources to enrich institutional and postrelease programs.[29]

The efforts of the Bureau of Prisons are to be commended. However, the bureau's goals and commitments must be considered in the larger context addressed by this book: Can we move in the direction of the elimination of prisons as we know them?

Reform of prisons and the elimination of prisons are two very different things. It is our position that the program embraced by the Bureau of Prisons is basically inadequate, in that it fails to confront the issue that is at the heart of the current controversy surrounding the state of our correctional system: Are prisons, by their very nature, more conducive to good or evil—in terms of the welfare of the individual offender, of his family, and of society at large?

It seems that the bureau's philosophy assumes that confinement is a necessary correctional technique for the treatment of the *vast majority* of convicts. There are no convincing data to endorse that assumption.

We recognize that there are some offenders who must be restrained for the protection of society. Any correctional system we develop in the future must have the capability to restrain—*where there is sufficient cause.* However, there are no data that indicate that the use of imprisonment as a primary sanction is of significant benefit to society; and there are data, cited elsewhere in this chapter, that indicate that imprisonment does significantly contribute to the development of antisocial attitudes and behaviors.

Reformation

Albert Morris, who edited a pamphlet on reform for the Massachusetts Correctional Association, wrote: "Reform implies the drastic correction of something defective, vicious, corrupt or depraved."[30] Reform cries out for action in the here and now; the concept implies urgency. Advocates of the status quo counter reformers' arguments with a demand for additional analysis and research. In most cases, this is an honest stance; however, it should be kept in mind that such a position can be nothing more than an intellectually corrupt defense against change.

"The reforms sought," Morris wrote, " . . . may range from the limited and specific to those with the broad and basic; the most extreme of which would do away with criminal trial procedure, sentencing and corrections as we now know them."[31]

Since the reformer is generally faced with a tense and emotionally disturbing situation, his natural wish is for the instant cure. Some reformers, those who suggest the simplest, most direct, and concrete remedies, may be acting on this wish. Their arguments are easily refuted, both scientifically and politically.

Constructive reform of any scope is seldom easy to contrive, always difficult to put into effect. It is, by its nature, experimental; and it involves risk. The fact that a practice has proven its worth in Scandinavia, Italy, or Japan does not necessarily mean that it would be effective in Puerto Rico, California, or Alabama. However, this argument does not qualify as a defense against reform, either.

The fact is that we have considerable data as to which techniques have worked in America and which have failed. Obviously, the most intelligent course is for reformers to join hands with advocates of current systems, to discuss the statistical data available, and to work toward rational compromises based not on expediency or political volatility, but on scientific principles.

Our chances of reaching this level of rationality in the near future appear slim, and that is a tragic observation to make.

But jobs and prestige are at stake. Political power and control are at stake. And attempts at reform are seen by administrators of existing systems not as evidence of the inadequacies of their own operations, but as disruptive activities intended to sabotage systems whose failures are due to inadequate support.

Not surprisingly, most efforts at prison system reform come from within established systems. Reform is a matter of degree; and one can readily see (for example, by reading the Bureau of Prisons white paper on reform) that reforms introduced by administrators are generally directed toward improvement of existing program facilities. They are not addressed to fundamental change. They do not attack the basic premises on which the existing systems are based.

Millions of dollars have been spent by would-be reformers in and out of government to investigate, develop, and evaluate correctional programs that do address themselves to fundamental change. Countless pilot studies have been made and painstakingly judged. American libraries and the federal Department of Justice have banks of information concerning programs that have shown promise, programs that should be more thoroughly studied. Yet the administrators of prisons systems continue to ride through this storm of suggestion without accepting challenge. Indeed, it appears that such suggestions have only strengthened their resistance.

One of the most serious obstacles to penal and correctional reform is the still unresolved conflict between the philosophies of custody and of treatment.

Sometimes community programs, by the nature of their leadership, impose more restrictions on those receiving treatment than do closed prison programs. The requirements of custody and treatment are at conflict throughout our nation's criminal-justice system. Because the legal mandate for custody (and control) is clear and the mandate for treatment is clouded, far greater amounts of money and energy have been devoted to solving the problems related to control than to solving those related to treatment, which are far more pressing in a moral, philosophical sense.

A comprehensive discussion of reform is contained in a bulletin published by the Massachusetts Correctional Association in November 1972, entitled, "Correctional Reform: Illusion or Reality?" edited by Albert Morris.[32]

Should Prisons Be Abolished?

If we have been correct in asserting that the existing American prison systems are totally inadequate as treatment complexes, then we must further assert that reform is mandatory. If we have been correct in concluding that the existing systems are significantly destructive of personality, and actually contribute to the development of pathology, then it follows that reform must be drastic, and must address itself to the basic worth of imprisonment itself. Therefore, we conclude that the use of imprisonment as a primary sanction ought to be eliminated.

Prisons do serve two legitimate functions: the protection of persons and property, and the punishment of persons who have caused significant harm and suffering to fellow human beings.

The first of these functions is of great importance. Governments have a sacred duty to protect their citizens, and citizens have a sacred right to that protection. Therefore, prisons must be preserved as *a treatment alternative of last resort.* Imprisonment should be a secondary and extreme sanction in our society. It should be incumbent upon government prosecutors to prove, in accordance with established, specific rules of law and procedure, that imprisonment is necessary for the protection of the public, in order for imprisonment to be imposed. An efficient system should be created within the judiciary to supervise the execution of imprisonment as a sentence. Our penal codes should be rewritten to reflect the belief that the imposition of imprisonment upon an offender involves a very grave governmental responsibility.

The second legitimate function of prisons, to punish those who have broken the law and harmed their fellow citizens, has no firm basis in American law, but seems to be an accurate reflection of American culture. We do not believe it should become a basis for new law. We do believe, however, that if it is to remain an effective variable in the administration of justice in America, we have no choice except to incorporate it into our law. We do not believe the American people would endorse such a suggestion as a point of law.

Among the recommendations of the American Assembly were these:

States should abandon large congregate institutions for sentenced offenders. Few offenders require confinement in maximum security facilities. If incarcerated at all, most should be assigned to a diversified network of smaller group facilities and nonresidential community-based services.

It must become firm policy to avoid further construction of adult prisons, jails or juvenile training schools. Resources should be allocated for more adequate alternative programs and services as well as for the repair of existing facilities to make them more habitable. Present changes in correctional policy have not run their course. Plans for new construction must be deferred.

The federal government and states should subsidize or initiate the placement of offenders on probation or in other community-based programs. Such services require standard setting, regulation by state correctional agencies and extensive use of volunteers.

The management of offenders must not be exclusively a public function. All correctional agencies should reserve funds to purchase services from other public or private agencies on a contractual basis. By creating a competitive environment, the quality of services can be greatly improved.

Young people have special needs and provide special opportunities. We need, therefore, to be certain that, if we institutionalize them at all, we do so only if we are prepared to provide professional and adequately funded services in their behalf.[33]

We feel that this is a well-motivated and worthy program for reform, but, given its context, an overly cautious and unimaginative one. It does not confront the fact that imprisonment has not, in our national experience, proven its merit.

It is our contention that one and only one course of action will significantly improve our system of corrections by accomplishing the collateral purposes of helping the offender and benefiting American society—the virtual elimination of imprisonment as a criminal sanction in the United States.

We believe America can become a nation without prisons as we know them—institutions whose administrators mouth slogans about rehabilitation and offer only confinement.

Those few prisons which would remain would serve society by restraining the "incurably criminal." Their primary function would be to protect society from such men; their secondary function would be to do so with a minimum of cruelty.

And the vast majority of American offenders would be spared that cruelty by placement in community-based treatment programs—much to our honor as a nation.

References

1. Clarence Schrag, "Turmoil in the Temple of Justice," *Issues in Corrections*, Edward Eldefonso, Glencoe Press, Beverly Hills, California, 1974, p. 20.

2. American Assembly, *Prisoners in America*, Report of the Forty-second American Assembly, Columbia University, December 17-20, 1972, pp. 4-5.

3. Gerhard O.W. Mueller, *Imprisonment and Its Alternatives, Part I, The Present System*, from a presentation paper, New York University, 1974, pp. 4-5. By permission of the author.

4. Ibid.

5. Ibid.

6. Ibid.

7. Gerhard O.W. Mueller, *Correctional Reform, Illusion and Reality*, edited by Albert Morris, Bulletin No. 22, a publication of the Massachusetts Correctional Association, Boston, 1972, p. 18. By permission of the author.

8. American Correctional Association, 1971 Directory of Correctional Institutions and Agencies of America, Canada and Great Britain, College Park, Maryland, American Correctional Association, 1971.

9. Charles M. Friel, "The Jail Dilemma, Some Solutions," *The American County*, November 1972, pp. 9, 10.

10. Albert Morris, ed., *Correctional Reform: Illusion and Reality*, Massachusetts Correctional Association, Boston, pp. 4, 27, 28. By permission of the author.

11. William G. Nagel, "Should Any New Major Correctional Institutions be Constructed?" A paper by William G. Nagel, presented before the National Conference on Criminal Justice, Washington, D.C., January 1973, p. 5.

12. John Martin, *Break Down the Walls.*

13. Ben Bagdikian, *Shame of the Prisons* (New York: Pocket Books, Inc., 1972).

14. William G. Nagel, op. cit.

15. Ibid.

16. Ibid.

17. Ibid.

18. Ibid.

19. Ibid.

20. Stephen Schafer, *The Victim and His Criminal* (New York: Random House, 1968), pp. 15, 16.

21. William G. Nagel, op. cit., p. 3.

22. Norman Carlson, Speech before Rotary Club, Houston, Texas, 1974. By permission of the author.

23. Ibid.

24. Ibid.

25. Ibid.

26. Ibid.

27. Ibid.

28. United States Department of Justice Bureau of Prisons, *Current Assignment*, White paper dated February 1, 1974, p. 2. By permission of Norman Carlson, Director, Bureau of Prisons.

29. Ibid., Unnumbered p. 1, section entitled "Future Thrust."

30. Albert Morris, op. cit.

31. Albert Morris, op. cit.

32. Massachusetts Correctional Association, Boston, Massachusetts, Bulletin No. 22, November 1972.

33. The American Assembly Report, Harriman, New York, December 17-20, 1972, p. 6, 7.

Appendix

Appendix
Section-by-Section Analysis
of U.S. Senate Bill 3309
"Community Supervision
and Services Act"[a]

Sec. 1 Short title—The Community Supervision and Services Act.

Sec. 2. Findings and Declaration—Congress hereby finds and declares that the interests of protecting society and rehabilitating individuals charged with violating criminal laws can best be served by creating new innovative alternatives for treatment and supervision within the community; that in many cases, society can best be served by diverting the accused to a voluntary community-oriented correctional program instead of bringing him to trial; that such diversion can be accomplished in appropriate cases without losing the general deterrent effect of the criminal justice system; that the retention of the deferred charges will serve both as a deterrent to committing further offenses and as an incentive to complete rehabilitative efforts, and that alternatives to institutionalization which provide for the educational, vocational, and social needs of the accused will equip him to lead a lawful and useful life.

Sec. 3. (1) The definition as to whom is eligible for pretrial diversion generally excludes individuals who are charged with crimes of violence, who have been convicted of any two prior offenses of any kind, who are currently under any court or correctional supervision, or who have previously been diverted.

(2) The services available to an individual who is diverted into the program include job placement, vocational and other training, medical and psychological services, all types of counseling, and assistance in obtaining a suitable residence.

(3) The plan is a voluntary agreement made by each participant with the program director, the prosecuting attorney and the court as to the services he will need, and the efforts he will make, in order to be assured that he will acquire what is necessary to succeed in society when his period of supervision ends. The plan can be modified to meet new goals of the individual or new problems identified by the program staff.

(4) In general, the officer authorized to divert an individual into a program of community supervision and services would be the U.S. magistrate or district judge who would conduct the bail hearing for the same individual.

(5) The administrative head is the person who serves as the local director of a program serving a judicial district in the U.S. court system. He is recognized by the court as a source of information and progress reports for the use of the committing officer in making the diversion determinations.

---

[a]Hearings before the Subcommittee on National Penitentiaries of the Committee of the Judiciary Ninety Second Congress, second session on S. 3309, July 19 and 20, 1972. By permission. U.S. Government Printing Office.

Sec. 4. Each potentially eligible person arrested on federal charges would be interviewed to verify his eligibility for participation in the program, to counsel him as to the possibility that he may qualify for diversion to such a program and, if he wishes, to assist him in preparing a plan to be presented to the committing officer.

Sec. 5. When the director of a program believes that a person charged with a crime would be best served by diversion to a program of community services, he arranges for his appearance before the committing magistrate, together with the prosecuting attorney. Both would make their recommendations to the committing officer. The individual seeking diversion to a program of community supervision and services would make his own presentation of the plan. The director of the program would evaluate for the court the likelihood of the individual's success under such a plan, and the prosecuting attorney would evaluate the individual's past record and any concerns he might have for the welfare and best interests of society.

Sec. 6. (a) The committing officer has the discretion to release any eligible individual to a program of community supervision and services.

(b) A district judge may, in unusual circumstances and after making appropriate findings that the best interest of society would be so served, release an individual who does not fit the eligibility criteria into a program of community supervision and services. If the individual is presently under the supervision of any court or correctional agency in connection with a prior offense, arrangements must be made with that agency.

Sec. 7. The director of each local program is responsible for preparing a thorough evaluation and report to the court each ninety days on the progress of every individual diverted into the program. In addition, if at any time the prosecuting attorney or the officers of the program find any evidence that the individual is failing in the program or has been involved in new criminal activity, they would be obligated to report it immediately to the committing officer.

Sec. 8. The diversion of an individual to a program of community supervision and services shall be initially for a period of 180 days. However, this period of time can be extended up to three years, particularly in cases where an individual may be attending a trade or vocational school and the additional supporting services of the program would be a significant factor in making it possible for the individual to complete the training and qualify for employment. The committing officer may terminate the individual's participation at any time and under these circumstances the criminal charges which have been pending will be immediately taken up. If an individual completes his plan, including subsequent modifications, and if the committing officer finds that it would be in the interests of society to do so, the individual may be released and the charges against him dismissed by the committing officer.

Sec. 9. The participation of any U.S. District Court in a program of community supervision and services will be based upon a plan that has been prepared by an advisory committee appointed by the chief judge of the district. This advisory committee shall also continue to function to review the administration and progress of the program. The chief judge of the district is the chairman of the advisory committee, and the U.S. attorney for the district is automatically a member. The chief judge may designate any other judges or any persons residing in the district as members, and they shall receive no compensation except reimbursement for necessary expenses.

Sec. 10. The attorney general may use any means necessary to provide the professional services involved in a program of community supervision and services. Such a program may be carried out by employees of the Department of Justice, the U.S. Probation Service, a bail agency administered by a district court, or by a local public or nonprofit agency which might provide similar services for criminal defendants in state, county, or municipal courts. The attorney general must have the agreement of the chief judge of the district court in appointing employees or contracting for services, and all regulations and policy statements to implement the program must be concurred in by the Judicial Conference. The attorney general shall also serve at the cabinet level to coordinate the delivery of services from other federal agencies to the individuals diverted into the programs of community supervision and services, including such agencies as the Department of Health, Education and Welfare, Department of Labor, and others. This section also provides for the preparation of reports, auditing technical assistance, and other administrative services.

Sec. 11. An annual expenditure of $2,500,000 would be authorized to operate programs of community supervision and services.

Author Index

Ackerman, J., 207
Aledort, S.L., 207
Allenbrand, F., 34
Anttila, I., 46
Aubert, V., 50

Baer, D.J., 157
Bagdikian, B., 241
Bartley, D., 59
Boone, J., 74
Booth, M., 197
Brown, J.F., 33
Brown, J.S., 198

Cameron, G., 180
Carlson, N.A., 34, 186, 241, 243
Chapman, D., 42, 47
Clark, R., 99
Clements, H.M., 34
Coors, A., 166
Coughlin, J., 58
Cloward, R., 242
Cowden, J.E., 205
Cressey, D., 44

Deehy, P.T., 206
de Tocqueville, A., 8
Dodge, C.R., 197, 233
Doleschal, E., 37
Donahue, M., 59
Dorn, R., 34
Durkheim, E., 50

Elder, P.D., 206-207
England, R., 105
Evans, J., 176

Flynn, E., 34

Gaylin, W., 242
Gilliam, J.L., 206
Goffman, E., 242
Goldman, N., 43
Gordon, Alfred, 193
Gordon, Arthur, 171
Gordon, D.R., 79
Graves, H.R., 51

Harrison, E., 34

Hart, P., 44
Haynes, 241
Henderson, E.B., III., 197, 199
Heyns, G., 177
Hough, J., Jr., 65

Johnson, R., 34, 176
Jones, L., 34
Jones, M., 60, 207

Keller, O.J., Jr., 34
Kelly, F.J., 157
Killinger, G.G., 34
Kirby, B.C., 206
Klapmuts, N., 37, 101
Korn, R.R., 242
Kutchinsky, B., 40, 41

Lahti, R., 47
Langley, M.H., 51
Lawyer, G., 193
Leavey, J., 62
LeBlanc, M., 41, 47
Leenhouts, J., 133

Maas, J.W., 182
Maher, J., 198
Mahoney, M.J., 147-148
Maloney, F., 58
Martin, J.B., 241
Martinson, R., 95, 102, 241
McCorkle, L.W., 241
McCartt, J.M., 199,202
McGlynn, J., 59
Miller, J., 59
Moffitt, R., 213
Monsen, L., 205
Morris, A., 245
Mueller, G.O.W., 197, 235, 236, 237, 240, 242
Munger, R., 176

Nagel, W.G., 35
Nixon, R.M., 241
Nold, J., 155
Norris, B., 51

O'Grady, R., 35

Palmer, T.B., 206
Penn, W., 3
Powers, S.B., 35
Preiser, P., 35

Quinney, R., 51

Rauch, Warden, 187
Reich, C., 37
Robison, J., 39
Rothman, D., 73
Rubinton, E., 207
Rudenstine, D., 79
Rutherford, A., 57

Santarelli, D., 241
Sargent, F., 58
Sargent, J., 59
Sarri, R.C., 35
Schrag, C., 242

Schur, E., 51
Shah, S.A., 35
Simmons, R.J., 171-173, 175
Smith, G., 39
Sykes, G.M., 242

Talbert, E., 199
Tornudd, P., 46

Vorath, H., 60
Vos, E., 41

Wallace, J.A., 35
Wheeler, M., 35
Wilgosh, L., 206
Wilkins, L.T., 241
Wilpers, M., 155
Winship, T., 59
Wolfgang, M.E., 241
Wyne, A., 177

Subject Index

Alcoholics Anonymous, 137
Aldersgate Methodist Camp, 162
America
  greening of, 37
American Assembly
  42nd, on prisons, 225, 234
  recommendations, 247
American Foundation
  Institute of Corrections, 7
American Indians
  sanctions against, 239
Arizona
  Creative Living Foundation of, 158
Arkansas
  rehabilitation program of, 162
  research & training center, 161
  State Prison System, 29
Arrests
  "Hippie" Look, related to, 43
Auburn System, 5

Behavior Modification, 122-123
Boys Clubs of America, 158
Boston Herald American Newspaper,
  74

Caging Human Beings, 235
California
  assembly office of research, 105
  board of corrections, 102
  community treatment program, 114-
  117
  special intensive parole unit (SIPU),
  106
  State legislature, 110
  University of San Francisco Project,
  106
  Youth authority, 111
Case Management
  Washington, D.C. studies, 108
Celebrity Sports Center
  as aid to Partners, 214, 225
Cenacore House of Denver, Col., 200
Character Traits of Delinquent Youth,
  156

Chicago
  Brookfield Zoo, likened to prisons,
  235
  Dept. of Human Resources, 158
Child Care
  philosophies for delinquent, 18, 19
Church
  Presbyterian, 176
Cincinnati
  Roman Catholic archdiocese of, 199
  University of, 199
Citizen Volunteers, 120
Civil Rights
  deprivation of in Japan, 239
Classification Centers, 15-17
Collegefields Program, 119
Colorado
  Division of Youth Services, 158
  Golden Gate Youth Camp, 167
  National Guard as aid to Partners,
  Inc., 214
Community
  corrections center, 124-125
  corrections, the meaning of to Mas-
  sachusetts youth, 70-71
  delinquency control project, 116-
  117
  integration project in Easton, Pa.,
  113, 124
  oriented youthful offender program
  (COYOP), 111
  treatment project (CTP), 114-117
  for recidivists, offenders project,
  120-121
  wilderness training, 163-164, 172
Connolly Youth Center, 67
Constitution of U.S., 28
Contracts for Volunteers, 219
Convention, Constitutional, 4
Correction Centers
  youth, 12-14
Correctional Institutions
  Bridgewater, 60
  collaborative process for planning,
  32
  Florida, 199
  minimizing noise, 32
  planning for prisoners privacy, 32

Correctional Institutions *(cont.)*
  planning new, 30-33
Correctional Standards, 28-30
  court of common pleas, 29
  Federal court of appeals, 29
  Holt vs. Sarver, 29
  National bureau of standards, 28
  omnibus crime control and safe
    streets act, 28
  private groups, 29
  U.S. bureau of prisons, 28
  U.S. constitution, 28
Corrections
  dilemma of, 22
Costs of Institutionalization, 23
Council of Europe, 40
Consciousness, I, II, III in American
  belief systems, 37-38
Counseling in Partners, Inc., 222-223
Crime
  adult, definition of, 51-52
  control planning, New York office
    of, 94
  hidden in America, 40
Crime Studies
  American, 40, 42-43
  Canada, 41
  Finland, 41
  Germany, 43
  Great Britain, 44
  Helsinki, 42
  Norway, 41
  Sweden, 41
Criminal behavior
  factors contributing to, 4
Criminal Code
  Federal, 236-237
Criminal Justice
  Act of 1972, xvii
  Standards & Goals, 102-103
Criminals
  corporate, white collar, 44
Criminologist
  failure of, in solving prison problem,
    45-46
Criminology
  the classical school, 38
  the interactionist school, 39-40
  the positivist school, 38-39
  stages, 38

Dallas, Texas, 162-163
Darrow Hall, St. Louis, 158
Denver
  juvenile court, 216
  metro bus co. as aid to Partners,
    Inc., 215
Diagnostic Centers, 15-17
Differential Case Load Management,
  107-108
Differential Treatment Unit (DTU),
  118-119
Disadvantages of constructing prisons,
  26
Drug Scene as a Partners, Inc.
  training subject, 216-217

Elmira, N.Y. Reformatory, 12
Ex-Offenders Immediate Needs, 97-98
Essexsfields Rehabilitation Project, 119

Federal
  Bureau of Prisons, 241-244
  Youth Center, Englewood, Col., 158
Florida
  Ocean Sciences Research Institute,
    139
  Reception Center, 16
French, Stephen L., Forestry Camp,
  160

Government Grant Requests
  preparation of, 229
Great Law of Pennsylvania, 4
Group Homes
  California, 122
  Colorado, 121-122
  for delinquents, 121-122
  for those in trouble, 198
Group Counseling Services in Oakland
  County, Mich., 151-152
Guided Group Interaction (GGI), 117-
  119

Halfway Houses
  Attention Home, 121-122
  Cenacore House, 200
  councils of ex-offenders, 202
  Delancey Street Foundation, 198
  Dismas House of Kentucky, 200
  Dismas House of Missouri, 197, 200

Hope Hall, 197
Hopper, Isaac T., House, 197
House of Industry, 197
Quaker, 197
St. Anne's Church, 199
St. Edward's Church, 199
St. Leonard's House, 197
Silverlake, 121
Synanon House, 200
Talbert House, 198-207
308 West Residence, 197
Hamilton County, Ohio, 200
Harvard, Center for Criminal Justice, 62
Harvard Study, 72
Hidden Crime Studies, 40-41
Highfields Project, 117
Holt vs. Sarver, 29
Homeward Bound, 160
Houston, Rotary Club, 243

Illinois
Dept. of Children and Family Services, 162
State Penitentiary, 10
Impact Program of Newark, 158
Individualized Services, 139
Institutionalization
cost of, 23
Institutions
for women, 11-12
Juvenile, 14-15
Planning for, 23-28
the future of adult, 17-18
the future of youth, 18-22
Intensive Intervention, 112-113

Jails
American, 240-241
County, 16
Japanese Prisoner Rights, 239
Job Corps, 158
Job Therapy
benefits of, 180-181
incorporated, 171-177
sponsors, 180
John Howard Association, 102

Kentfields Project, 119

Lake Butler, Florida Reception Cen-

ter, 16
Lancaster School, 64
Latin American Penal Code, 239
Law
Great Law of Pennsylvania, 4
offenders, 101
L.E.A.A. (Law Enforcement Assistance Admin.)
as a source of "partners" funding, 226
Job Therapy, 176
Parole Study, 72
Safe Streets Act, 28
League of Women Voters, 59-60
Legal Systems
Anglo-American, 236
Los Angeles, California
East Side multi-service center, 166
Lyman School, 61

M-2 (Man-to-Man), 171-175
costs, 176
job advance, 189-190
job advisers, 188-189
job placement, 175
job prep services, 189-192
job success clinic, 188
other states, 192
recruiting, 174
screening, 174
M-2 (Job Therapy) Correctional Impact of, 186
research on, 193-194
Manpower Challenge, 166
Manwell Report, 64
Massachusetts
committee on children & youth, 57-58
correctional association, 245-246
dept. of youth services, 57-58
University of, 61
Michigan
council on crime & delinquency, 106
Kent County Program, 119-120
Oakland County
circuit court, 147
citizens advisory committee, 148
office of criminal justice
programs, 148
project, 120, 147
Office of youth services, 158

Michigan *(cont.)*
    Office of Criminal Justice Programs, 148
    Royal Oak Project, 138-143
    University of, National assessment of juvenile corrections, 122
Minneapolis Rehabilitation Center, 114
Montgomery Alabama Reception Center, 16

National Advisory Commission on Criminal Justice Standards & Goals, 103-104
National Conference on Juvenile Delinquency, 61
National Council on Crime & Delinquency, 102, 120, 147-149
National Guard, Colorado, 214
New Jersey
    Coalition for penal reform, 102
    Impact Project of, 158
New York
    Auburn System, 5
    division of parole, 79
    preliminary report to the Governor on criminal offenders, 94
    state commission of corrections, 98
    university of
        criminal law education and research center, 235
    urban league, 158, 164
Newspapers
    Boston Globe, 57-59
    New York Times, 79
    Snohomish County Tribune, 173

Oakland County Michigan Project, 147-153
Offender Classification, 111
    I-Level method, 115
Offenders, selection of for punishment, 41-42
Ohio
    prisons, 200
    university (State), 58
Outer Limits Project, 165
Outward Bound, 155, 157-160, 162, 164-167
    Barrio, 166
    Claims, 167-168

drop-outs, 159
drownproofing, 165

Parole
    abolishment, 95-96
    boards & panels, 85-88
    Elmira, New York, 82
    image of, 82
    long-term recommendations, 95-96
    New York board of, 85
    New York Governor's special committee on criminal justice, 84
    probation, caseloads, differential caseload management, 107-109
    racism, 81
    revocation in New York, 91-92
    therapy
        defects of, 93-95
    transitional recommendations, 98
    studies
        California correctional system, 94
Partners, Inc., 213-229
    objectives of, 213-214
    philosophy in funding, 226
    photographs, use of, 224
    preparing a budget for, 228
    recruitment, 214-215
    soliciting community "In-Kind" support for Government Grants, 227
    training evaluation of, 217
    training of, 215-218
Peer Group Dynamics, 117-118
Penal Code
    German Fed. Republic, 237
    Italian, 238
    Latin American, 239
Penitentiary, Eastern State, 4, 240
Penn, William 4
Pennsylvania Prison System, 3
Philadelphia, Court of Common Pleas, 29
Phillips Research Foundation, 162
Phoenix
    Arizona, creative living foundation of, 158
    house, 166
President's
    crime commission, 101
    task force on prisoner rehabilitation, 101

Prison
    construction & politics, 26
    design, 24
    location, 25, 240-241
    operation, 25
    planning, 23
    systems
        composition of, 234-235
Prison Reformation
    Italy, 245
    Japan, 245
    Scandinavia, 39, 245
Prisons
    Attica, 241
        report of special commission on,
        83
    Colorado, 240
    Illinois, 240
    Kentucky, 240
    maximum security, 6-8
    medium security, 8-10
    minimum security, 10-11
    Rahway and Holmsburg, 241
    in rural areas, disadvantages of, 26-
        27
    size of, 27-28
Prisoner
    classification, 8
    counseling, 28
    reform, 5
Prisoners
    planning cell size, 28
    sensory deprivation, 27-28
Prisons for Women, 11-12
Probation
    caseloads research, 106
    for serious offenders, 109
    individualized services, 139-140
    Offenders rehabilitation training
        (PORT), 123
    programs described, 105-106
    Santa Barbara, California, special
        supervision unit, 111
    STAT subsidy programs, 110
        California, 111-112
        Colorado, 112
        Pennsylvania, 112
        Washington, 112
    U.S. District Court for District
        of Columbia, 108
Probationed Offenders Rehabilitation

    Training, 122-123
Project Wingspread, 162
Provo Experiment, 117-118
Psychology as a Partners training sub-
        ject, 216
Punishment, selection of offenders for,
        41-42
Purdy, (Washington) Women's Treat-
        ment Center, 178

Reception Centers, 15-17
Recidivism, effects of job therapy on,
        192-193
Recidivists, Community Treatment
        for, 120
Rappelling as a training help for delin-
        quent youth, 157
Reformatories, 12-13
Rehabilitation
    centers, 114
    Essexfields, 119
    group dynamics, 202
    training for probationed offenders,
        122-123
Residential Community Programs,
        121-125
Restitution, 3
Riots
    American Prison, 241
Role playing as a training device for
        Partners, Inc., 217
Roslindale Youth Center, 67
Rotary Club
    of Houston, 243
    of Seattle, 175

Sachem Foundation, 148
Saginaw Project, 106
Salesmanship Boys Camp, Dallas,
        Texas, 161-162
Salvation Army, 199
San Francisco Community Treatment
        Project, 118
Saranac Village, 166
Screening in recruiting Partners, Inc.,
        219
Sensing Electronic, 7
Shirley Industrial School, 61
Silverlake Experiment, 121
Small Group Homes, 197
Society for Alleviating Miseries, 4

Soliciting Community Facilities in Partners, Inc., 224
Solitary Confinement, 5
Southern Illinois University
Outdoor laboratory "Underway Program," 162
START Project, xvii
State Subsidy Programs, 110-111
St. Louis
Darrow Hall, 158
Dismas House, 197, 200
Stockton Community Parole Center Program, 161
Synnanon House of Los Angeles, 200

Talbert House, 198-205
Task Force On Corrections
Recommendations, 103-104
Team Activities for Delinquent Youth, 156
Television Surveillance Controls, 17
Therapy
Friendship in, 178
Training Schools, closing, 57

U.S. Senate, Community Supervision and Services Act, 253-255
U.S. Supreme Court, 198
UTE Indian Tribal Court, 258
United Nations Prison Policy, 29
Urban Bound Program, 165-166

Vocational Rehabilitation, Bureau of, 201
Volunteer Programs, earning community acceptance for, 227
Volunteers
in criminal Justice System, 134-136
of America, 199

W-2 (Woman-to-Woman), 177-180
Washington, Closing large Institutions in, 125
Washington Correction Center, Shelton, 125-126
Western Correctional Center, 13
Westfield Detention Facility, 67
Wilderness
Solos for delinquent youth, 155-156
Therapy, 155
Wisconsin, Council on Criminal Justice, 101
Wisconsin's Community Based System, 102
Women's Treatment Centers, 11-12
Worcester Detention Facility, 67
Work Unit Concept, California, 107-108

YMCA
as aid to Partners, Inc., 214
free Membership for Partners, Inc., 227
Yellow Cab Co., as aid to Partners, Inc., 214
Young Life—National Christian Youth Organization, 213
Youth Correction Centers, 12
Youth Crime, as a lower-class phenomenon, 52

About the Editor

Calvert R. Dodge is a project director for the Kentucky Manpower Development Corporation. He received the masters degree in sociology from the University of Wyoming in 1957 and the Ph.D. in communication from the University of Denver in 1971. He was director of the Colorado Youth Workers Training Center, and served as Vice-President of the American Society for Training and Development from 1969-71. Dr. Dodge is also an instructor of sociology at the Jefferson Community College in Louisville.